GUINE

M000312510

PATRICK CHABAL
TOBY GREEN
(*Editors*)

Guinea-Bissau

Micro-State to 'Narco-State'

HURST & COMPANY, LONDON

First published in the United Kingdom in 2016 by
C. Hurst & Co. (Publishers) Ltd.,
41 Great Russell Street, London, WC1B 3PL
© Patrick Chabal, Toby Green and the Contributors, 2016
All rights reserved.
Printed in India

Distributed in the United States, Canada and Latin America
by Oxford University Press, 198 Madison Avenue, New York, NY 10016,
United States of America.

The right of Patrick Chabal, Toby Green and the Contributors to be
identified as the authors of this publication is asserted by them in
accordance with the Copyright, Designs and Patents Act, 1988.

A Cataloguing-in-Publication data record for this book
is available from the British Library.

978-1-84904-521-6 *paperback*

This book is printed using paper from registered sustainable
and managed sources.

www.hurstpublishers.com

Map on p. xxvi by Agostinho Palminha

This book is dedicated to the memory of Patrick Chabal,
a great scholar and friend

CONTENTS

CONTENTS

FOREWORD

In late 2012 and early 2013, Patrick Chabal and I met several times to discuss this book. I had been involved for several years in a project related to Guinea-Bissau, and have known the country well since 1995. Chabal's interest in Guinea-Bissau needs no introduction, meanwhile; he authored the definitive biography of Amílcar Cabral, leader of the country's revolutionary war, and indeed one of the most influential revolutionaries of the twentieth century. But Chabal had become saddened by the state of the country. In 2011, shortly after I began working with him at King's College London, I had sent him a link to an article I had co-authored about Guinea-Bissau for the *African Arguments* blog, to which he had replied, 'There is no point in hiding the truth any more.' This exchange was probably the seed of this book.

Thereafter, it was Patrick Chabal who drove it on with the quiet force of someone who sensed their time was short. Once his long-time publisher, Michael Dwyer of Hurst, had confirmed his interest, and the title of the book (which was Patrick's) had been agreed, some outlines and a couple of chapters came in during the second half of 2013. Chabal and I edited the pieces together; we discussed the purpose of the book during several further meetings, agreed the final list of contributors and how we would jointly edit each of the chapters. But then in early 2014 Chabal's long-term medical condition deteriorated unexpectedly, and he died on 16 January.

This was a very swift blow which left everyone in shock. In his last email to me he mentioned that his condition had worsened, but said he still planned to read some of the work that had come in as he did not 'want to delay the project, especially at this stage'. In consultation with his family and Michael Dwyer, we therefore decided that the book should continue. Given Patrick's heavy editorial input prior to his death, it was generally agreed that the most appropriate imprint should still be ed. Chabal/Green. And although some will feel the title is controversial, we decided to keep it as the quotation marks make it clear that the term 'narco-state' is an externalised label—Patrick was a lover of controversy, and as it was his title it needed to remain, to invite challenge and debate as he would have wanted.

Finalizing the preparation of this book has therefore weighed heavily, though in lighter moods it has also struck me how fitting it is that this should be the last book on which Patrick worked. A month or so before he died, he wrote to me that he did not want this to be 'just another book'. Keeping true to this aim has ever since been at the forefront of my mind.

TG   *Cambridge*, January 2016

CO-EDITOR'S NOTE AND ACKNOWLEDGEMENTS

Many of the chapters in this book refer to key events such as the independence movement, the 1998–9 civil war and the assassination of Amílcar Cabral. Rather than ask each of the contributors to introduce and contextualize these events at each point, a timeline and series of biographical sketches have been prepared. Readers should consult these in the first instance where a person or event requires further context.

This book would not have been possible without the help of so many Bissau-Guineans who, over the years, have made me feel so welcome both in their country and in their communities in Britain, Portugal and Senegal. They are far too many to be named individually, but they are all very much present with me.

Patrick Chabal's sudden death caused a great deal of sadness. I am deeply indebted to Farzana Shaikh and Emile Chabal for their welcoming hearts and strength of purpose in the face of their immense grief. Many people helped in ways big and small, and without even knowing it at times. I would especially like to thank Francisco Bethencourt, Federico Bonaddio, Catherine Boyle, Richard Drayton, Michael Dwyer, Serena Ferente, Emily Fowke, Christoph Kohl, Niall O'Flaherty, Jeanne Penvenne, Adam Sutcliffe, Marina Temudo, Peter Thompson, David Treece, AbdoolKarim Vakil, and Julian Weiss.

GLOSSARY AND ACRONYMS

ANC	African National Congress, South Africa
AU	African Union
Armazens do Povo	people's stores set up by the PAIGC after independence
baloba	religious shrine
bolanhas	rice paddies
Casamance	neighbouring region of Senegal with many cultural, historical and kinship ties to Guinea-Bissau
CFA	Communauté financière africaine, the major currency in Francophone West Africa, also used in Guinea-Bissau
cipaios	military policemen under colonial rule
convivência	'living together', the norm in Guinea-Bissau where people from different ethnic and lineage backgrounds live in the same region and/or village
CPLP	Comunidade dos Países de Língua Portuguesa
CSDP	Common Security and Defence Policy
CUF	Companhia União Fabril, major trading company in Guinea during colonial rule
dasa	hut tax under colonial rule
DEA	US Drug Enforcement Administration
djilas	itinerant traders who have been vital merchants in the region since the fifteenth century, usually of Muslim faith and Fula or Mandinga
ECOMIB	ECOWAS mission in Bissau
ECOWAS	Economic Community of West African States
EU	European Union

EU SSR	EU mission in support of the Security Sector Reform in Guinea-Bissau
FARC	Fuerzas Armadas Revolucionárias de Colombia
FN	Front National, France
grumetes	shiphands in pre-colonial Guinea-Bissau's Atlantic trading networks, usually of African origin
IDP	Internally Displaced Person
IMF	International Monetary Fund
INEP	Instituto Nacional de Estudos e Pesquisas, national research body in Guinea-Bissau
iran	spirit
Kriol	Creole, the lingua franca of Guinea-Bissau, originally spoken mainly in coastal trading communities but becoming widespread during colonial rule
Kyang-yang	a prophetic movement emerging under the Balanta during the 1980s and 1990s
lumo	weekly rural market
MFDC	Mouvement des forces démocratiques de Casamance—rebel separatist movement in Casamance, Senegal
MISSANG	Angolan Technical Military and Security Mission in Guinea-Bissau
MLG	Movimento de Libertação da Guiné, rival to the PAIGC in the 1960s
moransa	extended compound for families in Guinea-Bissau
mouros	marabouts, spiritual intermediaries between the living and the dead, held to have magic powers and associated with Islam
NATO	North Atlantic Treaty Organization
NGO	Non-Governmental Organization
OAU	Organization of African Unity
PAIGC	Partido Africano da Independência da Guiné (e Cabo Verde)
PIR	Rapid Intervention Police in Guinea-Bissau
PDG	Parti Démocratique de Guinée, of neighbouring Guinea-Conakry
pontas	plantation (not only of groundnuts)
ponteiros	planter-traders who established the groundnut industry in Guinea-Bissau in the nineteenth century after the turn to 'legitimate commerce'

POP	Public Order Police in Guinea-Bissau
praça	originally colonial fortresses, now used to describe urban spaces
PRS	Partido da Renovação Social, led by Kumba Yalá to victory in the 2000 elections
régulos	chiefs appointed by the Portuguese colonial authorities, apparently to maintain 'traditional' governance structures, but actually to co-opt them
RUF	Revolutionary United Front, rebel force led by Foday Sankoh in Sierra Leone in the 1990s
SAP	Structural Adjustment Programmes of economic liberalization introduced in the late 1980s.
SCU	Sociedade Comercial Ultramarina, company regulating trade in colonial times, transformed into SOCOMIN after independence
SSR	Security Sector Reform
tabanka	Village/settlement in a rural area
tchon	Kriol word for 'land', but also implying ethnic/national territory
UN	United Nations
UNDP	United Nations Development Program
UNIOGBIS	United Nations Integrated Peace-Building Office in Guinea-Bissau, from January 2010
UNOGBIS	United Nations Peace-Building Support Office in Guinea-Bissau, from March 1999

BIOGRAPHICAL SKETCHES

Amílcar Cabral Founder of the PAIGC along with five colleagues following the Pidjiguiti massacre in 1959, Cabral had developed a pan-African political consciousness as a student of agronomy in Lisbon, where he met the future independence leaders in Angola and Mozambique, Agostinho Neto and Eduardo Mondlane, at the Casa dos Estudantes do Império. He became a global figure of the Left and of Black power in the late 1960s and 1970s, publishing widely and speaking around the world. A recipient of aid from Cuba and the USSR, the PAIGC forces were on the cusp of victory when Cabral was assassinated by a PAIGC cadre in Conakry (headquarters of the PAIGC) in January 1973. The true instigator of his assassination has never been proven, although it was widely suspected that Portugal's dictatorship fuelled tensions between mainly Balanta troops and the predominantly Cape Verdean leadership of the PAIGC.

Luís Cabral A half-brother of Amílcar, and also a key member of the PAIGC during the independence war. Luís Cabral became the first president of independent Guinea-Bissau, but was deposed by Nino Vieira in the coup of November 1980. He died in exile in Portugal in 2009.

Carlos Gomes Jr Widely known as 'Cadogo', Nino Vieira's right-hand man in the later years of his presidency. Gomes Jr was prime minister at the time of Vieira's death, and remained in the role until March 2012 when he stood for president as the PAIGC candidate. On course for victory, he was detained in the April 2012 coup, lived in exile in Portugal, and now lives in exile in Cape Verde.

António Indjai A leading figure in the military over the past decade, with strong regional connections, Indjai has been widely fingered by international observers as a key figure in the drugs trade, and as responsible for several coup attempts. An associate of Tagme Na' Waie, he grew to prominence after the latter's assassination in March 2009. He was involved in a coup attempt against President Sanhá in December 2010, and Sanhá then reluctantly appointed him as Chief of Staff. A fall-out over a drugs shipment which landed close to his residence in Mansôa in December 2011 prompted a further coup attempt led by Bubu NaTchuto. He was said to be the leading figure behind the deposition of Gomes Jr during the April 2012 elections. The leading strong figure in the transitional government leading up to the 2014 elections, his strategy to get his preferred candidate elected failed, and he was subsequently removed from his post by President José Mario Vaz.

José Ramos-Horta East Timorese Nobel Peace Prize winner, and first president of the country following the end of Indonesian occupation, Horta was appointed by the UN to oversee the peace-building process in the country following the 2012 *coup d'état*.

Manuel Serifo Nhamadjo A Fula from the east of the country, Nhamadjo polled third in the first round of the 2012 presidential elections. Following the April *coup d'état*, he was installed as interim president by the military and shepherded the country to elections in April 2014, when he stood down.

Raimundo Pereira Speaker of the National Assembly during the second presidency of Malam Bacai Sanhá, Pereira became interim president after Sanhá's death in January 2012. He was detained along with Gomes Jr during the 2012 *coup d'état*, and now lives in exile in Portugal.

Malam Bacai Sanhá From a Muslim Beafada family, Sanhá became president in the 2009 elections after the assassination of Nino Vieira by the military. His rule was punctuated by strong tensions with the military, and especially Antonio Indjai and Bubu NaTchuto, and a failed coup attempt in December 2011. He died in January 2012.

João Bernardo Vieira (Nino) A key figure in the military campaign which saw independence in September 1974, Nino Vieira became president after leading a *coup d'état* against President Luís Cabral, Amílcar's half-brother, in November 1980. The coup was prompted by continuing resentment of Cape Verdean dominance of the country, and Nino became the dominant figure of post-colonial Guinea-Bissau's politics. Following external pressure, he held multi-party elections in 1994, which he won as candidate of the PAIGC, but was then deposed in the civil war (1998–9). Nino returned from exile in Portugal to win a presidential election in 2004, but tensions simmered between him and the army. On 1 March 2009 the commander-in-chief of the army, Tagme Na' Waie, was killed in a bomb blast and soldiers retaliated by killing Vieira at the presidential palace.

Tagme Na' Waie A leading figure in the independence war, and someone who fought very closely alongside Nino Vieira during the struggle against the Portuguese. After Nino Vieira assumed the presidency again in 2005, Na' Waie became Army Chief of Staff, but developing tensions between the army and the presidency—which rumours said were due to conflicts over the growing drugs trade—led to a crisis, and Na' Waie was killed on 1 March 2009 in a bomb blast in Bissau.

Kumba Yalá Known in the country as the man who 'walked his way to the presidency', Yalá was the first person outside the PAIGC to become president of the country in the March 2000 elections. A Balanta from Bula, Yalá led an increasingly divisive country and was accused by many of trying to shore up Balanta power. Deposed from power in 2003, he sought alliances elsewhere in the region; after converting to Islam, he hoped to challenge the PAIGC hegemony through an alliance with the Muslims who live in the east of the country, but repeatedly failed to win electoral breakthroughs. Some alleged that he colluded with the army in the 2012 coup, but he died shortly before the April 2014 presidential elections.

TIMELINE

1884–5	Berlin Conference and the establishment of Portuguese colonial claims in Guinea-Bissau
1915	Long wars of pacification lead to final conquest of the territory
1959	Demonstration against colonial rule by dock workers at Pidjiguiti leads to massacre by the colonial army. Formation in secret of the Partio Africano da Independência da Guiné e Cabo Verde (PAIGC) led by Amílcar Cabral
1963	Beginning in earnest of the War of Liberation
January 1966	Fidel Castro adopts Cabral as a protégé at the Tricontinental Conference in Havana and starts supplying assistance to the PAIGC, which is the party leading independence efforts in both Guinea-Bissau and Cape Verde
30 January 1973	Assassination of Amílcar Cabral in Conakry, Republic of Guinea
21 September 1974	Declaration of Independence of the Republic of Guinea-Bissau. The PAIGC is the ruling party in both Cape Verde and Guinea-Bissau
November 1980	Nino Vieira leads a *coup d'état* against the government of President Luís Cabral, Amílcar's brother. The PAIGC splits into two parties, one in Guinea-Bissau and one in Cape Verde (PAICV)
1985	Arrest of Balanta politician Paulo Correia and eleven others by Vieira on charges of leading Balanta factionalism

TIMELINE

1994	First multi-party elections in the country see Nino Vieira elected president as the PAIGC candidate
7 June 1998	The 'Bissau War' breaks out after clashes between factions led by Ansumane Mané and Nino Vieira; the armies of Senegal and Guinea-Conakry intervene
11 May 1999	Peace officially declared, after Mané ousts Vieira on 7 May. Malam Bacai Sanhá takes over as caretaker president
16 January 2000	Kumba Yalá of the opposition PRS party is elected president
November 2002	Yalá dissolves parliament and dismisses the government
14 September 2003	Yalá is overthrown in a military coup
28 March 2005	Parliamentary elections see the PAIGC re-emerge as the biggest party and Carlos Gomes Jr is appointed prime minister
24 July 2005	Nino Vieira is re-elected president
2008	Security sector reform is begun, sponsored by the European Union; in November the PAIGC win a landslide in elections
1 March 2009	Military Chief of Staff Tagme Na' Waie is killed in a bomb blast; Nino Vieira is killed in a retaliatory attack
26 July 2009	Malam Bacai Sanhá defeats Kumba Yalá and is elected president
Early 2011	Angola deploys a peace mission, MISSANG, in Guinea-Bissau
26 December 2011	A coup attempt against Malam Bacai Sanhá is foiled
9 January 2012	President Sanhá dies; Raimundo Pereira is appointed interim president
18 March 2012	First round of presidential elections sees Carlos Gomes Jr with a clear advantage over Kumba Yalá
12–13 April 2012	Army factions overthrow Pereira and detain Gomes Jr, claiming collusion with MISSANG. Manuel Serife Nhamadjo is appointed interim president
4 April 2014	Kumba Yalá dies unexpectedly
13 April 2014	Election of PAIGC candidate as president, José Mario Vaz

NOTES ON CONTRIBUTORS

Miguel de Barros is a sociologist and a researcher at the National Institute of Studies and Research (INEP), Guinea-Bissau, as well as a member of the Council for Development of Social Science Research in Africa (CODESRIA). He has co-authored the book *A participação das mulheres na política e na tomada de decisão na Guiné-Bissau: da consciência, percepção à prática política* (Bissau: United Nations, 2013) and co-edited the volume *Hispano-Lusophone Community Media: Identity, Cultural Politics, Difference* (London: Sean Kingston, 2014).

Manuel Bivar Abrantes is a PhD student at UNICAMP, Brazil, and his research is about ethnic transformation in Guinea-Bissau. Since 2008 he has been doing ethnographic fieldwork in Guinea-Bissau and has a book on oral history and territory in production that will be published by UFF, Rio de Janeiro.

Hassoum Ceesay is a Gambian historian, writer and museum curator at the Gambia National Museum. He attended Fourah Bay College, University of Sierra Leone; Saint Mary's University, Halifax, Canada, where he gained a Bachelor of Arts in History in 1999; and the University of Nairobi, Kenya, where he gained a Postgraduate Diploma in Museum Studies in 2003; followed by an MA in African history at the University of The Gambia, where he also lectures. He has published two books on Gambian women's history.

Patrick Chabal was for many years a Professor at King's College London, latterly as Chair of African History and Politics in the Department of History. He wrote and co-authored many key works on Africa, including *Amílcar Cabral: Revolutionary Leadership and People's War Africa Works* (with Jean-Pascal Daloz) and *Africa: The Politics of Suffering and Smiling*. He died in January 2014.

Joshua B. Forrest is Associate Professor and Chair of the History and Political Science Department at La Roche College, Pittsburgh, Pennsylvania. He has authored two books on Guinea-Bissau, including *Lineages of State Fragility: Rural Civil Society in Guinea-Bissau* (Athens, OH: Ohio University Press), and two dozen articles on Bissau-Guinean politics. He has also published studies of the rise of sub-nationalism in Sub-Saharan Africa and local policy-making in Namibia.

Toby Green is Lecturer in Lusophone African History and Culture at King's College London. He has written and edited many works about the history of Guinea-Bissau and the wider sub-region, including *Meeting the Invisible Man* (London: Weidenfeld & Nicolson, 2001), and most recently (as editor) *Brokers of Change: Atlantic Commerce and Cultures in Pre-Colonial Western Africa* (Oxford: Oxford University Press, 2012). He has also recently conducted a digitization project of precious oral histories in collaboration with the British Library and Gambian National Centre for Arts and Culture.

Philip J. Havik (PhD in Social Sciences, Leiden University, Netherlands) is Senior Researcher at the Instituto de Higiene e Medicina Tropical (IHMT), while also teaching at the Faculty of Social Sciences and Humanities (FCSH) of the Universidade Nova in Lisbon. His multi-disciplinary research centres on the study of public health and tropical medicine, state formation, governance, cultural brokerage and entrepreneurship in Sub-Saharan Africa, with special emphasis on West Africa. His recent publications include 'Virtual Nations and Failed States: making sense of the labyrinth', in Eric Morier-Genoud (ed.), *Sure Road? Nationalisms in Angola, Guinea-Bissau and Mozambique* (Leiden: Brill, 2012): 31–78.

Christoph Kohl conducted a 2005–9 PhD project on ethnicity and nation-building in Guinea-Bissau at the Max Planck Institute for Social Anthropology and Graduate School 'Society and Culture in Motion' in Halle (Saale), Germany; he was Research Fellow at the Ludwig Maximilian University of Munich (in a project on returned refugees in Angola), 2011–12; since 2012 he has been Research Fellow at the Peace Research Institute Frankfurt (PRIF) for a project on security sector reform in Guinea-Bissau.

Aliou Ly is Assistant Professor of African and World History at Middle Tennessee State University. His research concerns gender in West African liberation movements, and he is currently exploring the ways in which a focus on the perspective of women fighters leads to rewriting current historical narratives of the Guinea-Bissau national liberation war. His article 'Promise and Betrayal: Women fighters and national liberation in Guinea-Bissau' was published in *Feminist Africa*, issue 20, Fall 2014.

Simon Massey is a Senior Lecturer in the Department of International Studies and Social Science at Coventry University. His doctoral thesis investigated the political and ethical bases of all-African peacekeeping operations and he maintains an interest in conflict management and Africa's peace and security architecture. More recently, he has conducted research funded by the European Union into the mechanisms and impact of irregular migration from Africa to Europe. As well as Guinea-Bissau, Simon has published articles on politics and security in Chad, the Comoros and Madagascar.

José Lingna Nafafé is Lecturer in Portuguese and Lusophone Studies at the University of Bristol. He has extensively researched the region and has written widely on Guinea-Bissau, including work on Flora Gomes' film *Nha Fala*; 'Guinea-Bissau: Language Situation' (2005); 'African Orality in Iberian Space: Critique of Barros' (2012); 'Mission and Political Power' (2005); and a pre-colonial monograph on the region called *Colonial Encounters: Issues of Culture, Hybridity and Creolisation, Portuguese Mercantile Settlers in West Africa* (Frankfurt: Peter Lang, 2007).

Marina Padrão Temudo is a Senior Research Fellow at the Department of Natural Resources, Environment and Land, Forest Research Centre (CEF), School of Agriculture (ISA), Lisbon. She has conducted extensive ethnographic research on rural development and conservation in Guinea-Bissau, Cape Verde, Mozambique, São Tomé and Príncipe and Angola. Her most recent articles have been published in *Development and Change*, *Politique Africaine*, *Human Ecology*, *Journal of Agrarian Change* and *Conservation and Society*.

Ramon Sarró is Associate Professor of Social Anthropology at the School of Anthropology and Museum Ethnography, University of Oxford. He has published the book *The Politics of Religious Change on the Upper Guinea Coast: Iconoclasm Done and Undone* (Edinburgh University Press for the International African Institute, 2009), based on a decade of research on the coastal Republic of Guinea, and co-edited the volume *Learning Religion: Anthropological Approaches* (Oxford: Berghahn Books, 2007). Since 2008 he has conducted fieldwork on prophetic movements in Guinea-Bissau and, more recently, also in the Democratic Republic of Congo and in Angola.

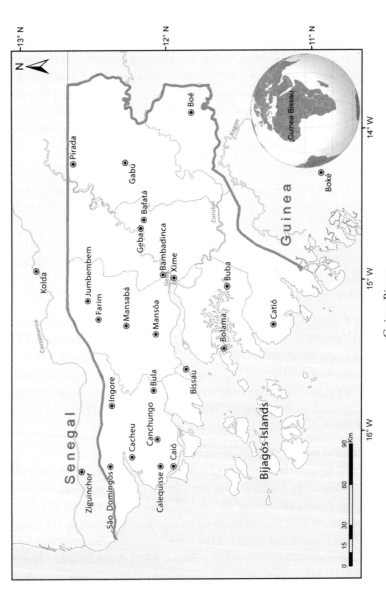

Guinea Bissau

INTRODUCTION[1]

Toby Green

Guinea-Bissau is one of Africa's smallest and least populous nations, and yet in the last decade it has become one of its most infamous. Following the civil war in 1998–9, the country was beset by numerous military coups, widespread civil and political instability and the accusation levelled at it from various quarters that it had become the world's first 'narco-state'. These events called into question the viability of the post-colonial state in a country such as Guinea-Bissau, which has no easily apparent and legally sanctioned 'rents'. Transnational organized crime, global security infrastructure and the concerns of the ongoing 'war on terror', all intersected in Guinea-Bissau with the crises of legitimacy of the post-colonial state. This makes the country a paradigmatic case study in the early twenty-first century for the analysis of Africa's recent past, and of the potential for peaceful and representative states in Africa's future. It also highlights the vital interplay of local dynamics and global securitization discourses, for while other countries in the region have been linked to the narcotics trade, the use of the 'narco-state' label for Guinea-Bissau alone has shaped aspects of subsequent interactions and debate.

[1] I would like to thank Mamadou Diouf, Richard Drayton, Richard Rathbone, Farzana Shaikh and Marina Temudo for their invaluable critiques of this Introduction; all errors of fact and interpretation remain my own.

So fast-moving has the situation been in the country that there have been only limited possibilities for consolidated reflection. The ramifications of events have been so widespread that it has been difficult for any single researcher to examine the meanings of the whole, and so this book has the purpose of attempting to bridge this gap through a collective effort. What does all this mean for Guinea-Bissau, and for understanding the nature of the state in post-colonial Africa? What links does Guinea-Bissau's instability have to questions of wider regional and global security? What would a stable state look like in Guinea-Bissau, and what are the conditions for its achievement?

Before introducing these questions, some specific reflections on the case of Guinea-Bissau are in order. The country is characterized by a unique human and physical geography. Over thirty languages are spoken, with Kriol—the Creole language born of African–Portuguese relations dating back to the early sixteenth century—the main lingua franca (Havik 2007b; Jacobs 2010). The Balanta are the largest group, with their heartland in southern and central areas of the country, and a strong tradition of resistance to outside invaders (Hawthorne 2003; Temudo 2009; Forrest, this volume). North and adjacent to the capital, Bissau, are the Pepels, Mankanhes and Manjakos, peoples whose languages and cultures are all heavily related to one another (Green, this volume). To the south of Bissau are the lands of the Beafada and Nalú, while offshore are the islands of the Bijagó peoples, some of the fiercest warriors in the region in pre-colonial times (Green 2012). Inland to the east, towards the border with Guinea-Conakry, the land is mainly occupied by Islamized Fulas and Mandingas, with the Fulas constituting perhaps now the largest people in the country;[2] most Fulas, however, are of relatively recent origin in the country, having arrived from the Fuuta Djallon in what is now Guinea-Conakry during political upheavals in the mid-nineteenth century (Green, this volume).

Historically, the country has for many centuries been a space for cross-cultural interactions through trade, marriage and warfare. After the thir-teenth-century arrival of the Mandingas of the Mali empire, there followed from the early sixteenth century interactions with Atlantic traders and the formation of mixed Creole communities characterized by a high degree of cultural and religious pluralism (Sarró and Barros, this volume). These Afro-Atlantic trading communities were largely confined to the coast and the rivers

---

[2] The most recent census involving ethnic data was compiled in 1991; subsequent to this, there has been substantial migration of Fulas from Guinea-Conakry, many of whom have gained Bissau-Guinean nationality, such that they may now constitute the largest group ahead of the Balantas.

of São Domingos in the north and Geba in the centre of the country. Further inland, political control was held by the powerful Kaabu federation (Lopes 1999; Green 2009), controlled by the Mandingas and reaching the height of its powers in the seventeenth and eighteenth centuries. In 1866 Kaabu fell to invaders from the Fuuta Djallon Islamic theocracy in neighbouring Guinea-Conakry, and the wars that followed for control of the territory in the later nineteenth century accompanied the rise of peanut plantations (Havik, this volume), and presaged the rise of formal colonial rule in the early twentieth century under the Portuguese.

Within this highly complex cultural and historical framework, the geography of the country is one that large political structures have always struggled to control. Many of the peoples who now live there first came to find a safe refuge from the incursions of the Mali empire in the thirteenth and fourteenth centuries (Green 2012: 47–8). The area was ideally chosen from this perspective, since Guinea-Bissau is criss-crossed by numerous creeks and rivers, many of which cross the border north into the Casamance region of Senegal, and have for centuries acted as conduits for trade goods and human migration (Green 2012). These creeks and the mangrove swamps by the coast form dense geographical networks for communication and passage which, during formal colonialism in the twentieth century, the Portuguese found impossible to control completely (Green 2012; Forrest 2003). It was only as late as 1936 that the Bijagó were finally subdued by the Portuguese empire; with the onset of the independence war in 1963—a war that lasted until 1974—the period of formal colonial control of the country was in fact very short.

Resistance, then, has always characterized Guinea-Bissau's relations with powerful outsiders (Mendy 1994). That the post-colonial successor to colonial states should struggle to embed itself here should therefore come as no surprise. What is at stake is the institutional and culturally-embedded resistance to external authority, something which has characterized the country's relations with global powers ever since the fifteenth and sixteenth centuries. As key African thinkers have shown, it is crucial to situate current events within the long historical continuum which has structured Africa's endemic inequality within the global economic system (Mbembe 2001: 9, 13, 69–70; Mbembe 2010: 24). Understanding the deep-rooted historical patterns of contemporary conjunctures was a deep concern of Patrick Chabal's (see e.g. Chabal and Vidal 2007; Chabal and Daloz 1999: xviii), and finds resonance in the broader need to understand crises not within an immediate causal framework, but as part of a global pattern of structural failure within the political and economic system.

Here one is reminded of Michel-Rolph Trouillot's pungent analysis of slave-owners' responses to patterns of resistance in the eighteenth-century Caribbean (Trouillot 1995: 83–4):

> planters and managers could not fully deny resistance, but they tried to provide reassuring certitudes by trivializing all its manifestations. Resistance did not exist as a global phenomenon. Rather, each case of unmistakable defiance, each possible instance of resistance was treated separately and drained of its political content. Slave A ran away because he was particularly mistreated by his master. Slave B was missing because he was not properly fed. Slave X killed herself in a fatal tantrum. Slave Y poisoned her mistress because she was jealous... [but] to acknowledge resistance as a mass phenomenon is to acknowledge the possibility that something is wrong with the system.

Similarly, focusing on individual causes and individual solutions within the ongoing problematic of post-colonial Africa fails to entertain the possibility that systemic issues will also need to be addressed, and placed within both a historical and a contemporaneous structural context. As Achille Mbembe puts it, 'African politics and economics have been condemned to appear in social theory only as the sign of a lack, while the discourse of political science and development economics had become that of a quest for the causes of that lack' (Mbembe 2001: 8).

It is for this reason that it is important to situate the current recurring crises in Guinea-Bissau historically: as the chapters by Green, Forrest and Havik demonstrate, 'ethnic', political and economic factors from the recent and not-so-recent past can all inform our understanding of why certain patterns have recurred in the country since the 1998–9 civil war. One of the fundamental issues in the construction of the nation state, the security of borders, requires the historical understanding that the Casamance region of southern Senegal and what is now Guinea-Bissau long formed a unified cultural space, for many centuries, and that some of the problems of rebellion in the Casamance, and instability of Guinea-Bissau, are related to the permanent porosity of this border, and the historical and kinship connections held by peoples on both sides of it.[3] Even the emergence of the large contraband drugs trade from South America to Europe via West Africa follows a long-standing pattern of contraband trade linking the two continents as far back as the sixteenth century (Green 2012); where in that era this was a trade in enslaved humans, now

---

[3] For instance, regular transport links the town of Ingore in Guinea-Bissau with the Goudomp department of Casamance, even though there is no manned border checkpoint.

it is the cocaine trade from South America that has taken centre stage in the global awareness of problems of governance in the country, and the clamour for solutions.

Guinea-Bissau's labelling as a 'narco-state' began to emerge shortly after Nino Vieira's re-election as president in 2005. Vieira had taken power in a coup in 1980 and been elected president during the country's first elections of 1994, before being ousted during the 1998–9 civil war. After the divisive presidency of Kumba Yalá (2000–3) was terminated by a coup, Vieira was re-elected, and the first rumours of Guinea-Bissau's new infamy began to surface (for more details, see Kohl, this volume). In 2007 and 2008, articles in major international media outlets such as the *Observer* and *Time* highlighted the country as a 'narco-state', emphasizing the hold of Colombian drug traffickers in Bissau and the impotence of Western observers to do anything about this (Vulliamy 2008; Walt 2007). Specialist observers concurred that the rise of drug trafficking through West Africa was a major security issue, and singled out Guinea-Bissau as the leader of the trend (Bernard 2008; Mazzitelli 2007; Ellis 2009). Throughout the following years, the country developed a notorious reputation as the centre of this illegal trade, with op-ed pieces in other leading global opinion formers such as the *New York Times* and *Der Spiegel* (O'Regan 2012; Smoltczyk 2013). The sting operation which led to the arrest in 2013 of Bubu NaTchuto, long renowned as a kingpin in the drugs trade, may in fact have deflected the vector of this trade to neighbouring Guinea-Conakry (Lewis 2014; Ellis/Shaw 2015: 2; see also Kohl, this volume), but the fact remains that globally the reputation of Guinea-Bissau as a leading 'narco-state' is second to none. Moreover, some commentators suggest that this pattern goes right back to the inception of the drugs route from Latin America through West Africa in the early 2000s, where there were apparently already strong links between the politico–military elites of Guinea-Bissau and Guinea-Conakry which enabled this to happen (Shaw 2015: 346–8).

Nevertheless, there are problems with the characterization of the country as a 'narco-state'. Shaw argues that the country offers an example of elite racketeering, and that the parlous condition of the Bissau-Guinean state makes the phrase 'narco-state' inappropriate. Certainly, the label falls within the tradition of the failed state paradigm, where Western-imposed narratives create stories of 'success' and 'failure' in Africa in order to shore up a hubristic self-image and entrench the status quo (Cravo 2012). Such narratives support the idea that successful change can only come from outside the country, whereas the realities are more complex: the real issue in the country is seen by many to be the imperative of nation-building from below, not externally-imposed state-building from without (Kohnert 2010), and just as the country's internal unrest is largely driven by internal factors, so the solutions are likely to come from within. Moreover, although Guinea-Bissau is widely held up to be a paradigm of a failed state, an African 'basket-case', comparisons of Human Development Indicators with other 'success stories' reveal the weakness of this analysis: Mozambique has very similar indicators, and is held up as a model of democratic transition and successful aid (Cravo 2012).

Even so, it is important to recognize in any book on Guinea-Bissau the depth of the current crisis in human terms. The indicators are bleak and are clearly related to ongoing political crises. After the 2012 coup (Kohl, this volume), GDP in the country—according to the admittedly fragile data-collecting techniques which are available (Jerven 2013)—fell by 6.7%; the latest World Bank report on the country meanwhile suggested that the country was unlikely to reach any of the Millennium Development Goals by 2015, while the numbers living below the national poverty line increased from 64.7% in 2002 to 69.3% in 2010 (World Bank 2014). Moreover, even according to traditional economic paradigms, the flash of optimism which came with the peaceful presidential elections of 2014 when José Mario Vaz became president (Kohl, this volume) has been short-lived: while external investment jumped to $46 million in 2014, it has already fallen back to $12 million in the year to September 2015 (http://www.worldbank.org/en/country/guineabissau, accessed 29 January 2016), testament to fears surrounding new political crises in Bissau (Kohl, this volume).

These desperate realities are reflected everywhere, from the mass migrations of Bissau-Guineans in search of a better life (Nafafé, this volume), to ongoing instability and migrations in the sub-region (Ceesay, this volume), to crises in gender relations (Ly, this volume), and to the global interest in security sector reform which has been ongoing ever since the crises achieved prominence in the early twenty-first century (Massey, this volume). They demonstrate that the depth of the problems goes far beyond the local, since they have both regional and global consequences.

Yet in the face of these stark problems, the manifestations of this crisis in the country are complex. Bissau-Guineans retain a good deal of autonomy in elements of religious and economic life (Sarró and Barros and Temudo and Abrantes this volume), and, in spite of attempts by some, the relations between the different peoples of the country have not been 'successfully' instrumentalized to negative ends through a crudely ethnicized narrative

(Kohl, this volume). Moreover, unlike some of their neighbours such as Liberia, Sierra Leone and the Casamance region of Senegal, the country has not slipped into a prolonged civil war or rebellion. Day-to-day life in the country remains peaceful, in contrast to the stereotyped image, and people frequently cooperate and marry across projected 'ethnic divides'. Understanding the way in which the country continues to operate in spite of its trumpeted collapse can therefore inform us in important ways about the potential both for the country and for the state in Africa.

This is how the events in Guinea-Bissau relate so closely to current paradigms of state success and failure in Africa. Although some leading analysts have expressed concern that the narcotics trade will become a new source of violent political competition and upheaval in Africa (Ellis 2012), in terms of political violence these events have had little effect in Guinea-Bissau beyond the political class. The state is thus an 'irrelevance' to ongoing daily security for most people, according to some (Bordonaro 2009). Certainly, on a daily basis it is in many ways a hindrance. As recent research suggests, supposed 'failed states' like Somalia with no state structure can in fact work better than when the 'state' was in operation (Ntephe 2012; Hills 2014). In spite of everything, as Chabal and Daloz would have put it, 'Guinea-Bissau works', and the key question to be answered here is how, why and what this means. For it shows that the problems in Guinea-Bissau are actually related to wider ideas about the crisis of the post-colonial African state in general.

* * *

Patrick Chabal's work on the place of the state in post-colonial African societies has helped to shape some of the key analytical categories regarding the subject. In the month of his death, January 2014, *African Affairs* carried two articles directly related to these ideas, one on neo-patrimonial politics in the ANC (Lodge 2014) and another on how 'Somalia Works' (Hills 2014). The neo-patrimonial paradigm has become a classic way of approaching questions of the state in post-colonial Africa: according to this view, the absence of sufficient state rents and the personalization of power sees political leaders accruing followers through patronage, according to former political paradigms which disrupt the functioning of the state. The fact that, like Somalia, Guinea-Bissau 'works', and yet is a country that to all intents and purposes has had no functioning state for a decade or so, is the subject that Chabal intended to address in his chapter for this book, in the afterword; it is certainly a subject that needs to be addressed here.

Chabal's major statement on the state in Africa, co-authored with Jean-Pascal Daloz, stressed that the 'generalized system of patrimonialism' was one shared in common by African states (*Africa Works*, 1999: xix). In this articulation, power was personalized and dependent on transactional links between the political patron and their clientelistic followers; while the emergence of modern functioning states required the end of patrimonialism and the construction of autonomous institutions, this was something that had not happened in Africa owing to a weak institutionalization following colonialism and independence (ibid.: 1–5). The fact that African state institutions remained personalized meant that they could not acquire neutrality and therefore legitimacy (ibid.: 13). The state in Africa was therefore a pseudo-Western 'façade' that served to mask personalized political relations and the state's role in resource extraction to the benefit of African and European elites (ibid.: 16; see also Rodney 1974).

This highly influential analysis retains many supporters. New research on African legal theory indeed draws directly on Chabal and Daloz, suggesting that the instrumentalization of disorder in African states is facilitated by a theory of the 'rule of law' imported from particularistic European systems into a different context (Ntephe 2012). Other African scholars systematically expand on the analysis of *Africa Works*, noting the role of the state as a system of private enrichment for political elites in many African countries, and the legacy of illegitimacy of authority which this creates (Ogaba Agbese/Klay Kieh Jr 2007). What has occurred is the 'privatization of public prerogatives' (Mbembe 2001: 32), whilst the ongoing relations of subjection introduced by the colonial state were extended (ibid.: 40); and it is worth noting in the Bissau-Guinean context how the conjuncture that has created a relatively low population through historical and geographical factors may itself prompt strong relations founded on patrimonialism.

One of the fundamental poles of analysis with which this view of the post-colonial African state has to engage is that of structural economic inequalities on the global stage. As Mbembe notes, post-colonial states were heavily shaped by long-standing patterns of long-distance trade and the ways in which African societies were integrated into world trade (ibid.: 41). The condition of what various scholars call 'extraversion'—trade between Africa and the outside world founded on unequal resource distribution and exchange (Cooper 1981; Bayart 2000)—had shaped these inequalities, which were in turn exacerbated by the increased control offered by the colonial system. After independence, these inequalities aggravated competition for access to

INTRODUCTION

resources, and thereby personalized the levers of the political system into what Frederick Cooper calls the 'gatekeeper state' (Cooper 2002).

Moreover, there is little evidence that the great new wave of enthusiasm about African economic growth popularized as 'Africa rising' is yet resolving these issues. The percentage of the population classed as rich in Africa did not change between 1980 and 2010, standing at approximately 5%; there has been very little change in income distribution in Africa in the past thirty years, indeed, with only a slight increase of approximately 10% in what is defined as a 'floating class', no longer classed as poor, while 60% of the population still fall into that bracket.[4] Thus recent policies have certainly not succeeded in breaking the poverty trap or the personalization of wealth within a small elite.

There have been demographic as well as economic triggers for this, especially the progressively younger population and the associated 'crisis of youth' or 'youth bulge', and the impact of HIV/AIDS in some parts of the continent. Nevertheless, this persistent paradigm suggests that what has really happened is that there has been an expansion of inequality within African societies in this period: with foreign portfolio flows into African standing at over US$20 billion in three of the five years to 2014,[5] and yet with little difference in income distribution, the inevitable consequence is growing inequality in many African nations, and with this comes a growing crisis in political representation, in Guinea-Bissau as in many other African nations.

This view becomes especially clear when we examine the place of patrimonialism within inequality. The economist Thomas Piketty has recently argued that Western countries are returning to a patrimonial economic system structured around massive inequality that is determined by the aggregated weight of inherited capital (Piketty 2014). This is in view of the continuing widening of the gulf in economic power between the top percentiles and the rest of the population. Such a pattern, of course, increasingly replicates those familiar from Africa where, according to Chabal and Daloz, neo-patrimonialism and the personalization of wealth and power are so acute. What can be suggested here is that their analysis in fact opens the door to thinking globally about the relationship of inequality and the erosion of political legitimacy: as inequality rises in the twenty-first century, there is a growing questioning of the legitimacy of the state not only in Africa but increasingly also in Western democracies, as characterized by lowering voter turnout and the rise in popular support

[4] *Financial Times*, 20 April 2014.
[5] *Financial Times*, 16 May 2014.

of protest parties such as the FN in France, the Freedom Party in the Netherlands, Syriza in Greece, Podemos in Spain, and UKIP in the UK. The structural factor of inequality is increasingly common, and therefore relates fundamentally to the growing problems of representation on a global scale, as many leading economists have noted (Stiglitz 2014).

This analysis illuminates much of what is wrong with the response of the 'international community' to events in Guinea-Bissau over the past fifteen years. After each coup, or associated political crisis, efforts are made by international actors to address the specific crisis and resolve it (Massey, this volume). But the structural issues which provoke the arena of crisis are unresolved, and indeed tend to be exacerbated by the growing inequalities both within Africa and outside it, which Piketty has now highlighted. Therefore, the instability continues. The crisis in Guinea-Bissau hence reflects problems of political authority of states widely seen as illegitimate across Africa; and the perception of illegitimacy itself is no longer an African problem alone, but a global problem of representation in the transnational era of rising inequality, almost unstoppable transnational border flows and the weakness of state responses to these issues.

Added to this problem in the current analytical approach to Guinea-Bissau is a second central issue, relating to the relationship between the state and the monopoly of violence. There is a large literature relating the rise of centralizing states in Europe, from 1500 onwards, to the military revolution and the monopoly of violence (Reinhard 1996; Glete 2002; Tilly 2000). In West Africa, too, the rise of centralizing states in the eighteenth century was historically related to the growth of standing armies and the legitimate power over violence in Asante, Dahomey and Fuuta Djallon. In order to exercise legitimate representative authority, a state has to be seen to have a legitimate monopoly of violence, and this has been one of the main problems for postcolonial African states which were, precisely, inheritors of an illegitimate colonial state (Ogaba Agbese/Klay Kieh Jr 2007: 9–10). A paradigmatic example of the sort of problem to result is in the Democratic Republic of the Congo, where state-building's management and monopoly of violence, as exercised through mineral extraction and economic and military coercion, has led to a crisis of legitimacy and resistance to the state emerging as a key feature of the state-building process itself (Iñiguez de Heredia 2013: 111–12). The consequence has been one of the deadliest wars of the past generation.

For Guinea-Bissau, the importance of this perspective emerges starkly in the comparative sub-regional context of the recent past. Zoe Marks has shown how far the devastating civil war in Sierra Leone emerged because of the crisis of legitimacy of the post-colonial state under Siaka Stevens (Marks 2013: 89, 100): it was the rottenness of the state and its loss of all legitimate authority to monopolize violence under Stevens which allowed the RUF's leader, Foday Sankoh, to mobilize his first supporters and draw in support from neighbouring Liberia. Thus the examples of Sierra Leone and the Democratic Republic of Congo both show that it is precisely in the resistance to the idea of the state as a legitimate monopolist of violence that many conflicts have emerged, especially when connected to the generational conflict and the crisis of youth in those arenas.

Yet this has not happened in Guinea-Bissau, for key historical and contextual reasons. The army—held up by many international observers to be the main destabilizing factor in the country—is proportionately larger than most of its neighbours, and has more legitimate authority as the inheritor of the army that won the independence war under the leadership of Amílcar Cabral.[6] It was built by Cabral, from the ground up, and was overwhelmingly composed during the independence war of young Balantas, who thereby reproduced the traditional resistance of the Balanta to outside forces (Forrest, this volume). After independence, most of the country's leaders were figures who had held significant positions within the independence war, such as Nino Vieira and Malam Bacai Sanhá. The army, therefore, is a source of legitimate authority and power in the context of a country where a successful independence war was fought against a violent and illegitimate colonial power.

This notably differentiates the country from Angola, for example, where there was more than one major rebel movement during the independence war, leading to a different post-colonial outcome. On this analysis the army, far from being a cause of instability in Guinea-Bissau, has through its size and inherited historical legitimacy been one of the key factors that has prevented the country descending into a bloody civil conflict. Certainly, during all the coups of the past fifteen years, wherever these have taken place, the army has been backed at every step by local politicians. Therefore, the army alone is not the cause of instability; though there are many problems with the army's use of power (Forrest, this volume), this needs to be borne in mind. Understanding the key structural relationship between states and the monopoly of

---

[6] Kohl's chapter in this volume, fn. 3: '[t]he ratio of troops to population between 1999 and 2004 was 10 times the ECOWAS average ratio of the region'. (United Nations Office on Drugs and Crime 2007: 14).

violence therefore reveals the fallacy of many external perspectives on the country: stabilizing Guinea-Bissau may mean working with the army, and helping to legitimate its authority, rather than identifying it as a proximate cause of instability.

It is therefore of central importance to understand the situation in Guinea-Bissau in both local and comparative perspectives. Civil–military relations may need to be reformed for the sake of stability (Embaló 2012), but this does not mean that the army is the root cause of the problems in the country. While in many cases of state collapse rebel groups have to deploy arbitrary and performative acts of violence to consolidate their monopoly of violence (Marks 2013: 140), this has not happened in Guinea-Bissau largely because of the strength and legitimacy of the army in the national narrative.

* * *

If the state is to 'work' in Guinea-Bissau, we have to have some idea of who it is to work *for*. What, then, would a successful state look like in Guinea-Bissau? This was the key question which Chabal intended to address in his chapter in this book, and a few general comments are therefore in order.

In the first place, it is important to identify elements which may *not* be necessary conditions for stability in the country. The place of the drugs trade is central to this analysis. It is likely that it has been a key factor in some of the violent transitions of power of the past few years (Kohl and Massey, this volume). As Ellis has suggested, competition for access to the rents of the drugs trade is a key driver of political competition, and, therefore, of the instability of Guinea-Bissau (Ellis 2012). Nevertheless, the role played by the drugs trade in the country is more complicated than generally acknowledged, as a few considerations show.

One of the striking features of contemporary Guinea-Bissau is the absence of large-scale NGO programmes in the country (Cravo 2012), although there are many smaller Bissau-Guinean run initiatives. This is something that interested Chabal, for in some of his earlier work he had noted how it was precisely access to NGO 'rents' which revealed the adaptability of African actors in gaining access to resources (Chabal/Daloz 1999: 22–5). However, the presence of the local NGOs alone does not guarantee development (Cravo 2012); and, as Chabal and Daloz note, if there is a reduction in viable means to sustain neo-patrimonial networks through the larger programmes, the linkage of a country's politics to 'increased disorder, either war or crime' becomes marked (Chabal/Daloz 1999: 162).

This prescient analysis places the current situation of Guinea-Bissau in a new context. As Shaw has recently noted, the 'drying-up' of external flows of cash in the 1990s meant that 'the Bissau elite were open to approaches that would bring new money' (Shaw 2015: 346; see also Ellis/Shaw 2015: 16). Given the condition of the state in Africa, war or illegal trades were the most likely outcomes following the programmes of structural adjustment which reduced the rents open to governing elites. There is no question, of course, that the drugs trade can contribute deeply to violence, as the case of the links between drug-trafficking and instability in Mali (Kwesi Aning/Pokoo 2013; Ellis/Shaw 2015: 16–7) and indeed Mexico show. Nevertheless, the case of Guinea-Bissau is somewhat different, and participation by some of the country's elite in the drugs trade was certainly a preferable option to the civil wars which engulfed neighbouring countries such as Sierra Leone and Liberia. It is not, therefore, that the drugs trade is itself a destabilizing factor, but that growing inequality itself created destabilization within the neo-patrimonial paradigm, with a rise in trades such as the drugs trade a likely consequent outcome. As the chapter by Ceesay in this volume shows, drugs trading does not cause failed states but is a symptom of them. In this light, the emergence of Guinea-Bissau as a 'narco-state' is no surprise at all: it was one of the few options available to the country in the 2000s.

Dismantling the drug networks alone will not therefore lead to a stable and successful state in Guinea-Bissau. Nor, as the chapters by Green and Kohl in this volume make clear, will focusing on growing ethnic divides in the country as a cause of war. This partial 'ethnicization' of politics is a symptom of the neo-patrimonial nature of the political system, and the competition for access to rents. It has historical links to the colonial war and the aftermath, with divisions between ethnic Cape Verdeans and 'authochtonous' Bissau-Guineans plausibly related both in the assassination of Cabral and Nino Vieira's coup of 1980 (Green and Kohl, this volume). As analyses from other parts of Africa make clear, however, the focus on ethnicity as a divisive factor often leads to ethnicity being presented as a catch-all for the many other issues related to inequality (see for instance the Burundian case, as analysed by Russell 2013: 20).

Rather than focusing on the issues which are not necessarily helpful in their own right, it is worth concluding by making some concrete suggestions. In the first place, there has been some notable work directed at reconciliation conferences in the country in the past few years. This is a laudable starting point, recognizing the failure of the state as a representative force and the divisions which have emerged in consequence. Such a process, built from within the country, might lead to the process of nation-building from the ground up identified as important by some (Kohnert 2010). Crucial to this programme is not only the content of reconciliation agreements, but also the process itself; in peace processes, it is the experience of the process itself as much as the content which can shape the possibility of a final agreement (Schomerus 2013). Hence, it is vital that all parties be able to contribute to the formulation of the process as well as the content of any agreement.

Further, not only must such a process of reconciliation be built from the nation upwards, but it must also bring in actors from the sub-region. As Hassoum Ceesay's chapter in this volume demonstrates, the failure by national and international actors to bear the sub-regional context in mind is a serious strategic error; moreover the rise of the drugs trade in Guinea-Bissau does appear to have contributed to the instability in Mali which led to the 2012 crisis there (Ellis/Shaw 2015: 16–7). Culturally and historically, Guinea-Bissau shares many links with neighbouring Guinea-Conakry and Casamance in Senegal, with The Gambia, and (to a somewhat lesser extent) with Mali and northern Senegal. Indeed, as Christoph Kohl's chapter makes clear, the initial coup that triggered the civil war in 1998–9 was triggered by disputes over cross-border arms-smuggling to the rebels in the Casamance, while the porous border is linked by some to the current drugs routes linking the country with Europe. Bringing regional actors into the search for both peace and development is a fundamental prerequisite for a lasting reconciliation process; moreover, such a regional cooperation could be part of the first step in the intellectual re-imagination of the post-colonial nation, reaching back to the ideals of pan-African unity so much in vogue when Amílcar Cabral first led the development of nationalism and national unity in the country.

This national and sub-regional process can be the only starting point for the rebuilding of the state from the ground up in Guinea-Bissau. It chimes with the calls which some analysts have made for a renewal of a popular constitutional base as a starting point (Ogaba Agbese/Klay Kieh Jr 2007: 27). This could build the legitimacy of the state as a governing institution. Rather than stripping the state away further, this would recognize instead the role of the state in economic stability, furthering both formal employment and the starting of private businesses; in the case of Mozambique, many private traders first develop capital through state employment (Brooks 2012). If after all the state is deemed not to be 'working', it is because its resources are not equitably shared, and this needs to be addressed so that more people can benefit from its establishment, which will enhance legitimacy.

Moreover, it is only a legitimate state that can drive forward some of the key policies that will help to address many of Guinea-Bissau's problems. Agricultural self-sufficiency is a basic starting point: though Guinea-Bissau has historically been a rice producer, and even a rice exporter (Hawthorne 2003), much of the payment for the cashew export crop on which small producers now depend is instead bartered for rice imports (Temudo/Abrantes this volume). This reduces the possibility for economic consolidation and stability, given that it is through the use of surplus profits from agricultural production that cycles of economic growth have often started (Green 2012: 109). In a nearby country, The Gambia, government-led initiatives have dramatically enhanced rice production, and thus this can be achieved through the establishment of a state with legitimate authority, and the development of this key policy. However, such a move would require significant recalibration of policies surrounding land use and economic productivity, and therefore requires strong work at local, national and sub-regional levels to build consensus (Temudo/Abrantes this volume).

Such steps may seem comparatively small in themselves. But the deeper structural problems and Africa's historical relationship to global patterns, which underpin many of the deepest problems in the country, cannot be addressed without them. Peace and a full stomach are prerequisites for the larger project, as identified by Mbembe, of the creation of intellectual surplus value to drive forward the transformation of the continent (Mbembe 2010: 28). There is an urgent need dramatically to reform Guinea-Bissau's educational infrastructure, given the growing lack of trained people within the country, and the consequent lack of preparation among even teachers at work there (Nafafé, this volume). The coup of 2012 (Kohl, this volume) meant the lack of payment for teachers throughout 2013 (World Bank 2014); increasingly, schools in the villages are 'private', built by the parents, who then pay the teacher, and although this changed in the aftermath of the 2014 elections and teachers were paid by the state, the most recent 2015 crises may lead to further problems in these areas. Meanwhile, the country's very few higher education institutions are chronically underfunded and access to study materials is negligible. Yet without the broader project of re-imagining intellectually what the nation of Guinea-Bissau should be, long-term stability will be hard to achieve. This requires institutional foundations in which such work can be done, which should be prioritized.

Here we can hear a strong echo of Cabral, who held decisively that no change could be brought about without a guiding ideological framework

(Chabal 1983: 68). This view rejects decisively the call of purely humanitarian responses to an absence of peace, and the reality of hunger, since as Mbembe notes such responses address immediate need at the price of the wider historical process that underpins these problems (Mbembe 2010: 29). Moreover, the development of this institutional intellectual framework should not ignore the sub-regional context, as suggested above: a sub-regional cooperative effort could play a key role in providing greater regional integration, stability and the sort of 'intellectual surplus value' prized by Mbembe.

The creation of autonomous African solutions is thus a longer-term prerequisite to the continent's future, and indeed to the global security which underpins the interest of international actors in the crisis of Guinea-Bissau: as Mbembe notes, without addressing these problems, 'our world's ... security will more than ever be seriously mortgaged' (ibid.: 29). Fundamentally, it is inequality, hunger and lack of opportunity that drive political instability in the country (Massey, this volume) and migrations to the West (Nafafé, this volume), and that creates fertile ground for the nexuses of the drug trade and jihadist movements that have already destabilized Mali in recent years. Resolving these problems requires enormous political and intellectual efforts; but in resolving them, Guinea-Bissau can yet move from the label of 'narco-state' to the sort of state that Cabral envisioned during the long years of the independence war from Portugal which gave rise to the nation.

PART ONE

HISTORICAL FRAGILITIES

1

DIMENSIONS OF HISTORICAL ETHNICITY IN THE GUINEA-BISSAU REGION

Toby Green

All colonialisms in Africa created and reinforced divisions by essentializing ethnic categories and then assiduously promoting their divisions.[1] The best-known example of Rwanda masked the truth that this was a general strategy of European colonial powers in Africa (Jefremovas 1997; Gourevitch 1999). As elsewhere, this makes historical dimensions of ethnicity in the Guinea-Bissau region of vital importance in understanding the current political crises in the country. This is not only because ethnic conflict and political disorder are strongly linked in many analyses of post-colonial Africa, since the colonial state and its inheritors systematically exacerbated difference and conflict between ethnicities (Mamdani 1997). It is also because many of the tensions

[1] I am very grateful for the support of research grants from the British Library (EAP 536) and the Leverhulme Trust (West Africans and Atlantic Empires: 1589–1700), under which some of the interviews and research used here were conducted. My thanks to Joshua Forrest, Philip Havik and Christoph Kohl, who all read drafts of this chapter and provided very helpful critiques; and to Patrick Chabal, who helped to delineate the main research questions to be addressed.

in the country today are continuities of distinct phases of ethnicization which go back to the sixteenth century and before.

A wide body of literature indeed recognizes that the very idea of ethnicity was itself largely constructed by nineteenth- and twentieth-century anthropologists, though strongly influenced by African colonial subjects and their disruptive interventions in categories and problems devised by the colonial states (Amselle 1998: 22–6; Banks 1996: 158, 190; and on the development of 'ethnicities' in the Guinea-Bissau region, see Brooks 1993: 28; more broadly, see also Amselle/M'bokolo 1999; Chabal/Daloz 1999; Ranger 1993). In Guinea-Bissau this process was enacted systematically in the twentieth century, since the Portuguese colonial state required its administrators to produce ethnographic reports of their circumscriptions in order to achieve professional advancement (Heywood 2000: 95; Carvalho 2002: 95–6). Thus, writers such as António Carreira and Avelino Teixiera da Mota produced important texts on the ethnographic composition of the colony, and the social structures and historical backgrounds of peoples such as the Bijagó, Fulas, Mandinga and Manjako. These texts remain important starting points for understanding both ethnicity in Guinea-Bissau, and the ways in which ethnicity has historically been constructed in the country (Carreira 1947, 1961, 1964; Teixeira da Mota 1954, 1970). However, as Chabal and Daloz saw, it is not the case that affiliations did not exist prior to the colonial periods, but rather that they were reconstructed in the colonial period 'according to the vagaries of the interaction between colonial rule and African accommodation' (Chabal/Daloz 1999: 57): thus while ethnicity has been constructed by outsiders in conjunction with autochthonous responses, this does not preclude continuities between the present and distant pre-colonial times.

This chapter discusses how ethnicity in the Guinea-Bissau region has tended to be constructed by outsiders as a mechanism to understand, categorize and attempt to exert economic control over the peoples who live there (see also, on Angola, Heywood 2000: 3). Drawing on the names of lineages and on patterns of settlement, ethnic categories offer the sort of hard categorial ease which stands in opposition to what Jean-Loup Amselle described as 'mestizo logics', more fluid and malleable social norms through which identities have historically been constructed in the region (Amselle 1998; see also Farias 1985: 28). The ethnic categories which have resulted have the appearance of being hard, but Bissau-Guineans experience them often as soft. Exogamous marriages and alliances are frequent, and indeed, as this chapter shows, the sort of intra-ethnic alliances analysed so expertly by Joshua

B. Forrest for Guinea-Bissau have been a major feature of social relations in the region (Forrest 2003). Nevertheless, as this chapter also shows, it is in the manipulation of apparently hard ethnicized characteristics, constructed through the global influence exerted by outsiders, that many political tensions are to be found; such tensions tend to be found most in institutions which hold an authority buttressed by external forces, whereas in more informal settings they are less prevalent.

This chapter explores these relationships and their influences in the country today. We begin in the pre-colonial era, with evidence for the pluralism of Bissau-Guinean identities in the sixteenth and seventeenth centuries. In this period identity in the region depended on the intersection of attachments to lineage and kinship, to broad political structures, to class and to land (Bennett 2003: 6). Linguistic and so-called 'ethnic' categories were fluid, and people of the same 'ethnicity' spoke different languages. Indeed, many of these categories were externally constructed by outside proto-imperial groups—Mandinga and Portuguese—for reasons of their own political and economic advantage. Although many of the Portuguese observers were influenced by African identifications according to kinship and territory, and thus developed ethnic categories in dialogue with Bissau-Guinean actors, over time the influences of the Americas came to bear (Horta 2013). Here harder ethnic categories were in play, and the pan-Atlantic influences of the Americas in Africa shaped the constructions of ethnic identity and categories which Portuguese colonists developed with regard to the peoples living in the region (Green 2011). The construction of ethnicity attempted to create divisions, but even so this was for a long period a largely unsuccessful project, and in the depths of resistance to the programmes of Portuguese 'pacification' in the early twentieth century cross-ethnic alliances were the norm (Forrest 2003).

With the rise of Portuguese colonialism in the twentieth century, however, the success of outsiders at disrupting lineage-based identities and alliances became greater. European colonialism shaped new land-based borders which created divisions between 'Portuguese' Guinea and 'French' Casamance (Senegal), where hitherto this region had been politically and culturally connected. Such borders soon subverted traditional ideas of lineage and land authority. Ties of belonging and ethnic identification became increasingly linked to border-crossing of externally-shaped boundaries, and diaspora and displacement began to characterize aspects of ethnic identity. Many Bissau-Guineans migrated north to the Casamance region and to The Gambia, while displacement from the Cape Verde islands to Guinea-Bissau accentuated the way in which ethnic affiliations in Guinea-Bissau began to be shaped by displacement and diaspora as much as by the pre-existing importance which lineage and land had once held. At the same time, the alliance which the Portuguese imperialists formed with certain ethnic groups—especially the Fulas and the Mandinga to the east of the country, and the Cape Verdean administrators of the colony—created intra-ethnic tensions which endured after the end of formal colonialism in 1973–4.[2]

This historical dimension is fundamental to understanding much of the political history of Guinea-Bissau since independence, since it has strongly influenced both Nino Vieira's coup in 1980, and on some accounts the role of the Balanta in the armed forces in the 1990s and 2000s (for more detail on this coup, see chapters by Ceesay and Kohl, this volume; Chabal 2009: 5–6 on ethnicity as a cornerstone of political analysis in contemporary Africa). Ethnicity in contemporary Guinea-Bissau is thus shaped partly by historical dimensions of relations to outsiders, and partly by the ways in which Bissau-Guineans experienced and articulated these relationships through shared interests such as class and the experience of post-colonial urbanism in the era of structural adjustment and state frailty. As a once-externalized form of identity which co-exists with other forms of identity, ethnicity is easily manipulated in the formal political sphere buttressed by externalized forms of political authority; however, in informal and local-level relations, it coexists with other important markers of identity and belonging.

* * *

The Guinea-Bissau region's place in the global system began to formalize in the thirteenth and fourteenth centuries through connections to the trans-Saharan trade (Brooks 1993; Green 2012). During that time Mandinga peoples allied to the Mali empire—located in present-day Guinea-Conakry and Mali—emerged as traders linking the region to the trans-Saharan trade for gold and slaves, which connected Africa to the Maghreb and the Mediterranean. The Mandinga settled in the eastern part of Guinea-Bissau, in the Kaabu region, where their establishment required both military force and alliance-building with local lineages.[3] Already, the trans-Saharan trade was conceiving

---

[2] The PAIGC declared independence at Boe on 24 September 1973, and this was recognized by a 93:7 vote in the United Nations General Assembly in November; however, Portugal only formally granted independence on 10 September 1974, following the April 1974 Carnation Revolution.

[3] Innes (1976: 77–9) has a revealing story of the naming of a child born of such alli-

the structure of extraversion, through which alliances of African and outsider elites would export African surpluses to the benefit of the world economy beyond Africa (Bayart 2000; Rodney 1972). This extraversionary structure encouraged the categorization of peoples, as categorization facilitated the manipulative strategies of hegemonic power linked to world economic growth. Hence already in the 1450s, by the time that Portuguese trade began, Mandinga traders connected to Mali and the trans-Saharan trade had developed ethnic categorizations for the peoples who lived in the Guinea-Bissau region. Almost 600 years later, many of these categories still form the principal ethnic designators for the country.

As the Jesuit Manoel Alvares wrote in the early seventeenth century, it was the Mandinga with whom the Portuguese were most friendly in the region.[4] Hence, when the Portuguese arrived in the Guinea-Bissau region, they almost at once began to use the ethnic designators of the Mandingas.[5] It was, indeed, not a little useful to them that such categorial structures already existed, since this facilitated their own extraversionary game connected to the trans-Atlantic slave trade. These ethnic categories were thus externalized projections borrowed by the Portuguese from the Mandinga, who were the intermediaries between the Portuguese and other coastal peoples (Teixeira da Mota 1954: vol. 1, 144–5; Hair 1966: 14–15). Many of the ethnic categories had Mandinga origins, including 'Bainunk'—'he who must be hunted'—and 'Balanta'—'he who resists'. (On 'Balanta', see Havik 2004: 95; Hawthorne 2003: 32; Roche 1976: 47. On Bainunk, see Roche 1976: 22.) But these ethnic categories were certainly seen as inaccurate by Bissau-Guineans themselves and often ignored differences between some of the peoples to whom they were uniformly attributed: both Bainunk and Kassanké, for instance, claimed that the Portuguese used the names indiscriminately for several distinct peoples (Teixeira da Mota 1954: vol. 1, 144–5; Rodney 1970: 8).

---

ances, revealing the combination of force and compromise required. See also National Centre for Arts and Culture (The Gambia) [hereafter NCAC], Research and Documentation Division at Fajara [hereafter RDD], Tape 550A, transcription pp. 58–9, where the informant S. Manneh says that before the Europeans came 'there was only war. The Soninké [Kaabunké] (pagans) feed on that.'

[4] Sociedade de Geografia, Lisbon, Manuscript of *Etiópia Menor: Descripção Geographica da Provincia da Serra Leoa* (Manuel Alvarez), folio 10v.

[5] Horta (2013) notes that this view is less tenable for the Senegambian region north of the Gambia river, but certainly in Guinea-Bissau, as this chapter shows, this was the case.

Affiliations of identity in the Guinea-Bissau region in this early time were thus based primarily on lineage, not hard ethnic boundaries. This explains the fluidity of identity at the time. The lack of hard ethnic boundaries allowed for the regular patterns of intermarriage and exchange, as confirmed by the oral sources. Further south from Guinea-Bissau, once the Mane invasions of the Sape kingdoms of Sierra Leone had ended by the late sixteenth century, cultural exchange was so regularized that seventeenth-century sources described the peoples of the Magarabomba river region of Sierra Leone as 'Sapes Manes' (Biblioteca da Ajuda [hereafter BA], Lisbon, Codice 54–XIII–94, fol. 1v—from 1686). Such patterns were also common between the Bainunk and the Floup in the Casamance.[6] Although, as Robert Baum has shown us, the late seventeenth century was a period of conflict between Floup and Bainunk communities, there was also much continuity (Baum 1999). According to the seventeenth-century Jesuit Alonso de Sandoval, some Bainunk peoples could not understand each other, whereas some Bainunk and Floup could understand one another's language (Sandoval 1627: fols. 38v, 61r). Yet language, as oral sources reveal, was a key aspect of how identity was formed, with Bamba Suso in 1966 describing Bainunk as 'Mandingas who speak their own language'—that is, retained their distinct identity through their own language (NCAC, RDD, Tape 020, transcription p. 9). Given the importance of language to questions of identity and community, therefore, the fact that some Bainunk and Floup could understand one another's language in the seventeenth century is sufficient evidence of just how far ethnic categories employed for the region were external projections, and cannot serve as a model for understanding the building of structures of political authority in the precolonial era (building on Anderson 1991).

Yet if affiliation was based primarily on lineage and language in the precolonial Guinea-Bissau region, other forms of belonging also mattered. As Herman Bennett notes, these included for larger groups adherence to some quasi-state structures (Bennett 2003: 6; Horta 2013: 664–5). The Mandinga of Kaabu exerted a form of hegemony over the peoples of Casamance and northern Guinea-Bissau, with chroniclers talking of the Beafada of the Rio Grande, the Bainunk and Kassanké of Casamance, and the Brames as professing allegiance to the Mandinga by the end of the fifteenth century. José Lingna

---

[6] The Floup peoples are thought by some analysts to belong to the same ethno-linguistic group as those known as Jola today; in this book the ethnym 'Floup' is preferred.

Nafafé and Rachel O'Toole have talked of the Guinea-Bissau region as being something like a 'multicultural' kingdom of the late fifteenth and early sixteenth centuries, and this may not be too far wide of the mark (Nafafé 2007: 75; O'Toole 2007: 26). Meanwhile, as O'Toole has shown, birthplace was an important signifier of belonging and was often the first indication chosen by enslaved Africans identifying themselves to their interrogators on arriving in the New World (O'Toole 2007: 24–5).

Hence although outside observers perceived ethno-linguistic continuity in the Guinea-Bissau region stretching from the sixteenth to the twentieth centuries, this really reflected a continuity of ethnic categories, not of peoples (Hair 1967). Moreover, such apparent continuity masked an important process of fragmentation and change that was often influenced by the long-distance Atlantic trade. The best example of this comes when looking at changes to the 'Brame' group in the northern coastal regions of Cacheu and on Bissau island. The Brames constituted one group at the time of the Portuguese arrival in the sixteenth century, and yet by the time of the onset of colonialism in the late nineteenth century it had fragmented into Mankanhe, Manjako and Pepel. This was a process already apparent in the seventeenth century, when documents describing Pepel peoples begin to appear (BA, Códice 54-XIII-15, no. 94[a]; Anguiano 1957: vol. 2, 116).

It is significant that the process of disaggregation from the Brame category into Mankanhe, Manjako and Pepel reveals the coexistence of both the lineage structures and the importance of external factors in shaping ethnic categories into the nineteenth century. The pluralism of the lineage structure emerges in Mankanhe stories of their origins, which prioritize the alliance of lineages. Thus, one story ascribes mixed Fulas and Mandinga origins to their founding lineage, formed by one Fulas, Brahima (whither the ethnonym Brame), and Mbula, a Mandinga princess; another, meanwhile, describes how a Mankanhe king captured a Balanta slave in warfare, fell in love with her and married her, and that it was from her that many of the Mankanhe descended (Fonseca 1997). These formative stories are significant in providing a context for oral traditions. Regardless of the accuracy of the specific case, what they show clearly is the importance of exogamy and inter-lineage alliance in the construction of identities and ethnic categories in Guinea-Bissau (cf. Forrest 2003). Moreover, these stories show how these processes took place after the onset of the Atlantic slave trade—that is in the period leading up to the nineteenth century. The marriage of the Mankanhe king to a Balanta slave places the story at some point in the seventeenth or eighteenth century, since, as Walter Rodney showed, domestic slavery of this type was not a feature of societies in Guinea-Bissau prior to the Portuguese arrival (Rodney 1966; see also Green 2011).

Thus the emergence of Mankanhe and Pepel ethnic categories can both be placed to some point in the seventeenth or eighteenth centuries. By the nineteenth century, the Manjako had emerged as a separate group who were linked closely to Atlantic trade. Writing in 1849, the French official Bertrand Bocandé noted how the Manjakos all traded with the Portuguese, and worked as shiphands (*grumetes*) in all the small boats plying the river (Bocandé 1849: 340). Bocandé describes the ethnic designator as emerging from the repeated use of the phrase 'I tell you' (*je vous dis*)—'Manjako'—which is suggestive of commercial negotiations or discussion (ibid.). By this time they were known as great travellers, and many of them had visited England or France according to Bocandé, although they preferred their homeland (ibid.). Thus like the Kriston, who also worked as traders in the Guinea-Bissau region and were closely connected to the Atlantic trade networks, the Manjako emerged in a similar fashion according to the way in which they engaged with outside actors (on the Kriston see Havik 2004; Kohl 2009: 2).

It should be noted that this construction of a Manjako ethnicity was very much the work of outsiders. As Clara Carvalho notes, many Manjako speak dialects of a language unintelligible to each other, and have different political and lineage structures (Carvalho 2002: 96–7). Some anthropologists see the original analysis of the Manjako by António Carreira as flawed and constructing a supervenient ethnic category where there was local divergence, and ignoring in particular the place of religion (Gable 1995). Thus in many ways theirs was an ethnic category shaped through the economic priorities of extraversion; that the construction coexists with other forms of identification is shown through the ongoing importance of lineage and land—*utchak*—to Manjako identity, and the enduring importance of relations to kin ancestors in Manjako villages and communities (Gable 1996).

One can conclude that perceived ethnic continuities in the Guinea-Bissau region between the sixteenth and nineteenth centuries mask very important processes of change. The idea of ethnicity, though constructed interactively with Bissau-Guinean interlocutors, was deployed by Mandinga and Portuguese outsiders as a convenience of trade and the warfare necessary for the slave trade, and also because by the nineteenth century this fitted with the scientific ideologies of racism and human categorization exemplified in the rising discipline of anthropology. Changing patterns of trade therefore had shaped some aspects of the ethnic categories which emerged during these three centuries, especially in coastal areas of the Guinea-Bissau region. Thus the growth of extraversion associated with the Atlantic trade was deeply connected to the construction of ethnic categories. These categories continued in this pre-colonial phase to coexist with other forms of allegiance according to lineage, land, religious belief and political structure, and in these structures lay the pluralism which origin stories such as those of the Mankanhe relate. But the pluralism of mestizo logics was always in tension with hard imperial catego-ries, and the rise of formal colonialism in the nineteenth century would shape significant new directions for such ethnic categories in Guinea-Bissau.

* * *

As numerous scholars have shown, Portuguese 'pacification' of Guinea-Bissau in the early twentieth century was achieved with extraordinary violence (Bigman 1993: 52–3; Forrest 1992: 17; Forrest 2003: 85–117; Pélissier 1989). This violence took the form both of punitive expeditions led by João Teixeira Pinto and his lieutenant Abdul Njai—called 'unbridled state terror' by some analysts—and the intensification of strategies of economic extraction through the groundnut economy and the imposition of hut taxes (Forrest 2003: 106). Initially, as Joshua Forrest has shown, the Portuguese attempt to exert formal political control over the territory of Guinea-Bissau led to inter-ethnic alliances against the new imperialism (ibid.). However, once Portuguese imperialism had been formally established by 1920, policies directed towards Guinea-Bissau helped to establish certain divisions which are of great impor-tance in understanding some of the tensions in the country today. Funda-mental cleavages emerged linked to ethnicity and religion as a direct result of Portuguese colonial policies, the anti-colonial war and the consequences which followed after independence. In many ways, the tensions stoked in these decades can be linked to current events.

The legacy of the violence of pacification and its consequences is still con-tested today. Descendants of Abdul Njai and his lieutenants view this ancestry as offering a noble warrior past;[7] meanwhile, griot narratives offer a similar perspective on Abdul Njai as a triumphal new power in the region, resisted by local villages but ultimately forging marriage and personal alliances. These views of the past have to compete with the reality that the violence of the wars of pacification and its consequences were experienced in different ways by the different peoples of the country. Marina Temudo's research has shown that the

---

[7] Interview with Mamadou Njai, Banjul, 7 November 2013.

Balanta were seen as especially oppressed under the colonial regime, with one Nalú interviewee describing how the 'Balanta were those who suffered most with slaps and lashing ... the *cipaios* [administrative 'policemen', mainly from non-Balanta groups] beat them and slept with their wives, something they never did with the Muslims' (Temudo 2009: 53). Thus, it may well be that differential experiences of colonial violence leave a legacy of differential responses to the post-colonial inheritor of the colonial state.

Such evidence immediately adds context both to the colonial war and to the post-colonial era. As Temudo notes, Amílcar Cabral was especially struck by the Balanta adherence to the anti-colonial struggle, being the first people of Guinea-Bissau really to put themselves wholly behind the armed struggle in the 1960s (ibid.: 52). He attributed this, as Patrick Chabal wrote, to the decentralization of Balanta political structures, which explained their early support for the war where the support of other groups for the independence war, such as the Mandinga and Manjako, was initially quite weak (Chabal 1983: 74–6). Chabal argued also that the socio-political structures of the Balanta, and in particular the age-grade system, facilitated the rise of young guerrilla cadres and their training by the PAIGC for war (ibid.; on age-grades, see especially Hawthorne 2003). However, Temudo's evidence also offers a new explanation, that the experience of Portuguese imperialism was especially severe among the Balanta, who were therefore particularly willing to join the colonial war when it emerged. In consequence the Balanta developed a reputation as warlike, rekindling this view of them which stretched back to their resistance to the pre-colonial Kaabu empire, and this is something which may illuminate current discussions of the 'Balanta-ization' of the army (see chapters by Ceesay and Kohl, this volume). Seen in a deeper historical context, this may be the continuity of a long process, which relates to how different peoples in Guinea-Bissau experienced both colonialism and the independence war; and it may also tell us something about how the experience of ethnic groups in Guinea-Bissau is perceived by others in the country, which is also important.

The Nalú informant cited by Temudo above also contextualizes a fundamental aspect of the cleavages provoked by colonialism, which lay in the relationship between the Portuguese and the Fulas of the Kaabu region. This was a relationship which went back to the late nineteenth century, and the alliance between Portuguese forces in Bissau and some Fula leaders such as Cherno Cali (Bigman 1993: 51). The Portuguese favoured the Fulas, since they had already a highly stratified society, with a slave-owning aristocracy, at the time of Portuguese colonial conquest in the late nineteenth and early twentieth centuries.[8] The Fula theocracy of Fuuta Djallon (in what is now Guinea-Conakry) had risen in the eighteenth century, and had allied strongly with European slave traders, with victims of the Fula *jihads* in the region often sold to European slave traders in the ports of Guinea-Bissau, Guinea-Conakry and Sierra Leone.[9]

Hence, at the onset of Portuguese colonialism, for two centuries Portuguese and Fulas had already been allied to the detriment of many of the other peoples of Guinea-Bissau, and this was a relationship which continued in the colonial era. As Peter Mendy has shown, while the political structures of the peoples of the coastal regions were dismantled, with Beafada, Bijagó, Manjako and Pepel seeing their chiefs substituted by place-men, this was not the case among the Fulas and Mandinga to the east: here, leaders acted more as regents and continued to exert economic and political power (Mendy 1994: 322; on the Manjako chiefs as 'preferential middlemen of colonial intervention', see Carvalho 2002: 107–8). The racialist perception of ethnicity by outsiders was significant here, for the Fulas were stratified socially, and some of them were lighter-skinned, which created a situation of favourable treatment by the Portuguese owing to the pervasive racialist ideologies which were in vogue in the first half of the twentieth century in Portugal (Henriques 2012). Such was the hold of the colonial regime over African leaders that a study by Manuel Braga Dias carried out between 1969 and 1971 found that in thirty-two of the sixty regions where there was a nominated African political leader, the local population did not accept their authority (Carvalho 2003: 9–10).

The impact of these ideologies in shaping divisions among the peoples of Guinea-Bissau is nowhere clearer, however, than in the role of Cape Verdean migrants in the colonial administration. From the sixteenth to the eighteenth centuries, the Cape Verde islands had always given the Portuguese their strongest colonial outpost in the region, and this was to have important consequences. Owing to a strong education system dating to the late nineteenth century, Cape Verdeans had better educational opportunities than those available in Guinea-Bissau (Keese 2007: 497). The majority of them worked for

---

[8] Chabal (1983: 18) notes the importance of this stratification. As an example of stratification of Fula society, see NCAC, RDD, Tape 466B, transcription p. 5, interview with Al Hadji Ibrahima Cissé in Bafatá in 1977: 'A free Fula would never marry a Fula slave.'

[9] See e.g. ibid., transcription pp. 16–17: 'He said what was the cause of the friendship/between the White/Men and the Fulas/so that the Fulas/and the white men/united and fought against other tribes,/Bijohos, Papeloos.'

29

the colonial administration in the Bissau area, and many of them remained loyal to the Portuguese administration even during the anti-colonial war (Keese 2012: 131). Portuguese reliance on Cape Verdeans was due to a number of complex factors, but the impact of racialist ideas and the lighter skin colour of many Cape Verdeans should not be discounted.

Portugal's racist ideological framework during the colonial era therefore influenced both the Cape Verdeans presence in the country and the response of Bissau-Guineans to it. As a result, during the 1960s, many were suspicious of the fact that the PAIGC leadership was dominated by Cape Verdeans such as Cabral. The PAIGC turned to an armed movement following the Pidjiguiti dock massacre in 1959 (see Timeline), and the overwhelming bulk of the initial leaders were Bissau-Guineans of Cape Verdean origin. These tensions were crucial to the late colonial and post-colonial turns of events in the country.

Thus by the time that the anti-colonial war began in the early 1960s, the decades of Portuguese colonialism had served to harden ethnic and racial categories. Where before, as we have seen, these were in many ways outside projections which had little impact on a country where exogamy and inter-ethnic alliances were common, by the 1960s tensions based on ethnicity were rising. The Cape Verdean origin of the PAIGC leadership was a source of suspicion for many, and initial alternatives to the PAIGC as an independence movement, such as François Mendy's Movimento de Libertação da Guiné (MLG), were based as 'Guinean' alternatives to the Cape Verdeans: indeed, according to Mustafah Dhada, Cabral's opponents thought that the PAIGC was a 'vehicle for Cabral to liberate the Cape Verde islands without firing a shot' (Dhada 1993: 8). Indeed, the assassination of Cabral in Conakry in January 1973 was certainly related to resentment of the Cape Verdean leadership of the PAIGC, of whom of course Cabral was the most prominent figure (ibid.: 34, 46; Chabal 1983: 134–5). Such tensions continued into the immediate post-colonial era and, though other factors were also important, were key causes of the coup against Luís Cabral in 1980 and Nino Vieira's rise to power thereafter.

It is important to note that this growing tension between Bissau-Guineans and Cape Verdeans was a new phenomenon directly connected to the experience of colonialism. From the time of the first settlement of the Cape Verde islands in the mid-fifteenth century, there had been deep-seated connections linking the islands and the coast, and much criss-crossing of peoples between the two (Green 2012: 5). Economic activity in the Cape Verde islands and on the mainland in Casamance and Guinea-Bissau was interdependent, with a mixed trade in salt, kola, cloth, dye and slaves linking the islands and the coast (ibid.). Most of the 'Portuguese' traders in Casamance and Guinea-Bissau were in fact Cape Verdeans, like André Alvares d'Almada, and the presence of these traders led to the rise of mixed communities. There were tensions at points between these communities and other Bissau-Guineans, but by and large the two integrated and shared a trading language in Kriol.

Thus, in this context, it can be seen that a major impact of the colonial era was to harden ethnic categories and tensions which previously had been softer. Allied to this in conceptualizing the place of ethnicity in twenty-first-century Guinea-Bissau, moreover, must be the impact of the colonial war in terms of displacement and the formation of diasporic ethnic communities in the sub-region. While rice production remained a mainstay of many communities until the 1960s, production collapsed during the 1960s and 1970s, as Chabal noted (Chabal 1983: 23–4). In places such as Bula, heartland of the Mankanhe community, this was directly related to migration which followed the onset of the war, as many people moved over the border to Casamance in Senegal.[10] Many Mankanhe families in Bula today have relatives in Casamance, and the spread of the community was mirrored further south, where many Balanta migrated across the border to Guinea-Conakry (Temudo 2009: 53–4). This was indeed a commonality to the anti-colonial wars across Lusophone Africa, where many BaKongo in northern Angola moved to Zaire, many Ovimbundu in southern Angola to Zambia, and many Mozambicans relocated to Tanzania (on the BaKongo case, see Keese 2012; on the Ovimbundu, Heywood 2000: 78).

Displacement and diaspora therefore became a key part of ethnic identities in Guinea-Bissau during the era of the anti-colonial wars. Indeed, this process had begun long before, when owing to the extreme physical and institutional violence of the Portuguese system of colonialism, many people had already taken to migrating north to Casamance and The Gambia in the 1920s and 1930s (Forrest 2003: 137–8). The Gambia's sizeable Manjako community today dates from this period, when many people simply walked north out of Guinea-Bissau to find a less harsh environment.[11] It was especially Manjako men who migrated, and they married into Floup communities who were already sizeable in The Gambia; indeed, the growing importance of Floup and Manjako communities in The Gambia is testament to the alliances between them which began to be formed over a hundred years ago in

[10] Interview with Antonio da Silva Mango, Bula, Guinea-Bissau, April 2011.
[11] Interview with Martin Gomez, Banjul, 7 November 2013.

response to the rise of colonialism (NCAC, RDD, Cassette 434C, transcription p. 26: interview with John Mendy).

Migration was not a novelty in the region, and it had formed a major part of life for many centuries. However, the rise of the nation state and state influence over land tenure would change its context radically. Where there had always been cultural, commercial and social connections between the peoples of Guinea-Bissau, Casamance and The Gambia, the fact that migration in the area came to involve border-crossing changed the nature of ethnic identities in relation to the nation state. As with the hard ethnic categories themselves, which as we have seen were often externalized projections developed for the purposes of economic control by outsiders, these borders also had—famously—been developed by outsiders, in this case the European colonialisms. They were borders which took no account of existing connections, and the fact that ethnic groups now straddled them would make it far easier for those with grievances to seek assistance outside the boundaries of the 'nation state'. This has been a major cause of destabilization in the region: in time the rebels in Casamance would often hide in the bush in northern Guinea-Bissau during the 1980s and 1990s, just like the communities in Casamance who had often supported the anti-colonial guerrillas in the 1960s and 1970s.[12] Here the importance of colonial border-crossing, and the shared historical context in both Casamance and Guinea-Bissau of the interaction with Cape Verdeans and the rise of the shared Kriol language, are fundamental to understanding the cleavage which the nation state created across these connections.

Thus by the time that Guinea-Bissau achieved independence, there were several key conjunctures relating to ethnicity and ethnic identification that had been set in place. The favouritism of Cape Verdeans and Fula groups had created divisions between the peoples of the coast and those of the east, as well as with the leaders of the PAIGC. Ethnic identities had hardened as a result of a combination of these policies and the growing economic control exerted by the global economic system in the heyday of European imperialism, which favoured division according to hard categories as a mechanism for the extraction of resources. Yet these ethnic categories crossed borders both north and south, and this would facilitate ongoing divisions and supply of weapons and support to peoples of different ethnic groups in Guinea-Bissau during the post-colonial era.

* * *

[12] Oral interviews with Ibrahima Cardozo in Goudomp, Casamance, March 2000.

As the political philosopher John Gray notes, the rise of democracy in a post-autocratic system often coincides with separatism and cleavages (Gray 2014). Where minorities fear that their rights and share of resources may be damaged by larger groups who will have a greater say through the majoritarian voting structures of a democratic system, conflict and separatist movements often emerge. Though Gray's analysis focuses more on post-Soviet Europe, it is also highly pertinent to thinking about the shape of events in Guinea-Bissau since the end of the colonial era. In sum, since 1974, ethnicity has become a strategy of mobilization in order to cement a share of resources, and different ethnicities have mobilized in different ways in order to achieve this. Whereas in the east of the country Islamic Fula and Mandinga peoples have received assistance from the wider Muslim world in the construction of *madrassahs* and some social services, in the northern coastal regions the Manjako have depended on large-scale emigration in order to retain their social power, while the Balanta have asserted their rights through their predominance in the armed forces.[13]

It is a mistake to view these strategies as indicators of 'age-old' ethnic and religious divisions. Are such different strategies really symptomatic of ethnic conflict, or are they rather evidence of the importance of taking a historical view of the construction of ethnic categories and their strategies of mobilization for a share of resources? In each case, as this chapter has shown, the strategies of the Balanta, Fula and Manjako represent continuities from past conjunctures rather than a radical break, and show the extent to which ethnic categories, while constructed in a dialogue with external priorities, are internalized. Historically constructed understandings of both ethnicity, and the ways in which different groups in Guinea-Bissau have interacted with the global system for many centuries, offer an important added context to the ways in which these strategies and conflicts should be seen, and how important they may have become in the present conjuncture.

In the Manjako case, migration has long been a feature of their interaction with extraversionary economic forces. Bocandé's text from 1849 reveals that even at that time many Manjako were accustomed to travel to Europe in an attempt to better their lot, while the Manjako were the most important migrant group who moved to southern Guinea-Bissau in the second half of the nineteenth century to work the new groundnut plantations (Bowman

---

[13] By the early 2000s, for instance, there were said to be 360 people from the small Manjako island of Jeta in Europe: interviews, Jeta, March 2000.

1987: 96); indeed, as Eric Gable notes, Manjako emigrant communities are in some cases 150 years old (Gable 1996: 107). For the Fula, meanwhile, as we have seen also, the role of Islam as a strategy for mobilization and consolidation was very important, and can be traced back to the seventeenth century. Their ancestors came to eastern Guinea-Bissau from the Islamic theocracy of the Fuuta Djallon in neighbouring Guinea-Conakry; and moreover, as Boubacar Barry suggests, many of the founders of Fuuta Djallon were themselves Islamic scholars who migrated south from the borders of the Senegal and Mauritania after the religious wars of the 1670s (Barry 1985: 136). In the Balanta case, the question of the 'Balanta-ization' of the army remains controversial (Kohl 2012a: 644), and in many ways ignores the fact that Balanta soldiers formed the overwhelming core of the army in the anti-colonial war. Yet such analyses may not entirely be a product of an externalized view of identity. In this case, as we saw, during the pre-colonial and the colonial eras the Balanta developed a reputation for militarism and resistance, something which—as we have seen—goes right back to their originary Mandinga naming as 'he who resists'. Viewed historically, therefore, this analysis takes on a different light. Rather than a new projection, the place of the Balanta in the army, and the army's recent role in destabilizing the state, can be seen as a continuity with the Balanta's long-term role in challenging external structures linked to economic extraversion, and also of the perception which others have of them as occupying this role. Chabal and Daloz's analysis of the post-colonial state as a vacuous institution designed to mask resource extraction for the benefit of African and European elites remains highly pertinent here (Chabal/ Daloz 1999): if the post-colonial state in Guinea-Bissau has thus far been little more than a mask or a shadow, or even, as Lorenzo Bordonaro suggests, an irrelevance, the Balanta role in destabilizing it can be seen as part of a long historical tradition of their challenging external structures of economic power and political authority (Bordonaro 1999).

Certainly, continuity can be found in many of the ways in which Balanta leaders have sought to obtain power within the post-colonial framework. During the 1980s, they were on the receiving end of severe political repression at the hands of Nino Vieira, who feared that they could mobilize most effectively to challenge his power (Callewaert 2000). This was first countered by Kumba Yalá, who sought continuity with Cabral's strategy in his mobilization to win the presidential elections of 2000. Like Cabral, Yalá became known as the man who walked his way to power, moving from village to village to introduce himself to the people and persuade them to entrust him with their vote

(Chabal 1983: 68).[14] After Yalá was deposed in 2003, the increasing separation between heads of state and Balanta sections of the army, led by figures such as Tagme Na' Waie, can be seen as long-standing strategies of the Balanta to mobilize against externalised forms of authority, in this case the post-colonial state. While certainly many other groups within Guinea-Bissau had long practised resistance against the colonial and pre-colonial political systems, the role of organized warfare in Balanta resistance historically can be suggested as being linked to its current role in the army.

Such considerations emphasize the importance of adopting a historical perspective when considering questions of ethnicity in post-colonial Guinea-Bissau. Given the discussion above, it should therefore be no surprise that the ethnic character of post-colonial conflicts in Guinea-Bissau is most apparent precisely in relation to power structures whose authority is derived from external sources. Where they are so often constructed by outsiders, and in relation to priorities of economic extraversion, ethnic cleavages are indeed most likely to emerge in struggles over political authority granted by external political structures. This is indeed precisely the case in contemporary Guinea-Bissau, where the 'shell' of the post-colonial state is only granted autonomy through the intervention of the world powers in the form of ECOWAS, the EU and the UN. Thus it is here that conflict has the appearance of being ethnicized, for it is precisely these bodies who are the institutional inheritors of the forces that assisted in the construction of ethnicized identities in the first place. Yet ethnicity itself is merely a manifestation of shared interest groups mobilizing to gain a share of resources within the confines of a post-colonial nation state whose structures and premises are not founded in African political systems and legitimacies.

It is important to note, therefore, that such conflicts are still far from being the norm in the country. Many villages are multi-ethnic in character and are often distinguished by inter-ethnic collaboration over various issues related to agriculture, trade and inter-ethnic kinship ties. Recent research by Brandon Lundy provides the example of cooperation between Nalú and Balanta peoples over a range of issues (Lundy 2013). Such arrangements are also common in Bula, to the north of Bissau, long the heart of the Mankanhe community, where there is a large community of Fulas both from within the country and

---

[14] On Yalá, personal communication from David Stephen, former representative of the United Nations in Guinea-Bissau, and from Carmen Neto, Chairperson of the Guinea-Bissau British Trust.

from Guinea-Conakry, and also important communities of Manjako and Balanta peoples. In short, outside the formal state structures, the inter-ethnic collaboration which has long been a feature of Guinea-Bissau's social and political framework, working across lineages and lands, remains very much in place. Where the post-colonial state is supported, however, conflicts grounded in ethnicity seem more apparent.

When we look at political analyses of disorder and corruption in post-colonial Africa, it seems that they can often be channelled to ethnic normativity. However, experiences on the ground make it clear that this can be too reductive, and fails to take account of the complexities and pluralisms in which African identities are grounded. When, in February 2000, I visited the home village of Kumba Yalá just a few days after he had been elected as head of state of Guinea-Bissau, I was told by people from the nearby town of Bula that it would be worth my returning several years later to see how the village had changed, and how Yalá had taken advantage of his position to bring prosperity to his family and neighbours. Such a view did not emphasize Yalá's Balanta status, but rather his ties of home and kin, which related far more to the importance of land and lineage in historical identities in Guinea-Bissau than to a reductive ethnicity.

In point of fact, when I did go back to the same village eleven years later, little had changed. Yalá's grasp on power had not lasted long, and the Balanta mobilization for resources had taken a different tack, based far more on historical resistance to the predatory state than on the interests of their 'ethnicity'. The peoples of Guinea-Bissau were among the fiercest in resisting European colonialism in Africa, both during the early twentieth century and in the anti-colonial war. It is this historical continuity of resistance that is best represented in the ongoing crisis of the neo-colonial state, rather than anything as simple as the continuity of 'ethnic' conflict in a country where people's identities have never been reducible to ethnicity alone. Daily lives beyond the weak nation state emphasize intra-ethnic cooperation following local signifiers of identity and meaning, and it is these which can offer hope for the future; projects of categorizing 'ethnic' customs and judicial procedures, financed by outsiders (see chapter by Kohl, this volume), are by contrast only likely to exacerbate processes of division and the ongoing crisis of the state.

2

GUINEA-BISSAU'S COLONIAL AND
POST-COLONIAL POLITICAL INSTITUTIONS

Joshua B. Forrest

Introduction

Guinea-Bissau today has degenerated into what can be termed a failed state, riven by repeated army *coups d'état* and army rule, while serving as a global transit point for the narcotics trade (see chapter by Kohl, this volume). Government infrastructure is essentially dysfunctional and incapable of lifting the nation out of dire poverty. In this chapter, I suggest that state fragility in Guinea-Bissau is historically rooted in the character of the colonial state and the way in which the immediate post-colonial state emerged. Today's political instability, the poor performance of governmental organizations and the turn towards illicit international trade do not reflect any sort of cultural determinism or intrinsic national character, but rather the historical implantation of instrumentalist political values, as well as a strong tradition of popular defiance of centralized authority that harks back to the pre-colonial period.

Contemporary reliance on intra-state factional jostling and militarized rulership reflect political characteristics and behaviours that evolved out of force-based colonial politics; as a consequence, a colonial and immediate post-colonial government infrastructure emerged that was organizationally weak and lacked politically constructive, popularly legitimate or inclusive links to rural and peripheral areas. Despite the inter-ethnic cooperation and peaceful social interaction that marks Bissau-Guinean civil society, these problematic politico-historical legacies have significantly influenced the evolution of elite-level behaviour in the contemporary period—most notably reflected in the 'instrumentalization of disorder' (a concept introduced by Chabal and Daloz 1999 and further discussed below) among military and government leaders, along with a dysfunctional intra-state organizational structure.

Colonial state bureaucracy and civil service

In many respects, colonial Portuguese Guinea reflected a model of governance typical—in its broad formal outline—of colonial administration in other Portuguese colonies, such as Angola and Mozambique. The colonial bureaucracy was conceived as an intrinsic part of the metropole (indeed, as integrated into the Lisbon-based Ministry of Overseas Colonies); the civil service was appointed by Lisbon officials with professional service in mind, dedicated to rendering the colony fiscally self-reliant and prosperous for Portuguese companies and settlers. To do so, the civil service was tasked with the development of infrastructure such as road-building for the purpose of extracting agricultural resources for export and for collecting taxes to support the colonial state bureaucracy (Pélissier 1989; Forrest 2003).

However, the reality 'on the ground' in Portuguese Guinea would reflect a particular social and historical dynamic between the colonial state and the indigenous society intended for exploitation. While conforming to a number of generic aspects of colonial state formation in Portuguese colonial Africa—local officials appointed directly by Lisbon, a direct formal management style (like the French, rather than British-style indirect rule), and reliance on forced labour in the early colonial decades (1920s–30s)—the Guinean state would also reflect particular fragilities and idiosyncracies reflective of its unique political position and its distinctive human geography. These include the fact that Guinea was technically run as a bureaucratic appendage of Cape Verde; as such, priority was generally given to assuring that the most qualified officials were assigned to Cape Verde, and Guinea's bureaucracy was often staffed with less well-trained officials than in the other lusophone colonies (Carreira 1984: 118–23). Also, an extensive land confiscation programme never took place in colonial Guinea in contrast to Angola, for example, where Portuguese colonial settlers confiscated land and established large-scale cash crop farms. In Angola, such settlements were marked by strong ties between these lusophone settlers and their respective state bureaucracies; by contrast, without extensive inland farm settlements by Portuguese colonialists (apart from a number of riverine trader-farms, the *pontas*), the colonial state in Guinea was not rooted in extensive ties with European settler-farmers.

Officials from Lisbon did the best they could under their short-handed circumstances, but lacking adequate administrative resources or training they often turned to arbitrary, informal arrangements, especially in the rural regions of colonial Guinea where Portuguese (and sometimes Cape Verdean) officials were essentially given free rein over the local populace. As a matter of official policy (especially in the early period), the colonial state relied on forced labour to assure the completion of public projects by African labourers. But control over local agronomic production was at best incomplete compared to other Portuguese colonies, or compared to neighbouring Senegal; observers suspected that Portuguese administrators in Guinea inflated crop export figures (Forrest 2003: 170–1). Some travellers remarked that state bureaucrats seemed consumed with assuring their own personal well-being rather than focusing on bureaucratic office work, tax collection or completing infrastructural projects. In short, Guinea-Bissau eventually inherited a civil bureaucracy best described as a weak or fragile state in regard to basic administrative competence and public policy capacity, or lack thereof (Forrest 2003: 176–7).

As a result, colonial Guinea's bureaucratic infrastructure, which has been described as 'antiquated and cumbersome', even in relation to other Portuguese colonies such as Angola and Mozambique, did not succeed in constructing many public projects outside the capital city of Bissau, and failed to provide social goods (as had been done in other African colonies) such as education and health care to the majority of the populace (Chabal 2002c: 43). Moreover, the colony was among the most economically underdeveloped in colonial Africa, characterized by 'socioeconomic and infrastructural backwardness' and dominated by a state administration that had not created a foundation for political, social or economic development in the post-colonial period (Chabal 2002c: 49).

Post-colonial state bureaucracy

In the initial post-colonial years (1970s), the state bureaucracy of newly independent Guinea-Bissau had inherited much of the structure and some of the personnel that had staffed colonial-era ministerial offices (apart from the Portuguese officials who had been at the higher echelons of the ministries). Although PAIGC officials with only revolutionary war experience had been appointed to supervise most of those offices, those officials quickly became bogged down in bureaucratic competition over resources and personal power grievances (Lopes 1982: 83). As their commitment to the 'bigger picture' of national development goals dissipated, and bureaucratic staff members perceived their own professional survival to depend on strengthening informal networks and surviving informal power scuffles, the bureaucracy became divided into a number of different factions based on loyalty to a particular individual and on increasing the power of a narrow band of social networks (Lopes 1982: 75–6). In some cases these factions reflected adherence to a specific spiritual sect; indeed, there were officials who were known to refuse to carry out their official duties at times, or switched their political loyalties, based on fear of retribution by a spiritual force and others who seemed ready to mobilize for a certain political activity based on a particular spiritual affiliation (Mendes 2011: 254). In a broad sense, the overall institutional impact of the growing predominance of factional and sectional networks was to continue the 'weak state' institutional practices that had marked the colonial era, albeit more dramatically divided and increasingly dysfunctional.

Moreover, by the 1980s–90s corrupt practices—such as illegal export sales of stores of rice by administrators—began to percolate with ever-greater frequency and then became common practice by the 2000s (Forrest 2010: 184, 188). Subversion of the law was also contravened by the sale of marijuana across the Senegalese border, a practice which expanded in the 1990s. Also in that decade, some members of the Bissau-Guinean armed forces were suspected of illegally selling weapons to a separatist group in Senegal's Casamance region (personal sources; see also chapter by Kohl, this volume). Subsequently, in the 2000s–2010s, according to international agencies, some government officials came to be suspected of increasing involvement with trading international narcotics, especially cocaine (Hoffman 2014; see also chapter by Kohl, this volume), to the point that international observers now commonly refer to Guinea-Bissau as a 'narco-state' (Tovrov 2014; O'Regan 2012; Vulliamy 2008). Yet while this often seemed to such observers to be a radical and dangerous new departure, in many ways it represented only the culmination of a long-standing, many decades-long flouting of the existing legal framework in favour of independent economic operations outside the purview of standard civil service procedure, from the colonial era through the early post-colonial period and into the present day.

All the while, the international development community (the World Bank, USAID, UNESCO and other UN organizations, etc.) continued to deliver substantial tranches of development aid to help shore up failing administrative structures and government-provided social programmes. Such development tranches included, for example, a $2.5 million World Bank provision in 2003 to help pay teachers' salaries; a special fund of $18 million set up by the United Nations Development Programme (UNDP) in that same year to cover civil servant salaries and to improve financial management in government offices; $13 million provided by the World Bank in 2004 to enable Guinea-Bissau's national bank to remain solvent; $5.9 million from the European Union in 2005 to help pay Guinea-Bissau's civil servant salaries; and $309 million in World Bank disbursements in that same year for a broad variety of Bissau-Guinean programmes in public administration, energy, health, mining and other sectors (Forrest 2010: 194–5). International aid agencies, especially the United Nations Peace-Building Support Office in Guinea-Bissau (UNOGBIS) but also the EU, Portugal, France, the African Union and the World Bank sought to improve managerial practices within the administrative structures of the state and to forestall intra-state political conflict through the holding of multiple conferences, training sessions and meetings with the country's civil servants in the mid-2000s, focusing on the rule of law, human rights, improving administrative efficiency and reducing bureaucratic malfeasance (Forrest 2010: 180, 185, 192–3; see also 'Special Report of the Secretary-General on the Situation in Guinea-Bissau', United Nations Security Council, 2012).

Throughout this period, there was a growing fear in the donor community that Guinea-Bissau was on the precipice of complete state collapse; but, given the relative day-to-day civility of the general populace and the upbeat attitudes and optimism of many of the country's civil servants, there was also a sense that greater and more targeted attention by the global development community regarding administrative management and state-run social programmes, while encouraging political negotiation, could forestall such a collapse. In hindsight, it is indeed likely that many civil servants are committed to good management practices and the rule of law within their respective state units, but it also appears evident that some key players at the highest levels of state power, and crucially within the armed forces, did not share such a commitment. As a result, these external efforts had little effect on coup prevention, overall state capacity or fiscal probity (although UN agency personnel in Bissau suspected that they at least helped to prevent total government paralysis or civil anarchy) (personal sources, 2007). While at an individual level many Bissau-Guinean state servants shared a commitment to appropriate fiscal and organizational management, important power-holders embraced a much more narrowly framed set of priorities. Ultimately, the colonial state legacy of personalized, arbitrary, self-serving political behaviour became ingrained in the post-colonial state's *modus operandi* and continues negatively to impact on the country's development potential and overall state capacity.

Political culture, the state and the armed forces

The inheritance of a problematic elite-level political culture and of fragile political institutions from the colonial era opened the political door to challenges from within the established state structures themselves. Indeed, the 'rules of the game' had shifted towards a 'winner take all' attitude, while certain leading individuals within the ruling political party (the PAIGC), the state government offices and the armed forces seemed to be motivated at least in part by a sense of entitlement for having suffered through the colonial era and/ or for having made sacrifices during the war of independence. The revolutionary unity that had been forged during the liberation struggle of the 1960s–70s had dissipated by the 1980s, particularly after the *coup d'état* of 1980 but also in the face of prolonged social and economic suffering by the general populace which seemed unrelieved by a variety of policy shifts (Forrest 2003: 200, 228). All of this precipitated a rise in political factionalism, increasing skepticism towards reliance on electoral mechanisms for political change, and a growing sense among certain elites that a *coup d'état* is a theoretically distasteful but not necessarily illegitimate means of securing political power.

The single greatest challenge to political stability arose from within the armed forces. This took two forms. (1) Nearly constant political tension between the armed forces chief of staff (de facto ruling commander of the entire armed forces of Guinea-Bissau) and the president of Guinea-Bissau (regardless of which individual happened to occupy those two high-powered posts); suspicion of the mobilization of a cabal by the chief of staff in order to plot a coup against the president pervaded the political regimes of Guinea-Bissau's post-independent presidents. (2) Factionalism flared up within the armed forces, mostly reflecting shifting personal and ethnic alliances and competition for access to state-based ministerial resources (Forrest 2002: 251).

There is yet another aspect of political culture that significantly affected post-colonial Guinea-Bissau's political trajectory. This is the social impact of the revolutionary armed forces of the PAIGC having defeated a European colonial power in dozens of battles (during the 1960s and early 1970s), winning control of as much as 70 per cent of the territory of the country and leaving the people of Guinea-Bissau with the (not inaccurate) impression of having essentially forced the Portuguese army out of the country. Here, it is important to recall that during the eleven-year revolutionary struggle, the PAIGC won control of ever-larger segments of Guinean territory, both by augmenting the size of rebel fighting units after first convincing local villagers of the worthiness of the revolutionary cause, and by relying on ever-more-effective battle techniques (guerrilla tactics, ambushes, concentrated attacks on isolated Portuguese army posts) against the better-armed (and NATO-supplied) Portuguese colonial forces (Chaliand 1969; Rudebeck 1974; Chabal 1983). It was this growing military success which gave Bissau-Guineans confidence that they had the ability to confront and challenge unjust state power. When Portugal's own government was overthrown in a military coup in April 1974, and the newly elected leaders in Lisbon decided to withdraw colonial troops from Guinea-Bissau (and from its other African holdings) and to end direct colonial rule, this was interpreted by the majority of the Bissau-Guinean populace as resulting directly from their increasing battlefield successes against the colonial state.

This left Bissau-Guineans in general, and members of the armed forces in particular (including the next generation of leading officers), with a psychological legacy of activism, of personal competency and of confidence vis-à-vis perceived-to-be illegitimate state rulers, and with a historical legacy of successful armed intervention in national politics (Forrest 2010: 182). The contemporarily relevant value that became entrenched was a healthy skepticism of formal political institutions, and lack of hesitancy to rely on force of arms if this was perceived to be warranted (Forrest 2002: 250–51). These are not rules-based values, but rather reflect a manifestation of what Patrick Chabal and Jean-Pascal Daloz have termed 'the political instrumentalization of disorder' (Chabal and Daloz 1999). In the case of Guinea-Bissau, there are political actors—such as state bureaucrats, middle-and lower-level civil servants, educators and elected parliamentarians, many of whom were educated abroad—who are in fact fully committed to the law, to constitutional rule-following, and to the predominance of the legislature in policy-making. So the polity is not *entirely* characterized by the political instrumentalization of intra-state power. But this latter value came to be adopted by many army officials and a segment of state ministers and other high-level government officials, as well as some political party leaders sharing a questionable allegiance to standard civil service procedures and a greater allegiance to particularistic factional networks that circumvent or ignore the formal mandates of state organizations.

Those who hold such instrumental values appear to believe that in certain circumstances it is acceptable and even necessary to circumvent 'the system' and seize power by force. Here we may suggest that such values, while to an important extent deriving from the experience of the anti-colonial revolutionary war, may also, at least in part, derive from the arbitrary and too-often (very) violent use of state power during the colonial period by state officials. Indeed, the colonial state itself was created and established on the heels of a prolonged campaign of mass killings in the countryside in order to subdue the general populace in the 1890s to late 1910s (Pélissier 1989: 235–83; Bowman 1997: 131–67). Once established, state authority-related violence (which included forced labour) was wielded with sufficient frequency and arbitrariness (Forrest 2003: 105–41) to help craft an institutional legacy that may have legitimized the seemingly gratuitous and self-serving use of violence to obtain or consolidate power within the state.

In contemporary Guinea-Bissau, that institutional legacy may have helped to provide the structural context within which political competition would unfold. It now seems evident that many of those who managed to obtain the highest reaches of political power (most notably, the presidency) either have done so by using violence or, once in power, have ruled in part through the use of force against real or imagined opponents. The problem is that once political actors who are committed to only (or predominantly) instrumental values predominate over those committed to formal institutions, and government and armed forces officials do not feel impelled to follow institutional rules, then, in effect, the floodgates open and all manner of political activity becomes possible. This is a matter of a historically constructed political culture; without an overarching commitment to a universal legal culture and a deep-seated respect for peaceful political change, the path to violent change becomes ever more tempting. Each coup effort (and especially those that succeed) appears to further legitimize, reinforce and entrench the culture of instrumentalization, wherein direct action is acceptable as a mechanism of political change to assure the betterment of one's own army unit or political faction.

While many bureaucrats and politicians entering government in the optimistic post-revolutionary years of the 1970s–80s may have shared the late Amílcar Cabral's ideological commitment to national progress, social class, self-sacrifice and revolutionary consciousness (Galli and Jones 1989: 108), this ideological commitment swiftly dissipated and was replaced by reliance on the wielding of political power 'outside the box' of the democratic playbook. The institutional legacy of the violent colonial state combined with the legacy of the anti-colonial struggle to implant political values into the body politic that emphasized instrumentalism over constitutionalism. Having given up on—or never having become committed to in the first place—any particular ideological belief-system or nationalistic fervour, politicians, bureaucrats and soldiers increasingly interpreted 'the people' to refer to their own narrowly defined elite faction, or if not part of a particular faction joined one on the sole basis of personal opportunism.

Pre-colonial political values may also form a part of the values-based landscape in analysing post-colonial politics in Guinea-Bissau. For centuries, decentralized societies—the Balanta, Bijagó, Floup, Manjako, Pepel and others—flourished alongside the lengthy rivers of the country, trading peacefully with one another and frequently intermarrying. At times, those decentralized societies were confronted by centralizing powers such as the Kaabu kingdom, and established a tradition of crafting inter-ethnic coalitions to fight off efforts to subjugate these riverine peoples. The success of these coalitions helped to embed in the body politic a tradition of civil society cooperation, but also a sense of the political legitimation of anti-state violence in the face of an autocratic centralized rulership (Forrest 2003: 30, 96; Lopes 1999: 52–77, 201–17; Bowman 1997). Later, in the 1920–60 period of 'settled' colonial rulership in Portuguese Guinea, this attitude of rejecting illegitimate centralized authority would be reflected through localized rebellions in one region after another; refusal to work on colonial projects; flight out of the colony; refusal to pay taxes or to engage in state-mandated labour projects; and by systematically transporting (by foot through the forest) much of the country's harvested produce (its key source of wealth) out of sight of colonial tax collectors. Through such passive and active resistance, colonial rule would lack orderliness and economic growth, much less political legitimacy; indeed, the colony struggled repeatedly to gain enough receipts from import/export trading to remain solvent (Mendy 1994; Forrest 2003: 142–77).

This persistent rural defiance culminated in the aforementioned eleven-year-long anti-colonial war of resistance (1962–73), which built on the long-term tradition of inter-ethnic cooperation in the face of a shared external threat and that unified the peoples of Guinea-Bissau behind the rebel efforts of the African Party for the Independence of Guinea and Cape Verde (PAIGC). Despite the unity that marked the ordinary people participating in the anti-colonial struggle, some rebel guerrilla commanders were inclined towards spontaneous rebel fighting, and they notoriously ignored orders given by PAIGC commanders (Galli and Jones 1987: 58–9). Despite this independent behaviour on the part of some army commanders, the anti-colonial resistance movement was characterized by overall cooperation and unity. The PAIGC-led war of resistance ultimately proved successful, as Portugal abandoned its effort to keep control of Guinea in 1973; the pro-independence fighters assumed national power shortly thereafter (Forrest 2003: 182–202).

This history and political culture helped to shape the post-independence period, which has been marked by independent-acting army factions that confronted and challenged ruling autocratic presidents. Beginning in 1980, then again in 1998–9 and on multiple occasions throughout the first decade of the 2000s, army units led by ambitious military officers attacked the presidency and sought to overthrow a sitting regime, often enjoying dramatic success (see chapter by Kohl, this volume). Fortunately civil society actors have reflected the lengthy tradition of inter-ethnic cooperation, mutual support and intermarriage, creating a wide gulf between the relative peacefulness of ordinary Guineans in villages and on city streets as opposed to the periodic episodes of violence on the part of intra-state political factions and elite actors.

Thus, looking chronologically backwards, Guinea-Bissau's culture of skepticism towards centralized political authority may be said to hark back, at least in part, to the pre-colonial and colonial past, and to the experience of successfully challenging state power on the battlefield during the war for independence. Such legacies cast long shadows over the centre of political life in the contemporary period and culminate in the afore described political instrumentalization of intra-state factional competition and elite-level political disorder, while cooperation and peaceful interaction in civil society reflect a similarly long-standing historical tradition.

The presidency

In contrast to the state bureaucracy, the office of the president was an entirely new creation without a distinct colonial legacy. As Guinea-Bissau became an independent nation state in the mid-1970s, the presidency of Guinea-Bissau was more closely connected to the ruling political party, the PAIGC, than reflective of an institutional link to the erstwhile governor of colonial Guinea. That governor's office was created by, appointed by and beholden to the Portuguese colonial authorities (initially in Praia, Cape Verde, and later in

Lisbon); all the holders of that office had emerged out of the Portugal-based military officer corps or elite civil service training institutions. In contrast, the post-colonial presidency of Guinea-Bissau was an institution that was essentially created by the incoming PAIGC. It had been anticipated that this office would be held by long-time PAIGC secretary-general and founding member Amílcar Cabral. When he was assassinated in 1973, only months before the PAIGC's accession to national power, the presidency was accorded to Amílcar's half-brother, Luís Cabral: a loyal, stalwart PAIGC apparatchik but lacking the charismatic persuasiveness, speech-making prowess and towering intellectual capacity of his fallen half-brother.

The newness of the office of the presidency, without an historical legacy; its attachment to the ruling party, the PAIGC, rather than to the state itself; and the fact that Luís Cabral essentially came into the presidency because he was chosen by the party elite to replace Amílcar—all these factors imbued the office of the president with a relatively weak political base. The presidency lacked the strong institutional structure of the colonial governorship, and Luís could not claim a personal history of grassroots-level mobilization activities with the general populace. Therefore, the presidency in immediate post-colonial Guinea-Bissau more or less 'floated' above the state and the armed forces. This latter point is important, because Luís had not crafted a close rapport with the soldiers and commanders who had spent so much time in the trenches of guerrilla fighting, who had successfully fought the Portuguese and enjoyed deep popular legitimacy. Moreover, Luís Cabral did not have the type of personal temperament or political skills to weave together a socially deep and highly networked authority system (à la Nkrumah, Kenyatta, Touré or Nyerere) which could build upon the relative unity of internal politics forged during the liberation struggle.

Instead, President Cabral turned to a strategy of repression towards internal dissenters and intensified his links with top PAIGC officials, but not with the base of party supporters in urban and rural society (Galli and Jones 1987: 73, 94). Internal political divisions began to emerge by the late 1970s: between army commanders with close ties to rural partisans who felt excluded from political power circles and urban-based political elites connected to the president; between government officials with easy access to storages of rice [rice is the national staple food] and those lacking such access; between those allies of the president who had been appointed to a high-level bureaucratic office and long-time party activists who received no direct political advantage; between Cape Verdeans and Guineans. By 1980, these tensions rose to the political surface in the form of a military coup which ousted Luís Cabral as president and installed a leading military commander, Bernardo 'Nino' Vieira, as the new president (Galli and Jones 1999: 92–9).

Vieira entered office with a high degree of popular legitimacy (despite his violent seizure of power), having repeatedly proved his military mettle as field commander during the anti-colonial war against the Portuguese, and because the overthrow of the regime of former President Cabral was largely applauded in Bissau and the countryside. However, Vieira's popularity would soon diminish as he reshaped the presidency from a weak institution (in the late 1970s) into a powerful office (in the 1980s–90s) from which he would rule with increasing reliance on the threat of force, political intimidation and arbitrary, dictatorial decision-making. This is despite the fact that Vieira succeeded in civilizing his office, establishing a multi-party political system (as of 1991), overseeing multi-party nationwide elections (1994) and attaining international approbation for embracing structural adjustment reforms and for appearing to build a foundation for economic development (see below).

During his nineteen years in office, from the perspective of many Western observers and development agencies, Vieira appeared to 'right' the ship of state (or at least begin to do so), by initiating policy reforms to professionalize the bureaucracy, privatize the economy and democratize the political system. The holding of competitive presidential and parliamentary elections and the opening up of the system to a broad range of political parties enabled President Vieira to become ingratiated into the global family of pro-democracy national leaders and promoters. The fact that he barely survived the 1994 election, winning only 52 per cent of the popular vote, rather than making him appear politically weak in fact lent legitimacy to his rule in the eyes of international observers (along with the fact that this election was in broad measure verified as free and fair by global observers) (Forrest 2010: 255; Forrest 2002: 253).

Despite all these political reforms, some of the changes proved relatively cosmetic and obfuscated President Vieira's growing unpopularity, as electoral competitors succeeded in carving ever-growing swathes of popular support for themselves (and away from Vieira) with each successive round of presidential campaigns. A democratic facade notwithstanding, few 'good government' reforms went beyond the level of formal proclamations, and elite political behaviour did not conform to what one would expect in a democratic, transparent and inclusive political culture. Moreover, the external pressure to undertake the pro-privatization and democratic reforms may well have played at least a partial role in exacerbating internal political tensions and diminishing the president's standing in the eyes of the general public. Those economic and political reforms also helped to create ever greater ideological distance from the purportedly progressive, quasi-socialist and decidedly pro-African nationalist goals that had helped to consolidate the PAIGC's popularity at independence.

Indeed, by the mid-to-late 1980s, Vieira had begun to retreat into an ever more insulated and isolated political *modus operandi* and was increasingly relying on his secret police and on security agencies that were specifically devoted to the president (rather than under the institutional tutelage of the army or state bureaucracy). The president's security forces were strongly suspected of mistreating, jailing, harassing or executing political opponents or those who advocated greater political openness. Ethnic resentments rose sharply, including, most notably, among the Balanta—the backbone of the military from the war of liberation through to the present—who were now sensing that they had been to some extent shut out of key government leadership positions under Vieira. (The Balanta are the largest single ethnic group in the country, with slightly less than one-third of the populace, and they have intermarried with members of many other groups.) Moreover, Balanta military officers were accused of fomenting a failed military coup attempt in 1985 and were subsequently jailed. Combined with the growing autocratic style of Vieira's presidency and his prolific use of secret police and violence or threats to silence real or imagined enemies, this added to the alienation of the president from much of the general populace. Subsequently, tension rose between President Vieira and the armed forces, as he sought to replace popular generals with those he hoped would remain loyal to him, and the chief of staff and the president became increasingly frustrated with one another.

By the mid-1990s, most soldiers appeared to believe that their own institutional interests were at stake (the organizational integrity of the army itself and the job security of the top commanders) and that the country in general and the political system in particular would benefit from a temporary military intervention and (especially) the removal from office of President Vieira (Forrest 2010: 173; Forrest 2002: 251–2, 254). Ultimately, President Vieira had succeeded in transforming the office of the presidency from a relatively weak institution to an overly powerful, insular, unpopular and violence-prone leadership structure that appeared to lack political legitimacy in the eyes of many (if not most) Bissau-Guineans.

The military's dance with politics

By 1998, army–presidential tensions had reached a tipping point and a *coup d'état* was underway; President Vieira reacted by asking for (and receiving) support from approximately 4,000 Senegalese sharp-shooters who came to Bissau to back up Vieira's security personnel. This led to a prolonged set of street battles in the capital city, lasting nearly half a year, which not only produced catastrophic destruction of much of Bissau's infrastructure but also disrupted the import–export system and national trade networks, and generated massive migrations into rural areas by Bissau's residents. By spring 1999, President Vieira had fled to Portugal and army generals had seized national power, ending Vieira's presidency and initiating a year and a half of army rule (Forrest 2010: 256–7; Forrest 2002: 255, 258–9).

Technically this was only the second time that Guinea-Bissau had experienced an army-led overthrow of the national government. However, in hindsight it seems that in terms of political culture, despite temporary stability and recent formal democratization, from the point of view of political attitude and consciousness the military had never fully departed from the political scene following its role in the independence war. To a great extent, this failure to leave was a consequence of Vieira's autocratic style of presidential rulership and his large-scale reliance on personally devoted security forces, such that it was widely known in the country that sheer force was Vieira's true key to political success. But this also reflects a politicized military that harks back to the anti-colonial struggle itself—the birthplace of Guinea-Bissau's national army—which inculcated into the body politic a political value of rightful military action in politics in the face of de-legitimatized political leadership (Forrest 2003: 181–200, 232).

Once the military rebellion was initiated in earnest in 1998, this attitude of legitimate intervention (by force if necessary) was rekindled; and from this time forwards through the 2000s, it would be consistently and dramatically manifested, and largely in disregard to the holding of national elections (see chapter by Kohl, this volume, on the proliferation of army coups). Despite these interventions, it is difficult to describe Guinea-Bissau's political system as characterized by full-scale military rule, because soon after a *coup d'état* whichever army faction seized power sought electoral legitimation—not only from the general populace, but also from global observers and from the donor community—through competitive national balloting or a re-civilianization of presidential power and a gradual return to the barracks. Thus, from the mid-1990s through to 2012 there has been a see-saw of political power-holding from army leaders to civilians and back again, and a frequent and dramatic shift in how presidents obtain power (elections, then a military coup, then back to elections, then another coup, etc.). Such a frequent alternation of rulership and of the means of acquiring control of the country's cabinet and political system has made it clear that no matter how often multi-party elections are held and the political leadership structure is yet again re-civilianized, the armed forces, like sleeping lions, will awaken at a time of their choosing and decide to intervene with force in order yet again to re-take political control. This, then, is not so much a political system, nor a stable and entrenched system of army rule, but rather a political dance of instrumentalist power (à la Chabal/Daloz, discussed earlier) between civilians and soldiers that imparts an ongoing liminality to the country's political arena.

The involvement of army factions in illicit activities must also be mentioned, because it is clearly relevant to the predominant political culture that evolved in the post-colonial era. In the 1990s, as noted earlier, elements in the Bissau-Guinean armed forces are believed to have provided weaponry to Casamancian secessionists in exchange for marijuana. In hindsight, it is clear that such illicit activity by army personnel served only as a prelude to more overt participation in international drug trading in the 2000s, providing yet further examples of instrumentalist-oriented behaviour by the country's political and military elites.

Economic non-development

Since the advent of colonial capitalism in the late 1800s, and continuing to the present day, Guinea-Bissau has had two interlinked economies: on the one hand, an 'informal' system of agronomic self-reliance, artisanal fishing, inter-village exchange and barter trade; and on the other hand, a formal system of international trade based on the mass production of primary resources (especially rice, peanuts, cashews, oceanic and riverine fish), along with the importation of construction materials, oil (for energy use in recent decades) and luxury goods. These two economies are connected in a number of ways; for example, when international prices for cashews, peanuts and rice are relatively high, producers have more income which they can direct into bolstering the informal economy (Bigman 1993: 27–49; Galli and Jones 1987: 37–52).

Despite this linkage, the relatively low rates of agronomic productivity and of artisanal production, combined with weather-related or infestation-generated problems with agricultural harvests, tend to keep incomes at near-subsistence levels for the majority of Bissau-Guineans. There has been little durable progress in regard to national economic growth since the Portuguese initiated colonial rule approximately a century ago (in the 1910s). 'Development' programmes have assumed a number of different forms from the colonial era through the 1970s–2000s, but none of these programmes managed to generate significant or sustainable gains in per capita income, or create a viable manufacturing base, or provide Bissau-Guineans with a niche in the international economy that could generate meaningful external capital flows (Forrest 2010: 198).

Certainly, there have been temporary blips of economic promise: the expansion of peanut fields in the 1930s and 1940s; the construction of highways and paved roads in the 1950s; the mass production of export-oriented rice in the 1950s and 1960s; a burst of factory-building in the 1970s; the advent of widespread cashew production in the 1980s–90s. Despite the efforts of economic development advisers, first from Portugal (1940s–60s) and then from the United Nations and the European Union (late 1970s–90s), these programmes did not produce the hoped-for economic gains (apart from some temporary rises in national income limited to the vicinity of the capital city of Bissau and to a small number of local growers and exporters), nor did they succeed in establishing a structure for building a workable foundation for national development (Forrest 2003: 162–9, 224–7). Worse still, the fixation on export-oriented cash crop production may well have generated a number of 'development' programmes that produced widespread ecological decay due to excessive tree-clearing (and partial deforestation) and the over-planting of dry-crop areas (Temudo 2005).

Deepening the country's perpetual economic crisis was the 'structural adjustment' programme advocated by the IMF and the World Bank and adopted by President Nino Vieira and the government of Guinea-Bissau in the 1980s–90s. According to the logic of structural adjustment theory, national economic production had been hampered by too much government involvement in agricultural purchasing and government regulation of the food supply and import–export trade, and so it advocated wholesale deregulation. At the same time, according to the structural adjustment advocates, Guinea-Bissau's bureaucracy was too large in proportion to both its population and its expenses in the public sector, including price supports for basic food supplies such as bread and sugar, which were too high in relation to the government's overall income. Reduction of public expenses, so it was believed, would move the national government closer to a balanced budget, which in turn would provide greater incentives for outside agencies to invest in a hoped-for burgeoning private sector. Meanwhile, the World Bank and IMF promised to provide continuing tranches of economic support to the government for basic operating expenses so long as its pro-deregulation and bureaucratic-reduction recommendations were adopted.

As it turned out, structural adjustment reforms initially appeared to be promising—mostly because the IMF and World Bank provided assistance to government expenses in the 1980s, but also because the fledgling private sector succeeded in expanding the production and export of cashew nuts, which rapidly became the country's primary export crop. However, by the 1990s the positive effects of structural adjustment came to a grinding halt as it became evident that reductions in government expenses were having a negative impact on urban society, with the poor in Bissau unable to rely as extensively on price supports for basic grains (bread and rice) as they had in previous decades (Forrest 2010: 184). As a sense of social desperation set in, the government appeared increasingly indifferent to spreading social unrest. By 1997, this contributed to popular support for the mobilization of most of the armed forces in an attempt to unseat the existing president (Nino Vieira). As discussed above, there were a number of different causes of this armed forces rebellion, including and especially intra-army factionalism; but a growing economic malaise had gripped the national populace as a consequence of structural adjustment-imposed reductions in government support programmes, and certainly contributed to the popularity of this ultimately successful challenge to the existing president's rule. Hence, this particularly dramatic example in a long line of external interventions in Guinea-Bissau's economic and political infrastructure had helped to produce a further destabilization of the country, in line with both the colonial and earlier post-colonial eras.

Conclusion

Although national elections in 2000 brought a peaceful transition to a new president and parliament, we made clear above that instrumentalist politics characterized by factionalism and a continuing chain of violent military interventions would dominate the state-level arena in much of the 2000s. Such disorder is tempered by nationwide lack of interest in civil war (as in parts of central Africa, for example), by long-standing traditions of inter-ethnic cooperation within civil society, and by a periodic return to civilianized political leadership after outbursts of military intervention and brief periods of army rule. But unimpeded civilian rule has typically proven only temporary, until the next military intervention, resulting in an alternation between elected governments on the one hand, and violent takeovers by army officers on the other. As this book goes to press on the heels of another crisis in Bissau, it is as yet unclear whether a renewal of the alternation can be avoided.

The well-intentioned efforts by international donors, aid agencies and global political mediators to shore up the Bissau-Guinean state, to generate sustainable economic growth and to cultivate a bargaining-oriented political process have yet to yield long-lasting positive results. Meanwhile, the apparent increasing involvement of at least part of the armed forces and political leadership in illicit international drug trading adds yet another element which favours the politics of violent instrumentalism and makes the likelihood of stable political rule and economic development appear ever more distant and theoretical.

Ultimately, it is wise to recall the historical origins of Guinea-Bissau's politics of disorder, grounded in the formation of a violent and infrastructurally weak colonial state, and then a revolutionary independence movement which could not manage to live up to its promise of unity and democratization in the post-colonial period. The pre-colonial, colonial-era and post-colonial theme of attempted force-based political centralization thwarted by various forms of violent resistance is today manifested in defiance of a formalized rules-based political order, a spate of *coups d'état*, and the suspected involvement of some government and army officials in the global narcotics markets—all of which has helped to generate an ever more attenuated and dysfunctional government bureaucracy. These political characteristics are not intrinsic to the people of Guinea-Bissau, but rather reflect a history of zero-sum elite-level competition, intra-state political and military factionalisms and the inheritance of a culture of political instrumentalism that continues to wield its influence despite continuing efforts (by domestic and global actors) at political and economic reform.

3

GUINEA-BISSAU'S RURAL ECONOMY AND SOCIETY

A REASSESSMENT OF COLONIAL AND POST-COLONIAL DYNAMICS

Philip J. Havik[1]

References to Guinea-Bissau's economy have generally been dominated by a focus on the post-conflict situation following the war of liberation (1963–74). Distinct phases have been identified, generally associated with political upheavals and shifts in economic policies, i.e. 1974–80, 1981–6 and 1987–98, and 2001 to the present. Whereas the initial period focused on industrial production and import substitution, following a military coup in 1980 the second period saw the introduction of an Economic Stabilization Programme (ESP) followed by Structural Adjustment Policies (SAP) from 1987 onwards, which were interrupted by the Bissau war in 1998. The last period, from 2001 onwards, was marked by a volatile political situation and economic decline associated with the legacy of armed conflict and a military coup in 2012 (see Kohl, this volume). Although the mainstay of the country's economy is agri-

[1] The author would like to thank the editor and reviewers for their useful comments.

culture, accounting for 85% of the country's sources of income and 60% of the country's GDP (RGB 2011: 16, 26), the rural economy remained a peripheral concern until the mid-1980s when the country embarked upon a programme of economic privatization. The (re)introduction of cashew nuts refocused attention on local producers and their inputs, as it rapidly transformed into a crop export monoculture, currently accounting for 98% of commodity exports, thus replacing peanuts which constituted the country's main export crop until the end of the colonial period.

In the case of Guinea-Bissau, peanuts and cashew illustrate a pattern of economic policies centred on cash/export crop monocultures. Secondly, they also serve to epitomize a trend towards economic 'modernization' under colonial and post-colonial regimes and a marked negligence of subsistence agriculture. Thirdly, colonial and post-colonial periods show marked similarities with regard to land concession policies for export crop production. Fourthly, they also reveal a notable tendency of the colonial and post-colonial state to engage with private interests, in terms of crop cultivation, processing and export, crop price fixing and marketing. Fifth, these policies emphasize the country's linkages with and dependency on international markets, thereby raising the issue of externally induced change. And finally, the rural economy's trajectory demonstrates the key importance of understanding local dynamics of indigenous agriculture and producers' capacity to 'marry' commercial with subsistence production and income-generating activities.

The literature on Guinea-Bissau's rural economy appears to show a marked contrast between a focus on the role of planters and the state on the one hand, and the role of smallholders and petty traders on the other. This apparent dichotomy comes to the fore in historical tensions between the two sets of actors, which remain unresolved in the present day. This chapter argues that despite political and economic changes over time, there is a remarkable continuity in terms of export crop monocultures, first of peanuts in colonial times and thereafter of cashew from the 1980s. Despite the lack of organized state support and the activities of commercial farming which went (and still go) largely uncontrolled, smallholder-farmers showed a great, but severely tested, resilience and capacity for adaptation and innovation, whilst attempting to combine export crop with subsistence production and income-generating activities.

Guinea-Bissau's rural economy will now be analysed in historical perspective, taking into account the striking continuities from the peanut-based monoculture to the 'cashew revolution', despite periods of armed conflict and decolonization. In order to conduct this analysis, the ecological, socio-cultural and historical aspects of its evolution will first focus on a general outline of trends during colonial and post-independence periods, followed by an assessment of the organization of crop markets, the main actors and political constraints. The tensions between commercial farming and smallholder producers will be discussed, as well as the role of the state, trade networks and the feminization of the subsistence economy. The final section will take into account the impact of industrialization policies and export crop processing in the context of the cashew boom, quantifying the performance of the rural economy and providing comparisons between Guinea-Bissau and its neighbours, i.e. Senegal and Guinea-Conakry.

Political change and rural production

The (short-lived) peanut boom in the 1850s, its resurgence from the 1920s and the rapid take-off of cashew cultivation under SAP in the 1980s and 1990s appear to confirm the significant potential of export-oriented farming triggered by corporate and market incentives. However, these cycles were also interrupted by transitional phases primarily associated with armed conflict and political change. Whilst the inter-ethnic conflict in the 1880s and the war of liberation created impediments to the export-oriented economy, the immediate post-war policies implemented by the ruling party, PAIGC (Partido de Independência da Guiné e Cabo Verde), opposed private enterprise and a plantation economy. Nevertheless, marked similarities have been identified between 'modernist' colonial and post-colonial perspectives on agriculture and trade (Galli 1986, 1994), as well as in terms of land concession policies (Espinosa 1994: 28; Cheneau-Loquay 1995: 296), economic planning and industrialization (Paulini 1984: 49–59, 89–98; Schiefer 1987: 204–9) and the functioning of the state itself (Lopes 1982: 53–76; Lopes 1987; Rudebeck 1982; Chabal 1983b).

While the literature on Portugal's former African colonies does reflect some of these concerns, high-profile nationalist liberation movements and the chequered post-colonial trajectories of state and society in countries affected by decades of colonial and civil wars represent a notable 'niche' study in Africa. Countries such as Angola, Guinea-Bissau and Mozambique which experienced protracted political and civil conflict have been the subject of intensive study and debate (e.g. Chabal 2002b). The presence of nationalist liberation movements, their programmes geared to socialist reforms and 'people's power', and their ideological shifts towards economic liberalization and multi-party elections have strongly imbued the literature on these countries with a focus on the violent end of empire and decolonization, state–society relations and nation-building (Chabal 2002b: 3–134). Owing to the particular nature of the struggle in the case of Guinea-Bissau, the roles of 'rural civil society' (Lopes 1982; Rudebeck 1988, 1989, 2010; Forrest 2003; Temudo 2008) and the importance of rural livelihoods (Galli/Jones 1987; Galli 1987; Hochet 1983; Havik 1991; Cheneau-Loquay and Materasso 1998; Temudo/Abrantes 2013) have been singled out. Indeed, Guinea-Bissau stands out in this respect on account of the high profile of the nationalist movement's leader and agronomist, Amílcar Cabral (1924–73), and his widely publicized thoughts on agriculture, 'people's power' and the mobilization of rural populations (Cabral 1980: 119–54). His critique on past policy and practice and the movement's success in gaining a foothold in rural areas challenged the deeply rooted notion of a purportedly static indigenous economy and a dynamic 'foreign' settler community propagated in colonial circles (Duarte 1950; Carreira 1968: 73, 91–2). Nevertheless, the deeply rooted post-colonial tensions illustrate the serious problems faced by nationalist liberation movements and post-colonial governments to respond adequately to rural producers' expectations and interests (Rudebeck 1982, 1988, 1989; Havik 1991, 1995; Forrest 1998, 2003; Temudo 2008, 2009; Temudo/Abrantes 2013).

In terms of crop cultivation, Guinea-Bissau forms part of a region extending from The Gambia to Sierra Leone once known as the Rice Coast, with particular characteristics in terms of ecology, climate and human settlement. Its most characteristic feature, the coastal wetlands, are shared with surrounding countries such as Senegal (the Casamance region), The Gambia and Guinea-Conakry. The country can be divided in broad terms into four ecosystems: the Bijagós Islands off the coast, the low-lying littoral floodplains, a transitional area towards the limits of the tidal reach covered in dense forests, and the drier upland savannah regions in the interior beyond the tidal reach (Havik/Daveau 2010: 33–5). Dissected by a number of large rivers, inlets and a myriad of creeks, the alluvial soils, mangroves and higher rainfall in coastal areas make the densely populated littoral highly suitable for paddy rice farming (local varieties of *Oryza glauberrima* and imported varieties of *Orzya sativa*). The transitional area is more suited to crop rotation (e.g. of millet and sorghum, and also with peanuts), while the sparsely populated savannah plains are characterized by shifting cultivation (e.g. of upland rice and millet) and cattle farming (Havik/Daveau 2010: 33–5). During the colonial period, northern and easterly regions became the centre of peanut farming, the colony's principal export crop, while palm kernels (*Elaeis guineensis*) were extracted mainly in littoral areas in the west and north and in the Bijagós archipelago. With economic liberalization in the 1980s, peanuts (*Arachis hypogea*) were largely replaced and overtaken by cashews (*Anacardium occidentale*), while the supply of palm kernels dried up (see Graph 1). This process was accompanied by the stagnation and decline of rice cultivation in favour of cashew production, a phenomenon which accelerated with SAP, resulting in the 1990s cashew boom when the country became one of the world's principal cashew nut exporters (Barry/Creppy/Wodon 2007: 83–4). Currently, 80% of rural producers are engaged in cashew farming, which occupies 47% of farmland (RGB 2011: 26).

These shifts and continuities in the rural economy have tended to overemphasize the importance of cash crops for the Bissau-Guinean economy, and highlight the need for an integral view of subsistence and export-oriented farming rather than a sectorial analysis (Cheneau-Loquay/Matarasso 1998). They show that the commodification of export crop production occurred simultaneously with innovations in terms of soil management, cultivation techniques and income generation implemented by indigenous farmers (Richards 1985; Teeken et al. 2012). These and other authors underline the relevance of historical experience, which suggests that prospects for economic growth in rural West African economies are not solely or preponderantly

Graph 1

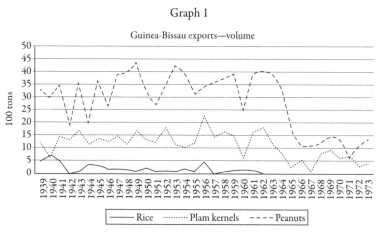

Sources: BACIAG 1963: 25–58; Boletim Cultural Guiné Portuguesa 1961-1971; Anuário Estatístico Ultramarino 1971; 1973.

externally driven but rather the result of indigenous adaptation and innovation. Indeed, in Guinea-Bissau the agency of smallholder farmers only began to be recognized in colonial publications from the 1950s, amongst others by Cabral himself (Castro 1950, 1951; Cabral 1956). Both the colonial authorities and the liberation movements were acutely aware of farmers' crucial role in terms of crop supplies, and actively vied for their political support in times of conflict.

The tensions resulting from colonial and post-colonial policies which favoured commercial farming became deeply rooted in the rural economy, influencing farmers' attitudes towards the state and crop markets. The politics of land concessions favouring export crop production was typified by the phenomenon of *ponteiros* or planter-traders that emerged in the mid-1800s with the introduction of peanuts in coastal areas (Bowman 1987). Thereafter, fluxes of free migrant labour engaged in sharecropping were directed towards commercial peanut-growing areas in what was then Portuguese Guinea, as well as neighbouring Senegal and The Gambia. Over time, in colonial and post-colonial periods crop production for export was regulated by means of land concessions, taxation and national farm-gate price-setting. Although commercial farming would experience periods of decline as a result of armed conflict, the Bissau-Guinean economy essentially remained a crop export monoculture.

Rice and peanuts: eco-systems, farming and ethnicity

Two violent upheavals occurred during the twentieth century that were of major importance for indigenous agriculture and trade in what was then still Portuguese Guinea: the so-called 'wars of pacification' which began in earnest in the early 1890s and continued until 1915; and the war of liberation (1963–74). Both were to leave a deep imprint on African communities, provoking migratory fluxes, regional shifts in cultivation patterns and the introduction of new rules of engagement with private actors and the state. 'Pacifying' the region's most densely populated areas did not merely serve political goals, but was above all inspired by economic and financial interests as a military administration, and from 1917 onwards a civil administration, were established (Mendy 1994: 185–256). African populations such as the Balanta, Manjako, Pepel, Mankanhe and Bijagó in fertile coastal areas were thereafter transformed into suppliers of internal and external markets, principally of paddy rice and of peanuts, in an effort to commoditize local production in a colony geared to economic extraction rather than European settlement (for ethnic relations see

Green, this volume). Laws governing 'native' labour, taxation, mobility, conscription, civil and penal responsibility, defining Africans' rights and obligations on the basis of racial criteria, were eventually abolished in 1961.

The protracted war of liberation that followed would wreak havoc in littoral areas, just as the 'pacification' campaigns had done in the early 1900s. These conflicts drove farming communities to migrate in large numbers both internally and across the border into neighbouring Senegal and Guinea-Conakry. The areas most affected by the war of liberation initially lay in the south, above all in the fertile, low-lying and mangrove-covered areas which, on account of large-scale Balanta migration from the north, had by the 1940s become the single major source of paddy rice. The liberation movement, PAIGC, privileged coastal regions and rice-producing areas (above all in the north and south) for its mobilization efforts and military interventions. By contrast, the main peanut-producing areas in the east, which mainly fell under Fula and Mandinga control, emerged relatively unscathed from these conflicts on account of the political alliances forged by resident ethnic communities with military and colonial authorities (see Green and Temudo/Abrantes, this volume).

Thus while the territory's main peanut producers, the Fula, acted as key allies of the colonial authorities from the 1890s (Mendy 1994: 185–256; Costas Dias 2008), Balanta (–Brassa) rice farmers would become the principal domestic support base for the anti-colonial struggle in the 1960s. This politico-ethnic dichotomy was also underlined by Amílcar Cabral in his writings, applying distinctions between centralized and segmentary societies proposed by British anthropologists in the 1940s to the Guinean situation (Cabral 1980: 37–8). The strong presence of the nationalist movement PAIGC in the south, where it established liberated zones depending heavily on local rice supplies, prompted Portuguese armed forces to target paddy fields for bombing raids, destroying crops and their intricate irrigation system (Drift 1992: 65–70), and to lay mines in rivers.[2] As farmers and trader-planters or *ponteiros* fled the area from the mid-1960s as the conflict intensified, rice production, above all in the south, was severely affected (Galli/Jones 1987: 44; Ribeiro 1989: 243–4; Drift 1992: 61–73). Then again, peanut cultivation in the east remained in colonial hands so was largely unperturbed, at least until the early 1970s, whilst production in the north suffered a marked decline on account of the war. These events were to have major consequences for the evolution of crop production in the post-colonial period.

[2] Interview with F. P. Brandão, Comebú, Guinea-Bissau, 17 March 1989 (interviewer: J. S. Sambú).

The case of rice is instructive. On the eve of the independence war, in the 1950s, the Balanta (–Brassa) were producing two-thirds of the total (paddy and upland) rice harvests, obtaining the highest yields in the Catió region in the south of the colony (Cabral 1956: 36; Mendes 1970: 276). It was estimated at the time that most of the rice sold in the colony was of Balanta origin (Baptista 1948: 897; Ribeiro 1989: 235); this situation continues to the present day, with the Balanta supplying about three-quarters of the country's total rice production. However, any attempt to determine the trajectories of rice production encounters obstacles in terms of the lack of accuracy of agricultural censuses. Comparisons between the 1953 and 1961 agricultural censuses appear to show that while the total cultivated surface area planted with rice and worked by smallholders was actually declining (by 25%) before the war of liberation, production levels doubled (Cabral 1956: 34, 237; Ministério Ultramar 1963: quadro VIII). However, distinct census methods and the absence of any significant improvements in farming infrastructures or rainfall suggest that the 1962 data are unreliable and probably inflated (Horta 1965: 391–4; Mendes 1970: 274–5); similar problems prevent comparisons with the 1988 census (MDRA 1990b). A number of paddy recovery projects implemented in the 1950s and early 1960s could have increased the total surface area for cultivation somewhat by the mid-1960s (Mendes 1970: 279). But the loss of rice-producing areas in the south to the PAIGC would have cancelled out this effort, illustrated by the end of rice exports in 1966 as imports rose rapidly (see Graph 1). Data from the late 1960s confirm a considerable decrease in rice production in areas controlled by colonial authorities to about one-third of 1953 production levels (Província Guiné 1972: 64; Chabal 2002a: 110–11).

An evaluation based upon data gathered after independence shows that production declined significantly after 1974 to a minimum of 25,000 tons in 1980—the year of the military coup which ousted President Luís Cabral—following low rainfall in 1977, 1979 and 1980, recovering thereafter to hitherto unattained levels in 1995 (see Graph 2). Nevertheless, average self-sufficiency in rice decreased significantly from the 1960s until the mid-1990s, i.e. from 95% in 1960–4 to 55% in the period 1989–96 (Oteng/Sant'Anna 1999). In the meantime from the mid-1960s onwards, a rice surplus—part of which was exported—was transformed into a chronic rice deficit (Temudo/Abrantes 2013: 579), resulting from the destructive impact of armed conflict on farms and the massive emigration of farmers on the one hand, and the lack of agricultural extension (for example to rebuild the fragile system of dykes and sluices), of credit and of incentives after independence on the other hand. Rice smuggling by farmers and by officials (see Forrest, this volume) accounted for an additional 'loss' of Guinea-Bissau's harvested staple crop.

As regards peanut production, it was responsible for 80% of the value of Guinea's exports in the 1950s, covering almost 94% of all arable land for commercial agriculture and occupying 21.8% of the total cultivated area, most of it worked by the Fula (36%) closely followed by the Balanta (25%) (Cabral 1956: 237). Often cultivated by smallholders as a rotative crop together with sorghum, millet and maize, the Fula supplied almost 44% of total peanut production in 1953, followed by the Mandinga (just under 23%) and the Balanta (18%); at the time the Fula were responsible for over half of the total production of (non-rice) staple cereals (Cabral 1956: 35). Of the total production volume of peanuts in 1953, one-third was exported; from 1964 onwards exports entered a sharp decline as a result of armed conflict and the PAIGC's opening of the northern front (in 1963) and the eastern front (in 1964), and its insistence on farmers abandoning peanut farming (Chabal 2002a: 111). With the sharp decline in peanut production and exports during the colonial war, a short-lived recovery in the 1970s (see Graph 2) and its virtual abandonment as an export crop in the 1980s as world prices declined and seed prices rose, ethno-political alliances forged during the colonial period were reshaped. While territories in the north and east that had formed the hub of the crop export economy were left without large-scale commercial crop farming and the monetary returns associated with it, at the same time the

Graph 2

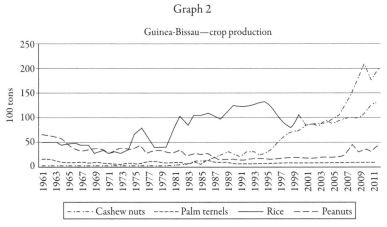

Source: FAOstat.

régulo system (i.e. of appointed chiefs) was abolished and ruling lineages were sidetracked (Carvalho 2000; Borszik 2008).

As crops were mobilized through long-standing trade networks, the competitive advantage remained with groups exhibiting a tradition of trade itinerancy and commercial acumen, such as the Fula and Mandinga *djilas* which formed itinerant trade diasporas throughout West Africa, as well as the Manjako out-migration network in the Senegambia (see chapters by Ceesay and Green, this volume). Given the agricultural geography of the territory, Lebanese traders and Islamised *djilas* from the east and from Senegal and Guinea-Conakry[3] would roam the coastal zones, and above all the south—the granary of the colony—for staple crops such as rice, which were in short supply in the eastern savannah zone.[4] During the liberation war a similar crop geography emerged when PAIGC-controlled areas in the south were fundamental for supplying the eastern and northern front with 'southern' rice (Dhada 1993: 75–7). The liberalization of trade in the late 1980s removed obstacles to the operation of these regional trade networks, which had been severely restricted during the colonial period and following independence on account of alleged profiteering and hoarding. As a result, the Bafatá and Gabú areas' considerable commercial potential came to the fore, strongly related to the existence of (covert) regional, cross-border trade networks, which also extended to cattle herds, as *djilas* were now able to move freely throughout the country in the wholesale and retail trade. Areas populated by the Manjako and Mankanhe in the northwest also benefited from new commercial opportunities to intensify their exchanges with the Casamance region in southern Senegal.

At the same time, the shift in land concession policies with SAP and economic liberalization was most emphatic in the densely populated north—the most affected area being the Biombo region surrounding the capital—and above all in eastern regions. By the early 1990s, these regions accounted for the majority of the surface area ceded to *ponteiros* for commercial farming (Pereira et al. 1992: 18, 20; Indjai 2002: 104–5). As credit facilities became available, albeit with patrimonial overtones, production shifted towards the cultivation of cashew and fruit—above all, mangoes—as a new intermediate stratum of small *ponteiros* emerged (Galli 1989: 41; Pereira et al. 1992: 20–31), while liberalization gave rise to farmers' associations and female producers

---

[3] Interview with J. P. da Silva, Paço d'Arcos, Portugal, 17 October 1995.
[4] Interview with J. A. Lopes, Catió Balanta, Guinea-Bissau, 17 March 1989 (interviewer: J. S. Sambú).

organized themselves for vegetable gardens and marketing foodstuffs (Dias 1996: 353; Havik 1998: 212–14).[5] The impact of land concession and extension policies following economic liberalization, which were recognized as policy concerns (MDRA 1990a: 16–17), would be much more limited in southern regions which were less affected by the large-scale influx of *ponteiros* (Pereira et al. 1992: 19; Indjai 2002: 104–5).

However, the transition from colonial rule to independence had a particular political significance in the less accessible south, where rice producers felt abandoned despite their decisive support for the nationalist movement and their crucial economic contribution in terms of rice supplies (Temudo 2009: 54; Havik 2012: 56–7). Far removed from the political centre, they failed to receive government support to repair their *bolanhas* (rice paddies) damaged during the war (Hochet 1983: 125). In the colonial period, above all from the 1940s onwards, *ponteiros* had provided transport, cement and tools at the request of Balanta, Nalú and Bijagó farmers in the Tombalí region, in order to recover and repair their paddies; once these were cultivated, farmers were expected to pay off the back-up services rendered with their produce.[6] However, during the war this infrastructure collapsed and was not revived after independence. Thus, during the early years of independence, communities operating an exclusively rice-based economy in a wetland environment largely relied upon earnings from productive (vegetables, poultry and fish) and resale trading activities carried on by women, who together with their dependants form the core of the *fogon* or hearth-hold (Hochet 1981: 12, 113–24). Over the next decades, the relevance of women's income-earning activities greatly expanded, both in urban and rural areas, as well as in the cross-border trade (Havik 1995, 1998).[7] Among the factors which influenced women's—and men's—income generation strategies were cuts in state subsidies, male unemployment as they lost their jobs in the public sector, and steep increases in the national reconstruction tax payable by adult women and men as a result of SAP policies (Rudebeck 1989: 56–60; World Bank 1994: 25).

---

[5] The Rede de Organizações Camponesas e Produtores Rurais forms part of the Réseau des organisations paysannes et de producteurs agricoles de l'Afrique de l'Ouest (ROPPA), founded in 2000, and provides a national framework for rural producers, but the main umbrella organization for local farmers' associations since 1993 is the Associação Nacional dos Agricultores da Guiné-Bissau (ANAG).

[6] Interview with F. P. Brandão, op. cit.

[7] Interviews with women *lumo* (i.e. cross-border) traders in Guinea-Bissau, 1990–5.

Once cashew farming spread across the whole country in the 1990s, alternative sources of income became available, also for families and communities exclusively dedicated to rice farming in areas where such crops do not tend to thrive or constitute a priority. Women in both rural and urban areas, recruited by *ponteiros* to harvest cashew fruit and nuts or farming orchards through kin and co-ethnic networks, seized the opportunity to gain additional income from the processing and sale of cashew nuts and fruit (mainly from cashew and mango trees)—part of which they are allowed to keep—and from the production and sale of cashew wine and *kana*, i.e. cashew brandy (Lea/Hugo/Cardoso 1990: 8–9; Havik 1995: 31–3; Havik 1998: 215–17; Domingues 2000: 303, 322, 450–1; Lourenço-Lindell 2002: 83, 102; Lynn/Jaeger 2004: 7–8). In the process, the south became the principal domestic supplier of fruit varieties, partly through projects promoting crop marketing but mainly as a result of farmers' inputs in banana, tangerine, orange, lime and kola orchards (Dias 1996: 366–9).

Thus, colonial and post-colonial periods illustrate the marked continuity of patterns of crop farming centred on the country's main staple crop, i.e. rice, and cash/export crops such as peanuts and cashew grown as a monoculture. Profoundly marked by the region's ecological make-up, relations between smallholder agriculture and commercial farming differed in accordance with regional and political factors. Whereas violent conflicts such as the war of liberation tended to exacerbate tensions and induce changes in the rural economy, they also brought to the fore ethnic distinctions and the regional division of farm inputs and crop trade. These considerations would play a decisive role during the colonial and post-colonial eras, also concerning the parts played by private actors and the state with regard to the production and marketing of staple and cash crops.

Commercial farming and crop trade: policies and constraints

From the late 1890s well into the 1940s, peanut and sugarcane *pontas* as well as distilleries to produce *kana* or rum were established by Cape Verdean traders in the Farim area close to the Senegalese border.[8] The main geographical focus of commercial farming would be reinforced during the 1920s with the rapid growth of peanut *pontas* in the east and north-east, i.e. in the Bambadinca,

---

[8] Interview with I. J. Semedo, Gã Vicente, Guinea-Bissau, 12 March 1993 (interviewer: S. Mané).

Bafatá and Gabú areas. Trade in peanuts, rice and sugarcane grown on these *pontas* was organized variously. The system of internal markets epitomized by the *centros comerciais* (or regional trading posts), which fell under colonial administrative control and where staple and cash crops were sold and stored, mainly concerned itself with the main *ponta* areas along the region's coast and rivers. However, the sparsely settled south (i.e. the Tombalí region) was essentially controlled by a few big *ponteiros* working closely with Portuguese trade houses. While peanuts were transported by road westwards from the north and east, paddy rice was shipped by boat from the south to the capital Bissau. Domestic and external trade networks were largely controlled by a Portuguese company, CUF (Companhia União Fabril), with interests in other African colonies such as Angola and Mozambique. By the late 1920s CUF exported more than half of all peanut and palm kernel production to be processed in its factories in Portugal (Havik 2007: 185). It shared control over import and export transactions and transport facilities with the Sociedade Comercial Ultramarina (SCU). Smaller firms were particularly active in the interior, such as Barbosas and Comandita, Nunes and Irmãos, Mário Lima, Aly Souleymane and others owned by Cape Verdean and Lebanese traders (Castro 1980: 361–3), the latter settling along the West African coast from the early 1900s. Just like the *Comités de Estado* and central store directors after independence, local administration and *centros comerciais* checked the sales, stocks and prices of company and *ponteiros*' stores. The latter were obliged to produce the required statistics or trade manifestos twice monthly, thus providing authorities with estimates of domestic crop production and trade.[9]

This tightly meshed private oligopoly was transformed into a dual state monopoly after 1974. Although some small traders were allowed to continue, after independence the domestic wholesale and retail trade was centralized under the control of the *Armazéns do Povo*, or People's Stores, while the SCU was nationalized and transformed into SOCOMIN, which remained in charge of imports and exports (Galli 1987: 113) until it was extinguished in 1989. The People's Stores would inadvertently 'copy' existing regional patterns by taking over trading posts and shops pertaining to colonial companies—as well as part of their personnel—during the war and after independence (Dhada 1993: 80, 197).[10] Interestingly, in the late 1970s and early 1980s the

---

[9] Interview with J. A. Lopes, op. cit.; interview with J. Atome, Catió, Guinea-Bissau, 16 March 1989 (interviewer: J.S. Sambú).

[10] Interview with J. P. Saldanha, Catió, Guinea-Bissau, 18 March 1989 (interviewer: J. S. Sambú).

major concentration of state shops was to be found in the south—the granary of the country—underlining the PAIGC's reliance on paddy rice farmers (Hochet 1981: 13). The liberalization of trade undertaken in the mid-1980s (Gomes 1993: 136–47) resulted in the privatization of the *Armazéns do Povo* and SOCOMIN, which thereafter operated in conjunction with a growing number of large and medium trading firms. The latter, such as Geta Bissau as well as local traders such as Mamadú Djabi and Sons, Djaguité, and Fara Heneni and Brothers (Lea/Hugo/Cardoso 1990: 11; Lea/Hugo/Ribeiro 1990: 41), tended to model their operations on the People's Stores—just as the Casa Gouveia inspired other trade houses in colonial times. At the same time, Mauritanian petty traders established shops in towns and the interior— much as the Lebanese had done from the 1910s in Portuguese Guinea—while also gaining an important share of the domestic cashew market.[11]

Despite the great impact of commercial *ponta* agriculture in colonial and post-colonial periods, the commoditization of crop farming in Guinea-Bissau has always been a local affair. The short-lived peanut boom from the 1850s to the early 1880s, as well as the re-emergence of peanut farming and the regional shift in rice production in the 1920s, essentially depended on local agency. Following the end of the military campaigns in 1915, Chinese immigrants and local Kriston planters (creolized Bissau-Guineans speaking Kriol as a vernacular), together with Balanta farmers, initiated the move from the northern Mansoa region towards the south of Guinea, i.e. to the Quínara and Tombalí regions, which led to a rapid expansion of paddy rice production (Cunningham 1980: 37–41; Ribeiro 1989: 234–5; Drift 1992: 38–61; Havik 2011a: 178– 81; Havik 2011b: 217–22). The first large rice pontas owned by Cape Verdean planters were to emerge in the 1920s in the Tombalí region in the south, soon to be 'copied' by commercial firms such as the SCU in the early 1930s (Indjai 2002: 185–7). In the Quínara region another group of mainly Cape Verdean *ponteiros* established large farms in the Fulacunda and Empada districts from the 1920s onwards, while a second wave of even larger large private concessions swept the Catió and Como-Caiar area in the 1940s and 1950s.

Thus, the transformation of the south into the granary of the country was based on local dynamics rather than being the result of colonial policies. Indeed, these changes were facilitated by the marked neglect of southern regions by colonial authorities (Havik 2012: 220). Hard-pressed by the negative impact of the world crisis on peanut production, they shifted their focus

---

[11] Interview with J. P. Saldanha, ibidem.

in the 1930s to increasing rice exports, which reached their peak in 1949 (see volume figures, Graph 1). The first state-funded and managed crop and seed storage facilities were set up in the south in the 1940s, in order to prevent the sale of entire staple harvests to traders, reduce post-harvest losses and guarantee a measure of food security; thereafter the network was extended to the whole colony. By the 1970s the colony boasted sixty-four rice and peanut granaries distributed across the territory, with a major concentration in the peanut-producing Bafatá region (Província da Guiné 1972: 166, 171–2).

In terms of land concessions, however, official concession policies wavered; and cadastral services (only created in 1942) were notoriously ill-equipped to cope with the demarcation and registration of estates, thus leaving serious 'gaps' in terms of their relations with local communities.[12] Thus these relations were often exercised outside the formal colonial sphere. In the 1960s, some of the most influential planters in the south clashed with the administration for monopolizing the sale and purchase of rice and exchange goods, thereby driving away farmers and traders. This prompted more assertive administrators to enforce the right of traders to deal directly with local farmers without planters' involvement.[13] Although *ponteiro* planter-traders maintained 'gentlemen's agreements' with local communities regarding their respective areas of intervention,[14] they did attempt to extend their concessions beyond the legal limits in order to 'capture' local farmers by convincing them they actually lived on the concession and treating them like 'their natives'.[15] Larger estates were generally left untouched; disputes were often resolved by favouring *ponteiros*' claims,[16] but generally local officials simply failed to intervene.[17]

These conflicts and abuses, often resulting from arbitrary informal rule (see Forrest, this volume), adversely affected production in the post-colonial period following liberalization. Tensions between local farmers and *ponteiros*, many of whom were of Guinean but also of Portuguese origin, over land demarcation, inheritance, control over resources, and the disputed legality of claims notoriously increased at local level as a result of uncoordinated govern-

[12] Mário Costa, Relatório da Inspecção Administrativa da Colónia da Guine, 1944–5: 67; Arquivo Histórico Ultramarino (AHU), Inspeccão Superior da Administração Ultramarina, ISAU, 2245.

[13] Interview with J. Godinho Gomes, Paço d'Arcos, Portugal, 9 May 1995.

[14] Interview with J. A. Lopes, op. cit.

[15] Costa, Relatório: 123.

[16] Interview with J. A. Lopes, op. cit.

[17] Interview with J. P. Saldanha, op. cit.

ment policies (Tanner 1991: 48–53; Cheneau-Loquay 1991: 33–40). With the advent of SAP and the shift towards economic privatization and deregulation in 1986, a major rise in *ponta* concessions occurred, many of them involving large surface areas (Espinosa 1994: 25–8; Indjai 2002: 102–11). As a result, new groups of planters emerged such as the absentee owners and the politically well-connected, while small and medium farms proliferated (Pereira et al. 1992: 24–8) as they had in the 1930s and 1940s.

Issues such as *ponteiros'* claims to village land, their transformation of these claims into legal titles, the access to water wells and the lack of compensation were often associated with the high-ranking positions held by *ponteiros* in the state bureaucracy (Tanner 1991: 46–58). In addition, wealthier *ponteiros*— then and now—were able to determine conditions on account of owning means of transport, e.g. big trucks, vans, motorboats and canoes. In the absence of a land law, the large extensions conceded to planters, which far exceeded the arable surface area, often clashed with local farming communities, without the latter having any means of redress (Pereira et al. 1992: 18). Whereas during the colonial period the concentration of concessions in the hands of planter-traders was already significant (Espinosa 1994: 25), between 1986 when liberalization policies took effect and 2000, the surface area of *pontas* amounted to almost half of all concessions made since 1946 (Indjai 2002: 103). By the early 1990s, 5% of planters held almost two-thirds of the total conceded area (Indjai 2002: 17; Espinosa 1994: 29).

The relevance of historical patterns for the post-colonial economy is shown most markedly in the context of relations between *ponteiros* and local producers. Both in colonial and post-colonial times, *ponteiros* exercised control over local transactions within the perimeter of their concessions, while colonial authorities, like their post-independence successors, set (maximum) farm-gate crop prices at the outset of the harvest season. In their concessions, which could include entire villages, *ponteiros* determined prices for the barter of crops and credit—during the colonial period usually at rates of approximately 100%—while prohibiting the sale of crops to third parties.[18] Then as now, the larger *ponteiros* also owned shops usually located close to transport routes and outlets catering for producers' basic necessities, such as locally distilled brandy or *kana*, textiles, tobacco and sugar.[19] Authorities' attempts at controlling the marketing of crops by means of licensing policies often clashed with farmers'

---

[18] Interview with J. A. Lopes, op. cit.
[19] Interview with J. A. Lopes, op. cit.

and traders' mobility, and induced them to smuggle produce under the cover of night.[20] These practices continued with the cashew boom, as part of harvests were rapidly smuggled across Guinea-Bissau's borders, which prompted authorities to reinforce frontier policing and custom controls. In a postcolonial setting following liberalization in the mid-1980s, cashew planters emulated colonial attitudes by obliging 'their' farmers to sell them their produce for less advantageous 'fixed' prices.[21]

The longevity of this system is indeed noteworthy. The Casa Gouveia and other colonial-era trade houses maintained regional stores in strategic locations in rice- and peanut-growing areas, operating networks served by trucks and vessels for the transport of crops from local trade centres and ports to Bissau, from which they were shipped to European destinations. The stores provided a selection of exchange goods (i.e. brandy, tobacco, textiles, fuel, tools, seeds, etc.) which could be bought on credit by traders and planters. The system dated back to the mid-1800s and consisted of the supply of imported commodities and seeds on credit at the outset of the rainy season (i.e. in May/June) in exchange for rice and peanut harvests and collected palm kernels.[22] The shop managers of the Casa Gouveia had margin for manoeuvre to concede—and even pardon—credit to traders and individual farmers if harvests were less successful, while sometimes giving presents such as rum or tobacco to their clients.[23] A survey of small traders showed that they were unable to cover their operating and maintenance costs (BACIAG 19 1959: 8–9) and that larger firms (e.g. ASG and SCU) maintained a stranglehold over small businesses in terms of commodities and credit (BACIAG 1 1958c: 30).

On paper the new state-owned network inaugurated in 1977 appeared to continue familiar policies, such as fixed consumer prices for imported goods including rice, fertilizers, pesticides and insecticides for agricultural use; minimum prices for local produce such as rice, peanuts and cashew nuts; while other, non-strategic commodities were left to a limited 'free market' (Guimarães 1992: 19–20). However, farm-gate prices for staple crops such as rice were

---

[20] Interview with J. P. da Silva, op. cit.; interview with, J. Godinho Gomes, Paço d'Arcos, Portugal, 10 March 1995; interview with J. P. Saldanha, op. cit.

[21] A distinction should be made here between the smuggling by big farmers and by smallholder farmers; it was an entrepreneurial strategy for the former and a survival strategy for the latter (Ka 1994: 72).

[22] Interview with José Atome, op. cit.

[23] Interview with José Atome, op. cit.; interview with J. Godinho Gomes, Paço d'Arcos, 3 March 1995.

often fixed at levels below world market prices, to the disadvantage of local producers, while price ceilings for imported commodities failed to take into account transport costs, causing serious nationwide supply problems (Alvesson 1990: 18–19). The failure to maintain adequate river transport, which was nationalized in 1974, was accompanied by a shift towards land-based routes much more sensitive to seasonal factors. The lack of basic and exchange commodities and credit facilities contributed to impairing the networks' incapacity to capture local produce, illustrated by a steady decline of the purchase of paddy rice (Cardoso 1986: 25; Forrest 1998: 14). As producer prices set by the state network after 1974 stagnated (Cardoso 1986: quadro 2) and the latter remained lower than those negotiated by private traders and in neighbouring countries, informal markets and cross-border smuggling flourished as the G–B peso introduced in 1976 lost out to the CFA, the official currency in Senegal and Guinea-Conakry and of other members of the UEMOA (the *Union économique et monétaire ouest-africaine* (Cardoso 1986: 25; Ka 1994: 96–7). This problem was by no means new: the differences in crop prices between Portuguese Guinea and its neighbours had already been denounced in the late 1950s (BACIAG 1 1958b: 9), above all in terms of determining the direction of cross-border flows of agricultural produce.

Whereas the colonial administration, through its guards or *cipaios* (military policemen), checked upon the transport and transaction of goods throughout the colony,[24] after 1974 the system of fixed prices, coupled with strict licensing as well as road checks (already introduced during the struggle), was continued, remaining in place until the mid-1980s. It has been described as a veritable lost 'war' on local private traders, above all the itinerant Fula and Mandinga *djila* traders (Hochet 1983: 18; Galli/Jones 1987: 113–14; Schiefer 1987: 246; Forrest 1998: 11–12). With economic liberalization these traders dramatically expanded their activities and became dominant commercial actors in rural areas (Forrest 1998: 15; Lundy, 2015: 118–23). Similar campaigns were also waged against itinerant female traders, whose networks continued to expand after 1974 despite state controls, engaging in a lively cross-border trade with their Senegalese and Guinean peers which rapidly grew after the mid-1980s. Sharecropping and selling their labour to *ponteiros* at crop-planting and harvest times provided alternative income for farmers, who largely depended on mutual intra-community assistance and informal networks. Small farmers and above all female producer-traders and itinerant traders, or *bidêras*, stepped

---

[24] Interview with J. P. da Silva, op. cit.

into the gap, selling their own produce and reselling products for more competitive prices at local weekly rural '*lumo*' fairs[25] in border villages (Havik 1998: 216).[26] Located along the country's extensive borders with Senegal and Guinea-Conakry, these fairs largely resulted from local initiatives by village authorities and petty traders wishing to provide outlets and cash in on the new trend. While the rapid expansion of women's vegetable gardens provided them with an important source of income, the proliferation of producer associations and rotating savings and credit associations (ROSCAs) or *grupos de abota* reinforced their organization and socio-economic impact (Havik 1998: 213; Domingues 2000: 445–9).[27] Guinea-Bissau's joining the UEMOA and the CFA zone in 1997 facilitated transactions whilst neutralizing the impact of high inflation on prices and the instability/devaluation of the peso currency (AfDB 2015: 15).

Therefore, implanted systems of cash crop economies over many decades did not make allowances for economic subsistence, which was virtually ignored until the late 1980s and early 1990s, when poverty-based assessments began to be carried out. These studies pointed at the constraints on productivity in agriculture in terms of human resources, migration and environmental factors, and attributed primary importance to the informal barter economy for rural populations' livelihoods (Crowley 1993). In addition, these reports recognized women farmers' key contribution to smallholder agriculture and income-earning activities (World Bank 1994: 28–30). Women were seen to fare better in relation to men in terms of poverty alleviation, owing to their informal economic activities (IMF 2007: 10) and their concern for the well-being of households and their dependents.

Industrialisation, crop-processing and the cashew boom

By the late 1950s, the principal local body representing traders and planters in the colony concluded that Guinea's economic system was outdated and trade

---

[25] Interview with J. A. Lopes, op. cit.; interview with J. P. da Silva, op. cit.

[26] See for example interviews with T. Nhando, Mansoa, 20 September 1991; R. Correia, Farim, 22 September 1991 (interviewer: J. M. Camará); S. Indjai, Buba, 26 August 1991 (interviewer: S. Q. Mané); M. Sané, Mansoa, 7 October 1991 (interviewer: J. M. Camará); M. Djau, Gabú, 7 November 1991 (interviewer: S. Q. Mané).

[27] On the importance of ROSCAs and microcredit facilities for women—and men—in rural areas in Guinea-Bissau, see Reis (1994) and Lopes (2011).

had stagnated, making insistent appeals for applied scientific research, economic planning, agricultural extension and credit, and reforms of the colonial bureaucracy and fiscal policies (BACIAG 1 1958a: 6–8; BACIAG 60 1962: 16–17). These appeals included strongly-worded criticism of large trading firms and planters; requests for stimuli for small planters; and help with small land concessions and credit facilities (BACIAG 78 1966: 44) similar to proposals made in the late 1980s and early 1990s with economic liberalization (e.g. Pereira et al. 1992: 37–53). One of the few advocates among the wealthy commercial stratum was a trader-planter of Cape Verdean origin, Mário Lima, a member of the colony's advisory board, the Conselho Legislativo, who associated himself with the nationalist opposition.[28] This critical stance was corroborated by the then deputy for Guinea in the National Assembly, Avelino Teixeira da Mota, arguing for the need to end the peanut monoculture and halt the process of 'senegalization' (Teixeira da Mota 1954: vol. 2, 164)—a concern shared by Cabral (1956: 42)—by introducing new crops like cotton, sugarcane and cashew trees while giving attention to the question of land tenure (Teixeira da Mota 1958: 913). Quoting studies on the negative impact of production of cash crops such as peanuts upon the natural environment in neighbouring territories, the need was recognized for social research into indigenous (above all rice) farming, thus far disregarded (Teixeira da Mota 1958: 913), and for an innovative look at agriculture neglected by an inept administrative apparatus (Teixeira da Mota 1954: vol. 2, 166).

In the 1930s, as *ponta* agriculture rapidly expanded, the first crop-processing facilities emerged in the form of rice-husking machines, introduced by private planter-traders, soon followed by larger trading firms such as ASG, SCU and Camacho and Correia (BACIAG 78 1966: 40). In the 1950s and 1960s, strong criticism was voiced with respect to the lack of industry and local processing capacity in the colony; besides lacking quality in terms of crop-processing, Guinea was in all likelihood the last colony in Africa to initiate the export of shelled peanuts (Teixeira da Mota 1958: 912; see Graph 3). The few rudimentary industrial units were distilleries producing *kana* or rum from sugarcane, palm kernel crushing machines, and presses for manufacturing palm oil, peanut oil, fish oil, soap and lemonades (Horta/Sardinha 1966: 146–52). Strong criticism was also forthcoming from the nationalist leader Amílcar Cabral: the backwardness of 'traditional' farmers, the lack of develop-

---

[28] Processo CR 72/65, Bissau, 24 June 1966, PIDE (Portuguese Secret Service) Archives, Instituto dos Arquivos Nacionais Torre do Tombo (IANTT), Lisbon.

ment policies and programmes of agricultural extension, of agronomic research and investment, all inhibited progress and the improvement of living standards (Cabral 1959: 534; Galli 1986: 57–62; Galli 1987: 85–9). Rather than recovering its paddy fields (Cabral 1959: 534), Portuguese Guinea urgently needed to modernize its 'backward' indigenous agriculture, including state-led mechanization (Cabral 1954: 399), and thereby increase the surface area under cultivation and intensify farming (Cabral 1954: 399–400). Guinean agriculture badly needed competent extension services for the support and training of local populations, to develop high-yield cash crop cultivation, to raise productivity of existing crops, and to establish a processing industry by means of state intervention (Cabral 1959: 535).

Although the Plano Intercalar de Fomento (1964–7) already envisaged government inputs in the establishment of cashew plantations and a processing capacity for cashew nuts (Mendes 1970: 127–35; Schiefer 1987: 199–121), investments failed to materialize (Horta/Sardinha 1966: 142). Reports concluded that reforms were needed in agriculture, to improve crop production levels and quality standards, to supply local industries with raw materials in a regular fashion, and to create a competitive market both domestically and within the Espaço Económico Português (Horta/Sardinha 1966: 162–3). At the time, the colony counted only three rice-husking facilities, all located in the

Graph 3

Guinea-Bissau exports—peanuts

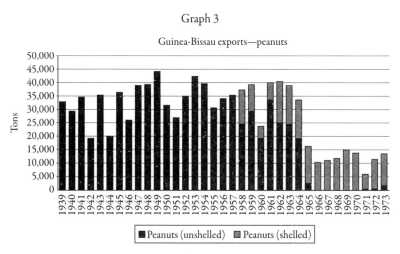

Sources: BACIAG 1963: 25–58; Boletim Cultural Guiné Portuguesa 1961–1971; Anuário Estatístico Ultramarino 1971; 1973.

capital, and seven peanut-shelling plants concentrated in the Bafatá region and the capital (Província da Guiné 1972: 118). As a result, the colony's capacity for exporting shelled peanuts notably increased during the colonial war (see Graph 3), despite the decline in peanut production. Indeed, the colony's sawmills, peanut and palm oil presses, distilleries, soap factories and bakeries were largely centred on the major towns such as Bissau or Bafatá (Província da Guiné 1972: 118). In order to develop credit facilities and capital investment, alternatives to peanuts had to be found, and one of the most promising appeared to be cashew nuts. First proposed as an export crop in the late 1890s (Carvalho 1944: 98–9), the first serious attempt to introduce cashew trees as a cash crop was made in the 1950s, when the colonial administration created the Bijimita colony in the Biombo region near the capital Bissau. Families from Bissau, as well as Pepel and Balanta farmers, were selected to settle the area; they were provided with housing, land, seeds and tools to grow a variety of crops. The seeds were supplied by the experimental farm or *granja* in nearby Quinhamel where cashew trees had been planted and harvested in the preceding years.[29] Until that point, the fruit of cashew trees growing in the wild was generally harvested to produce cashew juice and wine, as well as toasted cashew nuts for local consumption; this was done by women, selling from their homes and at markets. The fact that cashew harvests take place from April to June meant that strategic revenue could be obtained during the last months of the dry season and the beginning of the rains. Selected families were now expected to prove their capacity to farm the crops, otherwise they were replaced. The project was an initiative of the local administrator at the time, who had served in Angola where such policies had proved successful.[30]

The shift towards agro-industrial projects in Portuguese colonies in the 1960s (Baptista/Chaves 1961; Esteves 1964), strongly influenced by export-oriented companies such as the CUF, would also have an impact upon the Guinean economy. Government and specialist reports stressed the importance of cashew nuts for Portuguese Guinea's future economic prospects and the need for expanding its value-adding capacity for the husking, drying and cashew (fruit) processing (Oliveira 1966; Província da Guiné 1972: 124; Mendes 1972). Plans for the systematic introduction of cashew trees on thousands of hectares in the Bolama, Bissau, Cacheu and Bafatá regions were hatched in order to produce economic benefits for trade and exports. But

[29] Interview with J. Godinho Gomes, Paço d'Arcos, 9 May 1995.
[30] Ibidem.

cashew farming was also considered advantageous owing to the plant's proper-ties with respect to soil conservation in a territory with a fragile ecosystem (Horta 1965: 407–10; Província da Guiné 1972: 68). Alternatives such as sugarcane and cotton production—the first grown for *kana* distilling, while the latter had seen failed trials in the 1920s—were shelved for being too con-troversial. The production of kola nuts, which would become the PAIGC's main export crop during the war (Dhada 1993: 81), and sesame seeds was also advocated by the colonial government (Horta 1965: 423). Similarly, both sides also set their sights on the production of sweet potatoes, manioc and fruit, which were seen as essential for diversifying and improving the popula-tion's diet (Horta 1965: 402–4, 417–20; Província da Guiné 1972: 66–7; Dhada 1993:78).

These policies would be refashioned from 1977 onwards following the PAIGC's third congress, which adopted a contradictory, two-pronged strategy for 'balanced development': an industrialization programme, while giving priority to agricultural development (Chabal 1983: 199–201; Paulini 1984: 49–50, 89–97; Galli 1987: 89; Schiefer 1987: 210–35, 305–12; Okafor 1988: 127–32). Local agro-industries were established, such as the Titina Silá factory inaugurated on Bolama island in 1977 which was set to produce jam, mango and cashew juice; the Blufo milk factory in 1979; and the Cumeré agro-indus-trial complex for the husking of rice, the shelling and processing of peanuts, palm and cashew kernels, and the production of palm and peanut oil as well as soap (PAIGC 1980: 23–27). All this was accompanied by plans to raise peanut and cashew production, relying on the state's capacity to extract produce and supply its agro-industry with sufficient raw materials, as well as providing farm-ers with basic consumer goods and credit (Havik 1991: 283). It soon became clear that the industrialization drive had failed, in terms of mobilizing farmers into selling their tradeable surpluses (Rudebeck 1982: 13–14); their liveli-hoods further deteriorated as a result of successive droughts. But this failure also arose on account of the lack of a coherent strategy, which, by focusing on farming cooperatives and state farms, continued to ignore the need for incen-tives to the large majority of the smallholder farms (Okafor 1988: 133–4). In the process, the exports of peanuts and palm kernels rapidly diminished and entered into a continuous and inexorable decline (see Graph 4).

Also, these projects were characteristic of development strategies pursued by African states from the 1960s which increased dependency on foreign aid and credit, while failing to galvanize their rural economies (Okafor 1988: 136). Indeed, post-colonial economic policies in Guinea-Bissau need to be

Graph 4

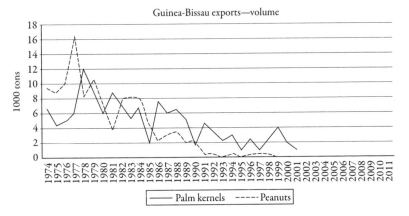

Guinea-Bissau exports—volume

Sources: Paulini 1984: 163; FAOstat.

situated alongside those of their neighbours. Curiously, the PAIGC's industrialization and import substitution strategy came as similar policies appeared to be failing in neighbouring Senegal in the late 1970s (Boone 1990: 343). Here the persistence of a peanut monoculture, despite its doubtful track record and the growing critique among colonial and nationalist actors from the 1950s, had revealed the persistence of neo-colonial approaches (Boone 1990: 346) infused with notions of a technocratic 'administrative developmentalism' (Barker 1977: 36–7) and underpinned by arrangements for 'economic continuity' with France (Boone 1990: 345). The Senegalese regime replicated tight state regulation from the colonial era centred on a peanut monoculture, and relied upon the perpetuation of political control and regulation of the economy (Ka 1994: 79–89), while political patronage was distributed through the single party, the UPS (Union progressiste sénégalaise), and the state bureaucracy (Boone 1990: 347).

Meanwhile in the case of Guinea-Conakry, its rural economy based upon the production for export of bananas, coffee and palm kernels was confronted with a serious crisis by the mid-1970s. After independence, President Sékou Touré and the PDG (Parti démocratique de Guinée) pursued a policy which gave priority to industrialization of the country and the modernization of agriculture through mechanization and training based upon farming collectives. These collectives focused on single crops for industry or export and state farms, and strict government controls existed over domestic trade circuits and crop pricing. Tensions ensued, demonstrating the problems faced by a 'traditional' smallholder-based rural economy expected to produce for a 'modern' agro-industry but obliged to import an increasing volume of staple crops (e.g. rice) (Denis 1976: 324–6). Attempts to introduce farm collectives in Guinea-Bissau (Chabal 1983: 206) were rapidly shelved during the war of liberation (Dhada 1993: 73–5) and post-independence efforts to revive them with ex-combatants failed. These experiences and those in neighbouring Guinea-Conakry may serve to explain government reticence in the 1980s following economic liberalization (Galli 1989: 28), as well as the shift of focus towards trade and farmers' commercial associations (MDRA 1990: 17).

Both neighbouring Senegal and Guinea-Conakry eventually embraced economic liberalization in the mid-1980s (Clapp 1993; Thioub/Diop/Boone 1998; Dahou 2008), i.e. simultaneously with Guinea-Bissau. While Senegal failed to diversify its peanut economy and Guinea-Conakry increasingly relied on investments in mining, neither combined a rural barter economy with a substantial upgrading of its crop export economy in the way that Guinea-Bissau did with the rapid expansion of cashew farming in the 1990s and 2000s. Barter trade between *ponteiros* and local farmers became based upon the exchange of cashew nuts by smallholder producers for domestically produced rice and—increasingly—imported rice (Lea/Hugo/Cardoso 1990: 41; Lea/Hugo/Ribeiro 1990: 29; MDRA/FAO/PAM 2007; Barry/Creppy/Wodon 2007: 78; Temudo/Abrantes 2013: 226). By the late 1980s cashew nuts already represented 44% of total exports in volume and over 60% in value (Lea/Hugo/Cardoso 1990: 19). By 2002, Guinea-Bissau had become the world's fifth largest producer (in volume) of cashew nuts, almost equalling Brazil's production levels (see Graphs 2 and 5).[31] In neighbouring Senegal cashew production centres on the Casamance region in the south, which has similar characteristics in terms of ecology, farming and human settlement as northern Guinea-Bissau. The Senegalese system consists mainly of smallholder production, illustrating local agency in the absence of direct government intervention—and even outright lack of interest—and agricultural extension in terms of selection of crop varieties, seed and crop quality and protective

---

[31] In 2000 the Comissão Nacional de Cajú (CNC) was set up in order to improve government coordination and planning in the cashew sector and annual cashew campaigns, to increase the efficacy of value chains, and to carry out studies on the employment of human and material resources in cashew production, marketing and export. The Agência Nacional do Caju da Guiné-Bissau (ANCA-GB) is currently responsible for regulating the cashew sector.

Graph5

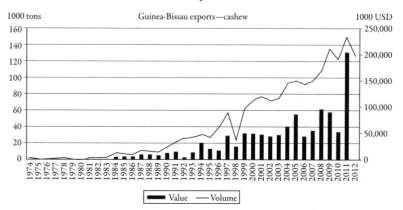

Sources: Lea, Hugo e Cardoso 1990: 20; app. 3; Aguilar e Zejan: 1992: 19; FAOstat; FAO Countrystat.

measures (Cambon 2003: ch.I). It strongly differs from Guinea-Bissau's active involvement of the state in terms of fixing prices—above all by setting the terms of the rice–cashew barter exchange—and taxing exports, but also in terms of the higher quality of kernels produced and exported from Bissau (Cambon 2003: ch.II; Kyle 2009: 6).

In recent years, Guinea-Bissau's processing capacity has increased on account of the establishment of a number of larger processing units in the capital Bissau, such as Agri-Bissau, Sicajú and BandB Cajú (Lynn/Jaeger 2004: 12; Kyle 2009: 7), while smaller units operate throughout the country, above all in the Biombo and Bafatá areas (Lynn/Jaeger 2004: 13–14).[32] In addition, the first cashew-drying plant was inaugurated in the country by a Portuguese firm in Safim (near the capital Bissau) in 2014. Despite the dearth of agricultural extension and credit for smallholders—85% of which grow the crop on an average farm size of 1.5 hectares (Carvalho/Mendes 2012: 23–4), often intercropped with other food and cash crops in the initial stages—they are

---

[32] In 1994, the Fundação Guineense para o Desenvolvimento Empresarial Industrial (FUNDEI) was established with support from the local and Swedish governments in order to modernize small and medium businesses in the country by providing credit and training facilities (e.g. in the Centro de Promoção de Cajú in Brá/Bissau) and improve product marketing, above all directed towards the cashew and fruit sectors.

largely responsible for cashew production, which in recent years represents 98% of export revenue (Kyle 2009: 2) and more than 10% of total tax revenues (Carvalho/Mendes 2012: 125). Although the cashew monoculture which emerged after economic liberalization has far outstripped its peanut predecessor, the crop's cultivation across different agro-ecological zones and ethnic divisions—the main production areas are located in the north, followed by the east and the south—indicates a significant alteration of the colonial/neo-colonial context of crop production described above. Despite the emergence of new value chains, certain differences between smallholder populations persist owing to their social organization, farming techniques and resource management (Dias 1996: 333–74; Forrest 1998: 5–8; Temudo/Abrantes 2014: 224–6).

Comparisons between Balanta and Fula farmers show that whereas the former, specializing in paddy rice farming, tended to reinvest the proceeds from cashew nuts and fruit in their rice fields, the latter heavily relied upon barter exchange to obtain the staple crop whilst experiencing food shortages (Temudo/Abrantes 2014: 226–7). Attempts to create a rice-processing capacity, such as the Xayanga complex, were undermined by a high degree of mechanization, a lack of fertilizers and seeds, expensive transport facilities and inadequate management, thereby driving up costs and failing to compete with imported rice (RGB 2003: 18–19). Initiatives by local farmer associations such as Apalcolf and Guiarroz also suffered from a lack of adequate credit facilities, extension, training, protection against harvest losses and spare parts (ibid.: 19). The need for increasing local processing capacity for rice is also argued on account of alleviating women's inputs in rice-husking (RGB 2003: 20), thus increasing their availability to engage in income-generating activities and to stem the rural exodus of younger generations (ibid.: 22).

However, the rapid and widespread expansion of cashew as a cash crop is deeply affecting the country's fragile environment—as it did in the colonial era in the case of peanuts—leading to deforestation in upland and savannah areas (Temudo/Abrantes 2014: 224–5). Cashew plantations which largely emerge in a spontaneous fashion cover about 5% of the country's territory—a percentage that far outstrips any other major cashew producers—and are rapidly expanding into hitherto uncultivated forested areas, above all in the east and the south (Lynn/Jaeger 2004: 2–3). Distances between villages and fields is increasing, while a burgeoning land market and disputes over land rights—not just between farmers and *ponteiros*, but also among smallholders and ethnic communities—are producing renewed tensions at local level as land pressure increases (Temudo/Abrantes 2014: 228; and also this volume). The barter exchange of cashew for rice has also had repercussions for farmers' and rural communities' food security, as rice production failed to keep pace with demand and dependency on imports of the country's main staple crop rose (RGB 2003: 21–22; MDRA/FAO/PAM 2007: 6; Gacitua-Mario/ Nordang/Wodon 2007: 67; Barry/Creppy/Wodon 2007: 83–4; Carvalho/ Mendes 2012: 120–5; Temudo and Abrantes in this volume; see Graph 6). In the meantime, peanut production increased somewhat on account of projects for improving seed quality, yields and incentives in order to raise farmers' incomes. In addition, given the almost total predominance of cashew in terms of production for domestic trade and export, fluctuations in farm-gate prices have an immediate and decisive impact on smallholders' income and their livelihoods (Gacitua-Mario/Nordang/Wodon 2007: 60–61; World Bank 2010: 2; AfDB 2015: 2–3).

Conclusions

'Single stories' of colonial and post-colonial economic 'modernity' and 'development' in Africa have been challenged from environmental, agronomic, socio-historical and anthropological perspectives. Guinea-Bissau forms no

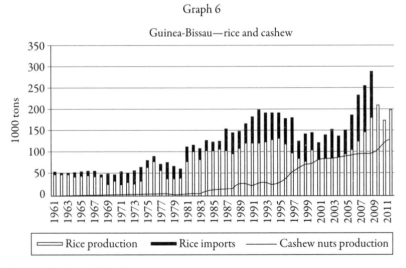

Graph 6

Guinea-Bissau—rice and cashew

Source: FAOstat; FAO Countrystat.

exception. But the country does occupy a particular niche in this debate, differing from its immediate neighbours, i.e. Senegal and Guinea-Conakry, on account of the particularities of its rural economy. The territory's ecology and history, its 'late' occupation, its complex ethnic mosaic, the tense triangular relations between the state, *ponteiro* trader-planters and smallholder farmers and the protracted war of liberation set it apart from other West African countries. The above analysis of the rural economy from the early 1900s onwards shows to what extent the country's course was characterized by a continuity of policies and practices geared to the production of a single export crop. The centralized fixing of prices for single crops by colonial and Guinea-Bissau's authorities well illustrates this historical continuity. Since the mid-1800s the rural economy has been dominated by two 'single' export crop cycles, i.e. peanuts and cashew, which almost exclusively depend on indigenous inputs by smallholders. Despite being determinant for the incomes of the large majority of the country's population, these inputs have received little attention from both colonial and post-colonial authorities. The advent of poverty alleviation studies in the early 1990s heralded a belated attempt at understanding the key role of indigenous farming. The tensions that emerged over time between commercial and subsistence agriculture—which remain unresolved—had and still have a crucial impact on rural communities. While the organization of the rural economy reflects these historical tensions and imbalances, it also confirms the longevity of the *ponteiro* model, as well as that of smallholder production of export and subsistence crops.

Conflict, migration, climatic and environmental factors all highlighted the fragility of the rural economy, whilst the lack of support and extension from the colonial and post-colonial state obliged producers to devise coping strategies in order to 'synchronize' cash with subsistence crop cultivation. Indeed, cashew is simultaneously a 'cash' and a 'subsistence' crop, like peanuts before it; on average, the proceeds from the barter/sale of cashew guarantee five months' food security for rural families (Carvalho/Mendes 2012: 130). Relations between smallholder farmers, commercial farmers, traders and the state were marked by erratic land concession and economic policies, which but for relatively short intervals failed to break the historical continuum straddling colonial and post-colonial periods. The lack of credit, capital, of a processing industry, of effective 'formal' trade networks and large variations in producer prices did not however deter producers from maintaining surprising levels of food sovereignty and marketable cash crop surpluses (Temudo 2013: 286) in what is essentially a barter economy. Indeed, given the high density of cashew tree-planting in smallholder farms, their productivity levels are considered to be higher than modern plantations (Lynn/Jaeger 2004: 5), while labour and material inputs are significantly lower than in the case of paddy rice cultivation, for example (Temudo 2009: 60; World Bank 2010: 2).

In contrast to colonial and post-colonial calls for modernization, which tended to ignore local inputs, the expansion of 'cash' crops was achieved without recourse to 'modern' agriculture as envisaged by colonial and nationalist circles. Whilst Guinea-Bissau is currently presented as a fragile, failed or 'narco-state', and figures in statistics as one of the poorest countries in the world, its rural economy demonstrates farmers' notable capacity to introduce new crops with a major impact on the country's output under unstable political and economic conditions. The feminization of the rural economy in terms of production and exchange also shows to what extent the consistent lack of state support and the inequalities deriving from commercial agriculture were countered—but not offset—by the remarkable dynamics of the country's 120,000 rural households and communities. Indeed, the fragility of 'modern' infrastructures in Guinea-Bissau contrasts with the buoyancy of its informal economy (AfDB 2015: 5). Despite the crop monoculture, the limited access to social, education and health services, widespread material poverty and lack of basic necessities (RGB 2005; RGB 2011), the wealth and diversity of economic, social and cultural resources remain the fundamental pillar of Guinea-Bissau's dynamic and resilient rural society.

PART TWO

MANIFESTATIONS OF THE CRISIS

4

RURAL LIVELIHOODS AND SOCIAL STABILITY IN GUINEA-BISSAU

THE END OF AN ERA?

Marina Padrão Temudo and *Manuel Bivar Abrantes*

In this chapter[1] we argue that until recently the resilience of Guinea-Bissau rural societies to cope with external shocks was high, mainly due to their food sovereignty strategies, and their customary rules of access to land and of solving land conflicts. However, the civil war of 1998–9, together with the full establishment of a cashew nut agricultural frontier, had a pivotal role in accelerating the pace of change in social and land use patterns, in a way that made societies less able to cope with political instability/crisis, market variability and climate change.

[1] Preliminary research was conducted under the framework of the project Carboveg-GB funded by the Guinea-Bissau and Portuguese governments, and subsequently funded by FCT (the Portuguese Foundation for Science and Technology) under the projects PTDC/AFR/111546/2009 and PTDC/AFR/117785/2010. The authors would like to thank Rosemary Galli, Vincent Foucher, Philip Havik, Alexandre Abreu, Eric Gable, the editors and the reviewers for their inspiring critical comments.

Wars in Africa have been well-known for causing hunger and famine. But the riots and social unrest associated with the recent increase in food prices made clear the link between food insecurity and the potential for the emergence of conflicts. As Hendrix and Brinkman (2013) emphasized, we may find a 'circular link' between conflicts and food insecurity. According to them, food security 'reduces conflict drivers, enhances social cohesion, rebuilds social trust, and builds the legitimacy and capacity of governments' (Hendrix and Brinkman 2013: 1). At the same time, both food security and seed security confer resilience to cope with social and natural disasters (e.g. Richards and Ruivenkamp 1997).

The land tenure question in Africa (e.g. ECA 2004; Cotula 2007) and the way access to land can cause social instability have also been under study. In the particular case of West Africa, Chauveau and Richards (2008) stressed the need to study the evolution of lineage societies in colonial and post-colonial times, mostly in relation to intergenerational tensions—associated with access to land and to women—that may be at the root of youths' motivations for insurgencies (see also Mokuwa et al. 2011). Major transformations in land tenure and the land structure are frequently associated with agricultural frontiers—linked with expanding cash crops and the settling of migrants. These changes can create social tensions between autochthonous communities and latecomers and between generations that can end up in conflicts (e.g. Chauveau and Richards 2008). But in the same way that competition over land—either between generations or between firstcomers and latecomers—can trigger violence, conflicts can further disrupt land tenure relations (e.g. Cotula 2007). Additionally, neo-liberal land tenure changes of land titling and the individualization of property increased the value of land and the competition over its control (e.g. Simo 2011). Recently, a growing body of literature has also emerged on land grabbing and green grabbing and their implications in terms of poverty (e.g. *Journal of Peasant Studies* 39, 1–2, 2012)—a common trigger of grievances and social unrest.

In the remainder of the chapter we are going to foreground our argument empirically, starting with a section explaining the reasons why Guinea-Bissau rural societies had been able to cope well with external shocks until recently. The following section will deal with the fast-track changes which have been happening over the last two decades, illustrating the way they are negatively impacting on rural societies' social resilience.

A long-term resilient social fabric

Food sovereignty and social stability

Up until recently most smallholders, while actively engaging with the market, had been able to access sufficient, safe and nutritious food, mainly through their own local production and exchange networks, and through hunting and fishing and the harvest of wild fruits, leaves and roots. The colonial intervention did not fully disarticulate smallholders' production systems, either through land expropriation or through favouring male migration (see chapter by Havik, this volume). Exploitation was largely based on the imposition of hut taxes, in order to force smallholders to produce and sell export crops (mainly peanuts and rice) and to collect wild products (e.g. palm kernels, rubber and beeswax). It depended also on forced labour for the construction of roads and bridges and on the control of trade (Chabal 1983: 21, 23, 25). But, while smallholders across the country considered the hut tax (*dasa*) 'small and easy to pay', forced labour—though minimal in relation to Angola and Mozambique (Chabal 1983: 21)—was fiercely resisted through migration and later through adherence to the liberation war (Temudo 2009).

The main export crop between 1846 and independence in 1974 was peanuts. Rice exports to Europe started in the 1930s, after the Balanta migration to the south, and continued through the mid-1950s, when contraband, a sequence of dry years and, finally, the anti-colonial war inverted this trend (Teixeira da Mota 1954, vol. 2: 151). Prices and seed credit policies (with local varieties) aimed to incentivize production for export, but smallholders used to smuggle rice and peanuts across the borders to Senegal and Guinea-Conakry when prices were higher in the French colonies (e.g. Teixeira da Mota 1954, vol. 2: 152). No improved seeds or fertilizers were distributed to farmers, and colonial efforts were mostly concentrated on reducing post-harvest losses (for a synthesis, see Temudo 1998, vol. 1: 207). In sum, the production of the two main export crops did not disrupt the local seed system.

Nonetheless, pre-harvest hunger of varying intensities has been described, at the compound and/or regional levels, since colonial times (Teixeira da Mota 1954, vol. 2: 54). With the exception of the Balanta—the only group who regularly produced surplus rice—self-sufficiency in cereals was rare. Until the end of the 1990s, however, food scarcity was generally site- and situation-specific, although cyclical at a country level, and related either to land scarcity due to population pressure (mostly in Oio, Biombo and Cacheu), to varied misfortunes (e.g. illness, difficulties in labour mobilization, poor harvests caused by droughts or pest attacks, exceptional expenses with ceremonies, among others) or to a greater investment in livestock raising and non-agricultural activities (mostly among the Fula and the Mandinga in the east). Frequently, at a compound level, food scarcity could be solved through networks of kith and kin, other local mechanisms of reciprocity (e.g. payments in cereals after 'unrequested' help during harvest), direct exchange of goods, non-agricultural incomes, harvest of wild foods and production of crops during the dry season (cassava, sweet potatoes, vegetables for consumption and/ or the market). In the case of the Manjako, traditional chiefs (*adju*) are commanded to support the most vulnerable in return for their subjects' tributary work in chieftaincy lands for rice production (see Abreu 2012: 187).

In general, we may say that the cultivation of cash crops did not disarticulate smallholder food production. The only exception was highlighted in the 1960s by Carreira (1960: 272; 1962b: 279), who noted a tendency to full market integration and economic differentiation in the main groundnut-producing area—the east. Smallholders reduced millets and sorghum production—the main staple foods in the region—and increased rice consumption, creating food insecurity, market distortions and a need for the colonial state to control prices in order to prevent price inflation by local merchants (Carreira 1960: 272). By contrast, after independence and according to eastern smallholders, in some villages the use of fertilizers in cotton production and the introduction of ox-ploughing induced an expansion of the production area of cereals.

Ethnic diversity (mainly in Quinara and Tombali provinces) corresponded to a kind of functional complementarity of livelihood systems, and cereals shortage was mostly mitigated by a complex system of inter-ethnic exchange mechanisms, reinforcing the inter-ethnic alliances emphasized by Forrest (2003). These included an exchange of work and other products (mainly groundnuts, palm oil and handmade soap, among others) for rice, and a system of loans based on strong social networks (e.g. Temudo and Abrantes 2012). In other regions, where both the social fabric and livelihood systems were more homogeneous, as in Gabú and Bafatá provinces, incomes from livestock, craftwork, honey, seasonal migration and commerce made it possible to earn the wherewithal to buy cereals. All around the country, though, hunting and/or fishing, and the harvest of wild roots, leaves and fruits constituted important sources of food, especially during the lean season. Moreover, up until today most smallholders produce local varieties, exchanging seeds through their kin and kith with no money transactions, and making a minute use of agrochemicals.[2] 'Multiplex livelihoods' (Bryceson 2002), then, had been a characteristic feature of rural life-worlds in Guinea-Bissau much before the liberalization of the economy.

All these aspects of rural livelihoods provided an extraordinary resilience to cope with the anti-colonial and the 1998–9 wars. Although throughout the struggle for independence the area under cultivation was reduced dramatically (Chabal 1983: 24; Galli 1995: 72) and migration to the neighbouring countries was high (Galli 1987: 90), smallholders in the liberated areas continued to produce surplus to feed the army and to be exchanged for some basic products (e.g. cloth, tobacco, matches, sugar). More recently, during the eleven-month period of the 1998–9 civil war, more than 200,000 urbanites found refuge in the countryside, where they were given food and shelter regardless of their ethnicity and the existence or not of kinship ties. The war started at the very beginning of the rainy season when cereal stocks were low, and some smallholders were forced to eat a part of their seed stock to face the increase in the number of household dwellers. Furthermore, humanitarian aid was insufficient and hardly effective (Tin 2002); and after the war seed distribution was unsuccessful, given a lack of knowledge regarding smallholder preferences, the delayed distribution and the fact that no information was given on characteristics of the varieties delivered (for a case study, see Temudo and Schiefer 2003). In sum, although rural societies were able to deal with the consequences of the civil war, their resilience to cope with future shocks was weakened.

Access to land and social stability

In Guinea-Bissau, the Portuguese state had never been able (or interested) to introduce a plantation economy (Mendy 1990: 38) and land remained largely under the control of smallholders (Chabal 1983: 20; see also chapter by Havik, this volume). Concessions (*pontas*) were mainly used as an instrument to ensure the monopoly purchase of smallholders' cash crops. At the time of independence there were 1,300 concessions, of which 212 covered 89% of the area attributed (Espinosa 1994: 23–4). Cultivation took place through a kind of contract farming, and exploitation was done via forced sales based on

---

[2] Contrary to what happened in other African countries, in Guinea-Bissau, before structural adjustment (SAP) rural development interventions were mostly unsuccessful (on this topic see Temudo/Abrantes 2012).

unequal terms of trade and a greedy credit system (e.g. Teixeira da Mota 1954, vol 2: 158, 9; Mendy 1990). Colonial land tenure laws were grounded on the assumption that the state owned the land. The so-called *'indigenas'* could not be granted land concessions and had only access to 'lands reserved for the exclusive use of the indigenous population'[3] and later to 'Indigenous reserves',[4] regulated by 'use and custom' (Espinosa 1994: 20–21). Despite this, the very preamble to the by-law regulating land grants, published in 1938, mentions the existence of conflicts between smallholders and land concessionaires around mangrove flooded land, suitable for rice cultivation—a fact also mentioned by many southern interviewees. Furthermore, fallows and forests were often considered 'vacant' or 'wastelands', and therefore could be granted to land concessionaires (see also Espinosa 1994: 23).

Land in Guinea-Bissau, according to Augel (1993: 229), is 'sacred ground', 'a place of identification' and 'one of the foundations of ethnic identity'. Indeed, many present-day provinces are still known by the Kriol label of *'Tchon* di [land of] Nalú', *'Tchon* di Balanta', *'Tchon* di Manjako', and so on. In each of these *'Tchons'*, the first ethnic group that allegedly settled in the territory has the right to allocate land to latecomers and to manage the use of natural resources. Furthermore, as many other scholars have stressed regarding other African countries (e.g. Mathieu 1996), land distribution to latecomers is mediated by a set of rules and by given ceremonies. These constitute a form of political and religious recognition of the authority of the firstcomers—the landlords (*dunu di tchon*).

Land tenure relations in Guinea-Bissau can be broadly described as being based on the right of any adult or household to provide for their sustenance, belonging or not to the same ethnic group as the landlords. Across the country, migrants who settled—called guests (*hóspedes* or *hospri*, Kr.)—had the same rights of access to and obligations towards land for agriculture, hunting, wood collection, wild food and medicinal plants as the firstcomers.[5] Until around 1999, access to land was not controlled by the market, but by the head of the founding lineage in each locale, be it a village, a chieftaincy, or a 'spirit province' (on this concept, see Crowley 1990: 223). In general, every household head possessed permanent holding rights to given parcels of land, which

---

[3] Regulamento para a concessão de terrenos, Portaria nº 27 (8/2/1938).
[4] Regulamento da ocupação e concessão de terrenos nas províncias ultramarinas, Decreto nº 43894, 207/61, Série I: 1103–28, 06/09/1961.
[5] Some differences could be found in relation to wild products, as mentioned by Crowley (1990: 230) for the Cacheu region.

could be passed to descendants. Leasing was uncommon, but in Cacheu and Biombo, Manjako and Pepel kings (*régulos*) have 'chieftaincy lands' that are frequently rented. Mortgage was also infrequent and only possible in the case of land where investments in labour and/or capital had been made. In Tombalí we observed some rare cases of orchards' mortgage, but among the Balanta (both in the north and the south) mangrove rice fields (*bolanha salgada*), where dykes and dams constitute major investments, had been traditionally mortgaged in cases where the need for cash (e.g. acute food shortage or prolonged illness) or cattle (mainly for mourning ceremonies) was urgent.

Usually slash-and-burn provided permanent usufruct rights to land, and it was on their own forest fallows that the majority of smallholders created orchards after independence. Some exceptions of major importance can be found, though. Among the Beafada, in some parts of Quinara, namely in the Tite and Fulacunda administrative sectors, smallholders had no permanent rights to shifting cultivation fields. In these cases, the area around the compounds where groundnuts were cultivated was given with permanent usufruct rights that could be transmitted to descendants, but every year it was the head of the founding lineage in each village who decided in which forest(s') patch(es) the villagers could slash and burn. In some Fula villages of Gabú, forest clearance did not give permanent rights of usufruct to a parcel of land, and after a field was left fallow anyone could occupy it. Moreover, in these villages, there was open access to forest land for village inhabitants.

Among the Balanta, access and rights to upland fields were also differentiated according to the specific history of land-use changes in each village and region. In old villages of the north where upland farming is still predominant, slash-and-burn gave permanent rights to land, and when smallholders started to plant orchards everyone knew the exact demarcation of his fallow fields. In southern Balanta villages of Quinara and Tombalí provinces 'upland fields had no owner' and could be appropriated either by men or women, because most smallholders were more interested in mangrove swamp rice cultivation. In fact, when the Balanta migrated to the south in search of rice fields they asked the Nalu and Beafada landlords for only mangrove swampy lands. They placed their houses in the savannahs surrounding the mangrove forests. In this land they established rice nurseries and the women sometimes cultivated cassava, sweet potatoes and vegetables. In sum, the village descendant of the first settler (*Fa ne botxa*) controlled access to mangrove swamp fields, but there was open access to the uplands.

Until quite recently, both the land and wild trees could not be sold, only the labour invested to transform them permanently. This means that a silk-cotton tree could not be sold, but a canoe could; a fallow field could not be sold, as the forest would still regenerate, but an orchard could as what was being sold were the fruit trees planted and cared for; a mangrove forest could not be sold, only the rice paddies created after the slashing of the mangrove trees and the construction of dykes. But among the Balanta, the mangrove rice fields stood apart. When the paddies had been 'sold' to a non-relative, many decades later, if anyone belonging to the lineage of the first owner who slashed the mangroves and built the dykes wanted the fields, he was entitled to 'repurchase' the plots by paying the same value (heads of cattle of a given age and sex, or tons of rice). Although the concept 'sale' (*bindi*) was used until recently to characterize this type of transactions, at present smallholders use the concept of 'mortgage' (*mpinha*) to distinguish it from what they now call 'true sale' (*bindi propri*).

In general, tensions around access to land between generations—which in other West African countries fuelled violence—were only high among the Balanta, whose initiations into manhood were sometimes delayed until they were very old men, and only after that could they marry and create their own household (*fogon*). Contrary to the Balanta, men in most of the other ethnic groups that comprise Guinea-Bissau's social tissue stayed in their fathers' extended patrilineal compound (*moransa*) after marriage. However, they could marry much earlier than most of the Balanta, and above all they were allowed to develop private for-profit activities, thus reducing tensions. Among all ethnic groups, in cases where tensions led to compound fission, if the young man was unable to get land in his own village, he could migrate to another village (belonging to his or another ethnic group) where eventually he would be granted enough land to provide for his family.

As other authors have highlighted (e.g. Berry 1993), women's rights over land in Africa are culturally defined and contextually specific but also depend upon each woman's bargaining power. Among Bissau-Guinean villagers it is commonly acknowledged that women do not usually inherit land parcels, as marriage is virilocal, but they have usufruct rights to parcels of land given by their husbands, family or friends. Muslim women's (mostly Fula, Mandinga, Beafada and Nalu) cereal production, however, belongs to the household and a big share of their cash crops (mainly peanuts and vegetables) is also oriented to family consumption at present. In case of food shortage, most of the income they acquired through cash crop production and trade is usually given to their husbands. By contrast, among the Balanta, men are the sole gender responsible for the provision of food for the household; women do work in the collective fields and in the household, but when they have money or cereals and the family is suffering from hunger they lend it to their husband, being repaid later. Balanta old women are the exception, as they frequently produce rice to feed their grandchildren.

Until recently land tenure conflicts between rural people were relatively rare and almost entirely solved without the intervention of the state administrative apparatus (e.g. Temudo 1998, vol. 1: 438–51). Indeed, according to Tanner (1991: 68), 'customary law has been shown to be effective at dealing with a complex and potentially problematic ethnic and culture mixture in most tabancas'. With independence the land was nationalized, but not only the colonial law continued to regulate the granting of new concessions (Tanner 1991: 10), but also colonial legal pluralism was practically kept intact. While the number of land concessions attributed between 1975 and 1980 was only thirty-one (with a total area of 1,084 ha), between 1981 and 1985 it rose to 296 (with a total area of 26.402 ha) (Espinosa 1994: 24–8). However, big changes started to take place after the mid-1980s with SAP.

The end of an era?

Changes in food security

As a result of government policies and also changes in the organization of labour, after independence agricultural production stagnated and the area cultivated with food crops never recovered to pre-war levels (Galli 1991: 55).[6] Especially after economic liberalization, youth aspirations of freedom and their consumption needs increased; as a consequence, the compounds (*moransas*) consisting of a single multi-generational household (*fogon*) started to lose cohesion and the ability to mobilize labour and create income that could be used for collective investments and the production of food. With the erosion of elders' authority, the age of marriage was progressively reduced and young people got the freedom to devote additional time to individual cash-for-profit activities. Furthermore, the village aid-groups that used to provide an important share of the households' agricultural work became rather expensive— partly because the availability of consumption goods increased the cash needs of the youth. As a result, the use of labour groups decreased, with negative

---

[6] Rosemary Galli made this statement in the early 1990s. Since then the area under cultivation increased with cashew nuts, though not with food crops—the only exception being the green belt created by the urban population around Bissau.

consequences in terms of the area cultivated by each household. In addition to a decreased importance of food production, the consumption of wild foods (yams, taro, leaves and fruits) also fell. In fact, the introduction by development agents of dry season vegetable production and wheat bread since the early 1990s, and the wide availability of such industrial foodstuffs as Maggi cubes, cookies and sugar, devalued the perceived importance of wild foods (see Temudo 1998, vol. I). The increasing importance of income from cashew nuts, available during food shortages (April to May) and which could be exchanged with imported rice by merchants, also contributed to reducing wild foods consumption and expanding the purchase of manufactured food. However, it was the political crisis of 1998–9 (Temudo 2008, 2009) that amplified the pace of social change, and many rural households became food-insecure.

During the civil war, most smallholders received internally displaced people; and in order to feed all household dwellers and to save most of their seeds, they adopted several nutritional and productive strategies (Temudo and Schiefer 2003: 407). Nonetheless, after the war, lack of enough seeds to boost production and a sequence of bad harvests weakened households' food security. Food shortage and vulnerability shifted progressively from being seasonal to being structural. There were political and economic reasons for this. After the return to 'peace', constant political unrest resulted from factional fights over the control of the state apparatus, of foreign aid, and of drug trafficking, along with a growing interference of the military in political affairs. This was compounded by the impunity of politicians and military involved in numerous and brutal killings and the mounting gap between the living conditions of the urban elite and the rural population. All contributed to the perception that 'the state only exists to exploit us', as phrased by many interviewees. Youth migration and school enrolment increased, creating a decrease in the availability of agricultural labour. Given this scenario, smallholders resorted to cashew nut production, because of its low labour demands, and with the proceeds they started to buy rice instead of cultivating it, thereby reversing long-standing strategies that had ensured local food security and sovereignty.

The civil war stands as a turning point, after which even those who until then had resisted cashew plantation started converting their shifting cultivation fields and land reserves into cashew orchards. Many smallholders interviewed across the country said that 'cashews brought laziness', because their planting led to a drastic reduction of cereal production and an increase in the use of wage labour. Most also stated that 'cashews are the source of money for everything: tin roofing for houses, marriages, feasts, funerals, bicycles, and buying rice'. The implication was that cashew production meant a total dependence upon its revenues, a reduction in other income-earning activities, a decrease in the use of household labour and a neglect of staple food production. In the east, the employment of wage labour, the rental of ox ploughing and tractors, and the use of herbicides increased with the income from cashew nuts, but at the same time many smallholders became more food-insecure.

While smallholders are now aware of the economic perils of exclusive dependence on one cash crop whose market is highly unstable and whose price has been declining, they still have no idea of the risks of mono-cropping in terms of pests and diseases. Despite this, in many regions the damages are becoming considerable. Additionally, the old age of many plantations and their high density are also main causes of low productivity. Facing adverse terms of trade and/or poor harvests, smallholders are often forced to acquire rice through high-interest loans from cashew merchants, thus incurring indebtedness before the harvest. Alternatively, they might adopt other adverse coping behaviours, such as reducing food consumption below nutritional needs and increasing sales of household goods in order to buy cereals. In both cases, their ability to respond quickly to prevent future calamities or grasp new opportunities is eroded.

Another factor complicating this picture is climate change. Smallholders are aware that the 'climate changed' and mention an increased variability in the distribution of rainfall, with the occurrence of long dry spells, the destruction of the mangrove swamp rice fields' dykes by exceptionally high tides, and an intensification in pest attacks.[7] In general the combined effects of labour shortage, investment in one cash crop, dependence upon the market for food supply, increased use of credit to solve pre-harvest food shortages, and climatic change have created a downward spiral of food insecurity and indebtedness among many smallholders.

The 2011 cereal harvest was very poor due to an irregular rainfall distribution, and most smallholders began to take rice on credit from cashew buyers very early in the 2012 dry season. In 2012, the Harmattan winds during flowering caused a reduction of the cashew harvest to less than 50% of the previous year's output. According to smallholders' and cashew buyers' testimonies, it may have reached only around 30% in some locations. The high cashew nut prices, however, were unable to compensate for the production

---

[7] On similar consequences of climate change on rice production in another West African country, see Bangura et al. (2012: 7).

fall. The military coup of 12 April 2012 delayed the start of cashew merchant purchases and disrupted the credit system they had created, because many smallholders decided to sell their cashews to other merchants instead of paying off their loans. Furthermore, the coup also caused problems in Bissau's port; and as a consequence, merchants were forced to sell their cashews to Indian exporters at a much lower price than that at which they had bought it from smallholders.

In terms of cereal production, the start of the 2012 rainy season was delayed by one month, so hard-working upland smallholders lost the seeds they had sown after the first rains. This led to the need for a second sowing. Yet, a worse food shortage happened during the 2013 dry season after smallholders had eaten their harvests. As many cashew merchants were unable to sell the 2012 cashews, the 2013 purchase campaign became compromised. Smallholders got their rice on credit from cashew merchants at very high prices and interest rates, while the price of cashews fell dramatically.[8] After paying their loans, there were few or no cashew nuts to exchange for rice. Facing the resultant hunger, many were forced to sell cattle and/or small animals at lower prices and exchange work for food with other smallholders. Again in 2014 and 2015 both cereal and cashew nut harvests were in general low, and the rice price increased dramatically after the fall of the new elected government.

Since 2007, when the direct exchange ratio started to drop below one kilogram of cashews to one kilogram of rice, the trend towards expansion of cashew production appears to be slowing somewhat in some locations. Moreover, some upland smallholders are increasing food production and, where forest reserves have been exhausted, a few have started treating their old orchards as planted fallow. That is, they slash and burn the orchards and inter-crop cereals with new cashew plants or with other fruit trees. In many Balanta villages smallholders mentioned that since 2008 the money, rice and wine obtained from selling cashews were used to pay and feed labour groups on rice fields. In fact, we observed across the country many mangrove swamp rice fields being repaired and even extended and new dams being constructed.

In sum, for most households in the country the move towards extensive cashew nut production intensified the involvement in markets for commodities, labour, land, credit and technology and reduced the investment in food produc-

---

[8] The market is rather fragmented across the country and prices and exchange ratios vary widely. In some remote locations, to get one kg of rice, farmers had to give four or five kg of cashew nuts in exchange.

tion and household food security. However, our recent empirical observations show that the trend towards increased food insecurity can be reversed or at least mitigated (Temudo and Abrantes 2012, 2015), either by slashing old orchards to produce cereals or by investing cashew revenues in expanding freshwater or mangrove swamp rice cultivation. By contrast, the land tenure systems—as we shall show in the following section—do not have this capacity to bounce back after the dramatic changes they have undergone, though legal reforms can be made to reduce conflicts and the potential for increasing land appropriation by the elite and foreign investors in village territories.

Land tenure changes

The recent changes in access to land, land rights, land use and the natural resource utilization strategies of Guinean society have been driven by a number of factors. Among these are some structural adjustment-associated measures, the new land law, the creation of national parks and reserves, the civil war (e.g. Temudo 2008, 2009, 2011) and the expansion of cashew nut production.

In the 1980s, during structural adjustment, credit was made available for large-scale 'modern agriculture', and in 1990 a commission was created for the development of a new land law. Tanner (1991: 30) argued that 'a relatively small group of people has been able, through close ties to state bureaucratic structures, to gain preferential access to information, credit and land'. The greed for land of the political and military elite grew after the liberalization of the economy, and during the following six years (1986–91) 1,430 concessions were granted, occupying an area of 230,516 ha (Espinosa 1994: 24–8). However, only about 3% of the land granted after the mid-1980s was being cultivated in the 1990s (Pereira et al. 1992: 15). Lifton noted (1991: 49) that smallholders were aware of the process of getting concessions, but that just a tiny number had the financial resources, education and availability of time needed to do this. As there was no cadastral of village territories, many concessions overlapped with village land, resulting in numerous conflicts between land concessionaries (*ponteiros*, Kriol) and smallholders (Tanner 1991).

In the 1990s, too, the process of demarcation of protected areas for parks began and triggered land security strategies and many conflicts over natural resource ownership and use (see e.g. Temudo 2012). Inside protected areas, former livelihood strategies and the expansion of the agricultural area had been curtailed by the creation of strict conservation areas and fauna corridors. At present, national parks and reserves cover about 15% of the country's area (with 8.8% more in the near future), which is particularly important since these areas are governed by a specific legislation and not by the land law.

In a report prepared for USAID-Bissau and meant to help the future formulation of a new land law, Tanner considered it impossible to formulate a law able to supplant the qualities of customary laws and proposed their integration in the future decree (Tanner 1991: 61). Approved in 1998, the law's main goals were the inclusion of the multiplicity of customary tenure and management arrangements, and the encouragement of investments by creating a market value for land. However, the land tenure by-law was only published in 2008 and the customary tenure systems were not integrated; there is still no land cadastre, and conflicts over land are rising due to the expansion of cashew production[9] and the increased number of land concessions. Nevertheless, it was the extensive cashew production that completely changed land tenure relations by increasing land pressure and introducing an emerging land market (see also World Bank 2006).

As already mentioned, slash-and-burn usually provided permanent usufruct rights to land, and the majority of smallholders created orchards on their own forest fallows. However, some exceptions of major importance can be found. When the rush for land started as a result of cashew expansion, in many Fula villages, where forest clearance did not give permanent usufruct rights, it was the hardest working smallholders and/or those (including women) with the biggest capacity to mobilize labour that were able to create the largest orchards.

In Quinara, among the Beafada, the first areas of cashew plantation were the savannahs around smallholder compounds, to which farmers had permanent usufruct rights; but when the land race started everybody tried to locate and claim rights to former slashed-and-burnt areas. In northern Balanta villages, where the cropping system changed through time and upland cereals cultivation was abandoned or drastically reduced a long time ago (in favour of mangrove or freshwater swamp rice cultivation), there was an open access to uplands. But cashew plantation induced claims to former cultivated areas, and as one farmer put it, 'brought that thing [of saying] this field was slashed by my father or my grandfather!' Thus conflicts over land ownership began. In both situations, some landlords were not willing to divide unslashed land among the landless or those with small orchards and they kept it for themselves, their kith and kin and/or for selling. In the southern Balanta villages of

---

[9] See also interview with Braima Biai, available at http://cplpfao.blogspot.pt/2008/05/entrevista-com-braima-biai-guin-bissau.html, accessed 22 August 2013.

Quinara and Tombalí, when settlements of other ethnic groups were close by, there was little upland territory. Individual Balantas had to negotiate access to the woodlands via networks of friendship with people of the neighbouring villages, in order to be able to increase or create orchards.

As a result of the land shortage that emerged because of rapid expansion of cashew orchards, a land market has been evolving and accelerating during the last few years. According to many interviewees, Manjakos were the triggers of the drastic change in land tenure relations. Facing land pressure in their homeland and armed with the remittances sent by kin who migrated to Europe, many Manjako moved to other regions of Guinea-Bissau. After having been given a plot of land, they wanted to expand their area under cultivation and started offering money to buy other plots.

In this context of a race for land, rural conflicts between smallholders are now seldom entirely solved by traditional authorities according to local norms and customs. The involvement of the police and the courts, however, makes process-solving long-lasting and rather expensive due to corruption. Outbreaks of violence often emerge when desperate smallholders completely lose confidence in the justice system's ability to solve their problems.

During the last decade, the political and military elite has taken over large tracts of land for private enterprises,[10] and smallholders feel they have no legal protection against the powerful. News has also been spread about land-grabbing involving the appropriation of allegedly 'unoccupied wastelands' for the plantation of several hundred acres of jatropha (*Jatropha curcas*) and oil palms (*Eleis guineensis*) for agrofuel production, but the projects were never approved by the government. The concession that, until recently, triggered most conflicts with villagers belongs to a Spanish company, and consists of several hundred acres of inland swamps for rice production. However, the forthcoming bauxite exploitation by Angola may give rise to major land expropriation of villages' territories around the mines, the railway trails and the roads to the future international port of Buba.

In sum, the expansion of cashew orchards has been changing land tenure rules and the land ownership structure, resulting in a still incipient but rising economic differentiation and numerous conflicts. However, given the decreasing price of the raw nuts on the global market, the absence of processing facilities in the country, the growing production in India (practically the sole importer) and rising international cereal prices, smallholders who stopped producing food in

[10] There are no published data on the concessions attributed after 2001.

order to live off big orchards maintained with hired workers are facing a downward spiral of indebtedness, forcing some to sell part of their land to be able to buy rice at critical moments. This fact is increasing land concentration in the hands of those who never reduced either household food self-provisioning or their labour input. Nonetheless, the appropriation of large concessions by the country's elite and potential future land-grabbing may create a much more worrying scenario of widespread landlessness and poverty.

Conclusions

The Guinea-Bissau 1998–9 civil war revealed the stabilizing power of a cohesive and socially embedded food regime and land tenure relations (Temudo 2008), while at the same time it was the straw that broke the camel's back and triggered the system's unravelling. Since then the country has been experiencing more and more intense, and longer, periods of food insecurity, as a result not only of poor agricultural and market policies, but also of inappropriate development and humanitarian aid approaches, the long-term political instability, climate change, and smallholders' decisions in the face of these events. Because cashews are a good land security marker and a land-extensive, low labour-intensive crop, they seemed a best-bet option in a context where plenty of land was still available, but labour was a constraint at peak moments. Moreover, the barter system at the farm gate is also a major advantage for smallholders, in a country where the road and transport infrastructure is very bad. Contrary to this negative trend in food security, the recent rise of rice prices is pushing many (mostly Balanta) smallholders towards an increase in cereal production. If nothing is done to support these efforts to increase self-provisioning at household and village levels, smallholders will fall in a downward spiral of food insecurity and indebtedness, which can easily make them more prone to political instrumentalization and thus increase the country's political instability.

The above-mentioned factors also promoted changes in who gains access to land and how they do so, contributing to the reduction of the solidarity and reciprocity that previously stabilized the rural social fabric. Furthermore, both the areas given over to parks and the recent land concessions—especially to the country's elite—deprive some rural communities of their most productive agricultural land and grazing areas, increasing the rural–urban economic gap and fuelling new grievances and tensions. The involvement of the rural population in the creation of a rural cadastral that protects a village's territory as inalienable land, the repossession by villagers of the land taken by concessionaires, the elimination of logging permits in a village's territory, and a more people-centred management of the parks can all help reduce conflicts and the potential for politicians making political capital out of them. Without this, the widespread perception of the state as cannibalizing the lives of the people will continue.

5

HISTORY, MIXTURE, MODERNITY

RELIGIOUS PLURALISM IN GUINEA-BISSAU TODAY

Ramon Sarró and *Miguel de Barros*

The 1998–9 military conflict represented for Guinea-Bissau a historical watershed widely discussed, in its many aspects, in different chapters of this book.[1]

[1] The authors thank the Fundação Para a Ciência e a Tecnologia, who funded the project 'The Prophetess and the Rice Farmer: Transformations in Religion, Gender and Agriculture in Guinea-Bissau (2011–2014)' (of which R. Sarró is the PI and M. de Barros an external adviser). This made it possible for them to conduct interviews together in Guinea-Bissau in March/April 2012, December 2012/January 2013, March/April 2013, December 2013 and March/April 2014, and to meet several times in order to brainstorm and to write the chapter, both in Guinea-Bissau and in Lisbon. Interviews with Muslim leaders, Catholic priests and Protestant pastors were conducted by the two authors together in Bissau, but the article also draws from research conducted by R. Sarró with the project's researcher Marina P. Temudo in the rural areas of Guinea-Bissau, especially on the Kyang-yang religious movement. We thank Marina for sharing her research and her data with us, and for her insightful comments on an early draft. Ambra Formenti and Inês Galvão made useful comments too. Most especially, we thank Toby Green for the invitation to write

It could likewise be interpreted as a watershed for the history of the relationship between religion and politics in the country. Whereas religion had kept a low profile in previous political situations, the role of religious institutions and ecumenical initiatives during the conflict was striking, as was the direct role religion played in the aftermath of the conflict and in the reconstruction of the political landscape. Note, for instance, the explicit role of the Catholic Church in putting forward the name of a candidate, Henrique Rosa, as a potential president for the republic (which he became in September 2003). However, the exact composition of the religious ecosystem of Guinea-Bissau and the relevance of religion in society in general remain fuzzy and underexplored. The increasing presence of religion in the public sphere is in sharp contrast with the bad reputation the country has gained over the last decades owing to its political corruption, social instability and international drug-related problems. So far, however, very little has been done to study what the connection between the two contrasting elements (the 'purity' of religion and the 'dirt' of corruption) really is.[2] In lieu of an impossible thorough survey (which would require a major collaborative research enterprise), in this article we review some of the work done on the topic, underlining a deep historical continuity in Bissau-Guinean religious culture, despite the above-mentioned watershed, and suggesting possible lines of research.

Let us start by questioning a tenet in social sciences: that cultural complexity is a characteristic of globalized urban settings. Some of the most innovative authors on cultural complexity (Hannerz 1992) or super-diversity (Vertovec 2006) seem to take for granted that multiculturalism is mostly a *consequence* of social change (produced by globalization and migration). Following them, many scholars and students today have a tendency to assume that traditional, non-urban settings cannot be culturally complex. Yet, the fact is that rural societies actually *are* extremely complex and multi-varied, as a genealogy of anthropological work has cogently established (Smith 1974; Burnham 1996) and our fieldwork confirmed.

Guinea-Bissau offers very good examples of this rural complexity. In some southern regions we have lived in villages in which people speaking Kriol,

---

for this book and for his rigorous feedback to earlier drafts. Comments by external anonymous readers were also very helpful.

[2] For a useful exception, see the work of Idrissa Embaló on the role of everyday religious institutions and ceremonies (whether Christian, Muslim or 'animistic') in the creation of a conflict-free atmosphere (Embaló 2008).

Nalú, Balanta, Beafada, Fulfulde and Susu cohabit and in which many of their inhabitants speak fluently several of these languages. In Entxale, a bigger but still rural village of 5,000 inhabitants in the east of the country, we counted eight different languages. This linguistic diversity is accompanied by an ethnic and a religious one. In Entxale there is one mosque, one Catholic church, one Protestant temple, many neo-Pentecostal young people who so far have no temple and pray elsewhere,[3] and many *balobas* (Kriol for traditional shrines). Till recently, there were also members of the Kyang-yang, a prophetic movement which mixes ritual and symbolic elements from Islam, Christianity and traditional Balanta religion (see below for a further discussion of this religious movement). This pluralism, common to many Bissau-Guinean villages, could make of Guinea-Bissau a model for scholars to understand the inner workings of religious pluralism in the complex world of today. This is certainly one of the key issues to be kept in mind when trying to understand the socio-cultural changes that have affected Bissau-Guinean society since the onset of the current chains of post-1998 crises. Although so far there is no direct recommendation by the international community referring to religious leadership, there is room to speculate that the entanglement between religion and governance in this country (so strongly connected, ethnically, culturally and historically, to neighbouring, mostly Muslim ones) may eventually become a worry for external experts and donors.

Religion in Guinea-Bissau: an encounter of frontiers

Like much of the Upper Guinea Coast, the region today comprising the territory of Guinea-Bissau was in the past the scene of a meeting between three religious frontiers. First of all, the African internal frontier, to use Kopytoff's category (1987), i.e. the reproduction, through segmentation and expansion, of indigenous groups, often accompanied by the expansion of their religious universes. The occupation of the land by the agriculturalist or agro-pastoralist groups of Guinea-Bissau (Balanta, Floup, Nalú, Tenda, Manjako, Mankanhe, Banhuns, etc.) followed a frontier model, perfectly studied by Eve Crowley

---

[3] 'Neo-Pentecostal' churches are forms of Protestant Christianity in which a strong centrality is given to the work of the Holy Spirit. The Holy Spirit can change individuals and communities in a way that is reminiscent of the transformation endured by the Apostles of Jesus the day they were celebrating the Jewish feast of the Pentecost, when the Holy Spirit descended upon them and imbued them with charismatic power (Acts of the Apostles, 2: 1–31).

(Crowley 1994, 2000). This expansion was accompanied by notions of spiritual contracts discussed in the next section. The ritual workings and cosmological contexts of 'animistic' societies have been well studied by a legion of anthropologists (for Manjako, see Gable 1990; Carvalho 1999; Teixeira 2001; Constantine 2006; for the Bijagó, see Henry 1994; Pussetti 2000; for the Floup, see Journet-Diallo 2007; for Nalú, see Temudo 2012).

The second frontier to consider is the Muslim frontier, spreading westbound since the thirteenth century through a combination of the military enlargement of Muslim empires and individual traders and clerics, some acting peacefully, some using violent *jihads* (see Gaillard 1995 for a relatively recent *jihad* among the Beafada). Particularly important for the understanding of the territory of what is today Guinea-Bissau was the so-called empire of Kaabu (Caroço 1954; Lopes 1999; Costa Dias 2004; cf. Green 2009 for criticism of viewing Kaabu as an 'empire'), and its internal fights between Mandingas and Fulas stretching back to the eighteenth century. These came to a head in the nineteenth century, with the collapse of Kaabu at the Battle of Kansala in 1867 following attacks by the Fula theocracy of the Fuuta Djallon in neighbouring Guinea-Conakry. Such historical conflicts offer an important background to the unstable relationship between Mandinga and Fulas, the main Muslim actors in the public sphere of Guinea-Bissau today.

The Muslim centres such as Fuuta Toro or Fuuta Djallon, or later the Islamized Kaabu, managed to control some coastal groups, such as the Nalú, whose rulers were subjected to the Fuuta Djallon during much of the second half of the nineteenth century (Sampil 1969). However, as far as coastal groups and Islam were concerned, the Nalú were more the exception than the rule. In most places in coastal Guinea-Bissau, the Muslim frontier did not reach the coast, even if individual Muslims were reported in early sources (Horta 2004), testifying to a very old co-existence of Muslim and non-Muslim agents even in the urban centres, largely inhabited by Catholics and Jews.

The third relevant frontier is the Christian Atlantic frontier, as old as the history of the arrival of the Portuguese in the mid-fifteenth century, when Catholicism began to be institutionally established. Both individual frontiersmen and Portuguese institutions collaborated in the making of a Christian community that established itself in coastal centres such as Farim, Geba, Bolama or Cacheu, home to the oldest Catholic church in Guinea-Bissau (Vicente 1993). A Christian Creole society, a sort of embryo of the colonial society, emerged in these sites, monitoring the Atlantic trade and entering, often through the mediation of Cape Verdean agents (Djaló 2013:149), into commercial connections with hinterland groups (Brooks 2003; Havik 2004). This proto-colonial society prefigured also a set of relations between Creoles and natives that, much later, would be legally enforced with the rise of colonial legal structures.[4]

Despite the fact that most early sources on the history of the 'Guinea of Cape Verde' (as this part of the Upper Guinea Coast was referred to) was Catholic in authorship and intention (for a thorough analysis, see Horta 2011), the literature on the establishment of a Catholic community in what is now Guinea-Bissau remains scattered across archives and colonial journals (see Vicente, n.d., for a thorough bibliography). Apart from the detailed historical survey by Father Rema (Rema 1982), there has been no other systematic work on the structure and transformations of the Catholic communities in pre-colonial times, colonial days or the post-colony. This is problematic, given the central place of religious practice in Guinea-Bissau, and the role of Catholicism in the formal colonial period; for such reasons, understanding contemporary conjunctures must engage with the religious dimension. As far as the post-colonial dimension of Catholicism is concerned, Koudawo (2001) offered a very good exception. Building upon previous work by de Fonseca (1993), Koudawo undertook a thoughtful synthetic analysis of the different phases Catholicism has been through from independence (when it was abhorred for its colonial past and foreignness) to a relative revival during the liberal opening of the 1990s, to the solid implementation (indeed a fully-fledged 'indigenization' with the nomination of a native bishop and priests) in the aftermath of the civil war of 1998–9.[5] An update to that seminal analysis by Koudawo does indeed seem necessary today.

The importance of Catholicism in the making of the Creole community has been the object of scholarly research (Brooks 2003; Havik 2004; Nafafé 2005, 2007; Sweet 2006) and is perhaps most visible in the Creole term for person: *pekadur* (literally, 'sinner'), today used by all Bissau-Guineans, Christian or

---

[4] The making of a Creole, originally Portuguese, community has too often taken for granted, wrongly, that, given the Catholic hegemony of Portuguese culture, this equals the making of a Christian community. This has rendered invisible the very important Jewish diaspora along the lusophone Upper Guinea Coast (Mark/Horta 2011).

[5] Because of the mediatory role of the civil war (Infanda 2009), it proved a true coming-of-age for the Catholic Church in the post-colony. Furthermore, it allowed religions to be present in the public, political sphere and consolidated ecumenical initiatives which, up to that moment, had kept a very low profile (Augel 1996).

not. Yet there was nevertheless a surprisingly limited pastoral activity in colonial, Catholic-driven Guinea-Bissau (Gonçalves 1960, vol. 2: 12–13; Trajano Filho 2004; Djaló 2013: 148–52). There were isolated missions in rural areas, as well as many individual converts among different ethnic groups, but overall, and beyond the Papel areas close to Bissau, the rural mission in Guinea-Bissau had little impact compared to the successful Muslim implementation in the hinterland or to the formation of robust Catholic communities in neighbouring countries. This historical context of the Christian Atlantic frontier is therefore important in understanding the religious composition of the country today.

The religious ecosystem of Guinea-Bissau has always been quite respectful towards 'animistic' groups left unconverted by both Muslims and Christians. Why? While explanations based on 'resistance' come easily to our mind (to explain, for instance, the relative non-conversion of Balanta to Islam or Christianity), we think that religious transformation has to be explained in a more holistic, regional model, without falling into overly heroic views of cultural resistance. It is not only the resistance of local groups to Christianity or to Islam that needs to be explained, but also the resistance of Muslim and Christian actors towards entering certain zones. For instance, Djaló discusses the explicit instructions that early Catholic agents must *not* leave the urban centres (2013: 148). A holistic, regional model, combined with a careful analysis of sources along the lines suggested by Djaló, would probably help us understand the advantages, for all the actors involved, of keeping different cosmological enclaves co-existing. This might explain why in certain zones some members of the local community converted to a world religion, while others did not.

The above-mentioned Balanta are a case in point. Despite the resistance model often imposed upon them by external observers (be they Muslim neighbours, colonial administrators, scholars or politicians), the fact is that many Balanta *did* convert to Islam, becoming the sub-group known as Balanta Mane. The Balanta Mane abandoned many customs and adopted Mandinga ways of life, and their language is now substantially different from both Balanta Nhakra and Balanta Kuntoe, the two main languages spoken by their animistic neighbours. Like those, the Balanta Mane live in the region of Oio, which has been a kind of 'buffer zone' between the Muslim internal frontier (populated mostly by Mandinga and Fulas) and the coastal Christian one. The Balanta, being mostly animistic, have been the object of both Christian proselytizing (quite successfully; the current bishop of Bissau is a Balanta Kuntoe) and Muslim efforts in the same vein (which have been very successful in the past among the Balanta Mane, and are quite successful today among the Balanta Nhakra). In Guinea-Bissau in general, Christians rarely attempted to convert in Muslim areas,[6] and Muslim proselytizers were rarely active in Christian centres except as traders, but the buffer zone of Oio along the Geba river and other interstitial frontiers were reservoirs for agents of both religions to search for converts.[7]

The existence of the buffer area of Oio (and other similar ones in the country) makes us think of an important element in the religious geography and political culture of Guinea-Bissau: the importance of mediation, negotiation and religious compromise. The Upper Guinea Coast has too often been analysed in terms of polarities (coast–hinterland, landlord–stranger, youths–elders, raider–refugee, animistic–world religious, male domain–female domain, etc.). In reality, these oppositions are ideal types, and many possible negotiations occur in between the two poles of each continuum. Guinea-Bissau has been quite a good example of successful opposition management, creating a hyper-complex cultural grid full of mediations and negotiations. Thus, to give just a few examples, today's bishop of Bissau, Mgr José Câmnate na Bissing (ordained bishop in 2000), is a Balanta Kuntoe, a group strongly perceived in the Bissau-Guinean public sphere as being animistic. The leader of the National Islamic Council is a Mandinga learned man who, despite his important role in the Muslim community, goes by the Christian name of Armando, because he grew up in a Catholic home and is proud of the name given by his adopting family. The recently deceased ex-president Kumba Yalá was a Balanta man who always wore the red bonnet (a symbol of animistic tradition), even after he converted to Islam, thus allowing his presence and discourse to bridge two different publics (in his last years, incidentally, he partially reconverted to traditional religion and boasted of new spiritual contracts).

This spirit of compromise underlies the co-existence and, if we may use a Portuguese concept often invoked in Guinea-Bissau, *convivência* (co-living).

---

[6] This could be nuanced by arguing that Protestant churches were already trying to convert Muslims in colonial times, as proved in the thorough and graphic article on communication, media and propaganda by Gonçalves (1966). However, we suspect their success was minimal.

[7] The 'fascination' with Islamic mores among animistic Balanta of Oio was a matter that worried Governor Sarmento Rodrigues, who, being well aware of the geographical distribution of religions in the province he was ruling, also noted the alliance that Christianity should establish with the animistic coastal dwellers (Rodrigues 1948).

This can take two forms: religious syncretism, or compartmentalized respect for the other's religion. Thus, when Muslim people invite Christian friends to a baptism, a funeral or a wedding, they provide alcohol for their guests. Muslims do not drink, but they know that their guests may want to do so, and they want them to be happy. *Convivência* means that all points of view must be given expression. When the late bishop of Bissau, Settimio Arturo Ferrazzetta, passed away in 1999, there were three funerals: a Catholic one, a Muslim one and an animistic one.[8]

This spirit of *convivência*, present both in the cosmopolitan *praças* and in remote hamlets, underlies the ecumenical dialogues that have been so important in the management of political crises over the last fifteen years. Perhaps the most visible example is the relationship between the Catholic priest David Ciocco and the imam of Mansoa (the capital of Oio), Abubacar Djaló. Fifteen years ago, when the latter returned from Qur'anic learning in Egypt to found a mosque in Mansoa, he invited Father David to place the first stone. Later the two signed an agreement so that the Catholic radio station 'Sol Mansi' (founded by Father David in 2001) and the Muslim Qur'anic station of Mansoa ('Recom') would work together, the former hosting Muslim programmes, the latter hosting Catholic ones, and the two sending ecumenical messages to the mixed public of Mansoa.[9]

But let us not be too romantic about *convivência*. It is in itself another ideal type, with its exceptions in everyday life, where clashes of religion do occur. It is all right, for example, for Muslims to proselytize in the eastern frontiers of the country (or in buffer zones such as Oio), but if they try to enter regions historically associated with either Christianity or animism, such as the coast or the islands, they may find themselves with a real or symbolic confrontation, and therefore will have to use their own real or symbolic violence, such as iconoclasm (destruction of sacred objects, sacred forests and shrines). There have been some recent examples of this on the coast and on the Bijagó islands. But iconoclasm may backfire. Take what happened in January 2009 between

[8] Ordained in 1977, Ferrazzetta was the first bishop of Bissau. After his death, Guinea-Bissau had two dioceses: Bissau and Bafatá. Ferrazzetta was a significant mediator in the armed conflict and an initiator of the ecumenical spirit continued by his successors.

[9] The importance of radio channels in the making of ecumenical religious publics in Guinea-Bissau is an underdeveloped area of research (already discussed by Gonçalves in colonial days, 1961: 27–32; and 1966). One of the authors (de Barros) has already started a contemporary systematic survey; future publications will follow.

the islands of Pecixe and Jeta, when a Muslim Mandinga man was preaching among the largely animistic Manjako. A boat departed from the port of Pecixe with the intention of taking the Muslim cleric and his followers to Jeta to continue their proselytizing. But halfway there the boat sank and more than seventy people died, probably because it was overloaded. The tragedy was later interpreted by animistic people as an example of the superiority of the local spirit over the Muslims trying to penetrate their territory. The land of spirits has to be trodden carefully. These kinds of events and beliefs reinforce the geo-spiritual divide and contribute to the tenacity of traditional religions in many parts of Guinea-Bissau.

Contract, prayer and negotiations

A contrast that often crops up in conversations and interviews with Bissau-Guineans is the distinction between religions of contract and those of prayer. Animistic societies share a cosmological matrix according to which the community is based on oaths and 'spirit contracts'. Spirits (*irans*, in Kriol) are the real owners of the place (*tchon*, a concept of particularly strong religious and political relevance in Guinea-Bissau). In order for humans to inhabit a place, a contract between the spirit and the first arrival must be 'signed'. This gives ritual and political seniority to first arrivals, who thus become the owners of the place (*donos do tchon*). Late arrivals (*hóspedes*) will need their authorization to settle and to have access to land (Temudo 2012). However, if the first arrivals do not keep renewing the contract with the *iran*, through periodic libations and sacrifices, the nourishing territory may turn into wasteland.

Islam and Christianity, in opposition, meet in prayer. Indeed, Guinea-Bissau might offer a paradigm in which to study the social-glue aspect of prayer, a concept used as a metonym for 'religion'. It is not unusual in Guinea-Bissau to hear expressions like 'I am going to prayer' as synonyms of either 'I am going to the mosque' or 'I am going to the Christian meeting'. Moreover, the expression 'the people of the prayer' is used to refer to the religious and human sameness underlying Christians and Muslims. This centrality of idioms around 'prayer' highlights the community-making aspect of this religious practice. At the discursive level, praying constitutes a common index for people to perceive themselves as equals ('the people of the prayer'), even if they belong to different world religions. At the practical level, some religious celebrations (important Muslim and Christian feasts) often bring people together in big ecumenical prayers. With prayer such a key defining aspect of people's lives, understanding the fabric of the contemporary country and how religion might be related to political projects of stabilization is extremely important.

Prayer is thus a very strong centripetal gluing force, but it can also become a centrifugal driver of exclusion. Individuals or groups who do not belong to the 'people of the prayer' category are more and more ostracized and excluded from the public sphere. This exclusion and marginality generates reactions such as the mimetic Kyang-yang prophetic movement discussed below, but it can also create resentment. It also creates tensions between Muslim and Christian proselytizers in their competition to convert 'pagan' people.

Religions of prayer abhor notions of spirit contract. In Christian theology, in particular, you can have a contractual relationship with the Devil (the 'Faustian' contract) but certainly not with God. In both Muslim and Christian theology, God is beyond practical obligations towards humans, and cannot be forced to abide by legalistic forms of contract. However, the strict opposition between 'prayer' and 'contract' may be another one of those ideal typical ones that work very well at the level of representations, but that in practice are divided in many in-between solutions and situations. Many of the Muslim practices associated with *mouros* (the Kriol word for what in many parts of West Africa, including eastern Guinea-Bissau, are referred to as *marabouts*) can be seen as a mixture of contract and prayer. *Mouros* are Muslim seers and diviners who offer their spiritual help to clients (today in exchange for money), helping them with all sorts of problems (related to jobs, migration, kinship, etc.), normally using verses of the Qu'ran as magic spells, and sometimes achieving a synthesis between Qu'ranic knowledge and traditional local lore. *Mouros* are criticized by reformist Muslim leaders because, according to them, the divining practices of the *mouros* often fall beyond the strictures of the Qu'ran. Yet, these diviners are so important in the Bissau-Guinean public sphere (as well as in the diaspora) that their existence, even if contested, is part and parcel of the religious *convivência*, and is not very aggressively tackled by anyone. The same can be said of Catholicism, a religion based on prayer, but whose practices are often subjected to the logics of contract, promises and *torna-boka*, as Bissau-Guineans refer to the rituals one must perform in a shrine in order to return a favour of the spirit of the place. Sometimes even migrants who live in Europe, who may be Muslim or Christian, must make a journey back to the most remote village in hinterland Guinea-Bissau to perform a *torna-boka*.[10]

---

[10] For a vivid description of how traditional religion is embedded in everyday Guinea-

Islamic trends: old and new

The history and workings of the expansion of Islam, sometimes referred to as 'the threat of Islam' in colonial sources (e.g. Franklin 1956), have in Guinea-Bissau been a topic of scholarship by colonial administrators (Rodrigues 1948; Teixeira da Mota 1954; Brito 1957; Gonçalves 1958, 1961, 1962; Carreira 1966), as well as by recent historians (Bowman-Hawking 1980) and anthropologists (Gaillard 1995, 2000; Johnson 2002; Costa Dias 2009). Nevertheless, despite some efforts by recent scholars, ethnographic work is still needed to assess the relevance of Islam in today's public sphere.[11] The available literature shows that the making of a Muslim community in Guinea-Bissau has been extremely turbulent and fragmented since the days of pre-colonial empires such as Mande, Kaabu or the two Fuutas and their fights (both internal and among each other), right through to today's controversies within the *umma*. It also shows that between the letter of the Qur'an and everyday practices there have been many possible compromises, negotiations and processes of cultural osmosis and symbiosis which, in their turn, have produced many reformist Muslim movements. This is true of most of West Africa; but perhaps due to its ethnic pluralism and the tenacity of traditional religions, as well as the ability of inhabitants to adopt multiple identities and make fluid alliances, Guinea-Bissau might offer a paradigmatic case in which to study the cultural logics beneath Muslim incorporation, expansion and internal debates.

The entanglement between Islam and the anti-colonial struggle has been tackled by Garcia (2000, 2004), and its relevance to understanding later post-colonial politics by Gaillard (2002) and Cardoso (2004). Cardoso argues that Islam, much like Christianity, was regarded with suspicion by the first independent governments, largely because of its 'verticality' (to use Cabral's formulation) and its association with colonialism (see chapter by Green, this volume). Religion, whether Christian or Muslim, was perceived as a hindrance in making the *homo novus* of the revolutionary future. In the 1990s, religion

---

Bissau and how it entangles itself with Qu'ranic notions in the case of *mouros*, see Green 2001.

[11] For some exceptions, see the recent MA thesis on early marriage among Muslim women (Borges 2009) or the UNICEF report (Einarsdóttir et al. 2010) on the problem of the '*talibé* children', i.e. young boys sent to undertake Qur'anic training in Senegal, where they are forced to beg, a big concern in both Guinea-Bissau and Senegal.

was, like associations and civil society in general (Barros 2012), starting to have a much more accepted presence in the public sphere. As the example mentioned in the introduction to this chapter, of the nomination of Hernique Rosa in 2003, this was accentuated after the conflict of 1998–9, when religious institutions became more engaged in the political landscape. As far as Islam was concerned, Cardoso argues that although the situation at the time he was writing (i.e. 2004) was not quite the same as that of Senegal (overt symbiosis between political parties and Sufi brotherhoods), Guinea-Bissau might be going in that direction, with similar symbioses between Islamic trends and political attitudes. Ten years after Cardoso's article, and basing ourselves in our field research among Muslim agents and associations in pre-electoral Bissau in December 2013, we are inclined to believe that the convergence between political leaders and Muslim publics he anticipated is becoming more and more likely.

Today there coexist in Guinea-Bissau different understandings of Islam. We have verified the existence of the following key categories: mainstream Sunni Muslims; Sunnis belonging to the Sufi brotherhoods Qadiriyya, Tijaniyya and Muridiyya (the last one mostly composed of Senegalese settlers, since this brotherhood is very important in Senegal); Sunnis belonging to the reformist movement Wahabiyya; Sunnis belonging to the Ahmadiyya (even if the initial foreign introducers of this movement were expelled from the country by Kumba Yalá in 2001, following misunderstandings with the National Islamic Council); Sunnis belonging to the Tablighi Jama'at (a movement particularly attractive to young people); and, beyond the Sunni sphere, Shi'a Muslims. The latter are probably recent arrivals, but they must be taken into consideration. Worries about Shi'a presence and actions have been firmly voiced by Sunni *ulema* of different trends.

The arrival of Wahabiyya and Shi'a over the last decade is attributed, by many of our interviewees and by the media,[12] to the proximity of Guinea-Conakry. A large number of Muslims from Guinea-Conakry have entered Guinea-Bissau since the Mandinga Alpha Conde took presidential office in the former 2010. Conde is a Muslim, but the Fulas of Guinea-Conakry have been massively persecuted since the beginning of his rule, which many Guineans describe as a

---

[12] See, for instance, the 2012 entry 'Muçulmanos guineenses que praticam o islão segundo regras xiitas preocupam chefes religiosos' in the blog *Ditadura do Consenso*, http://ditaduradoconsenso.blogspot.pt/2012/07/muculmanos-guineenses-que-praticam-o.html, accessed 11 April 2014.

'Manding-ization' of their country, often making parallels with the times of the first president, Sékou Touré (1958–84), who was also a Mandinga and under whose rule many Fulas had suffered discrimination and persecution. Many Fulas from Guinea-Conakry, including wealthy traders and some politicians, have established themselves in Guinea-Bissau, making alliances with religious (and probably political) agents. There is a great need for the dynamics of this diaspora and its politico-religious effects to be analysed.

When discussing new Islamic forms in the field, a notion that normally emerges is that traditional Islam used to be much more tolerant to local non-Muslim practices than the new forms of today. This is probably the case, though we should not romanticize past forms of Islam or fall into the problematic explanation that forms of 'Black Islam' were closer to African beliefs than to orthodox Muslim belief. The arrival of Islam in the past was also, on many occasions, violent to local socio-cosmological understandings, and 'orthodoxy' is too theological a concept to have sociological value anyway. Probably, a lot of devotees who practised so-called African (or Black) forms of Islam would argue, if asked, that they were perfectly in line with Muslim orthodoxy. And who would we be to dispute that?[13]

Age is a particularly interesting aspect of the debate. Some of our interlocutors argued that established forms of Islam in Guinea-Bissau had one very important thing in common: the gerontocratic order. According to them, in the past it was as difficult and long for an animistic young child to become a proper elder in the local community as it was for a Muslim Fula or Mandinga to become a properly learned Muslim elder. Both processes of maturation were, indeed, time-consuming (for the confluence between Islamic and traditional systems of religious training in West Africa, see Brenner 2000). Newer forms of Islam, by contrast, try to bypass the 'in-between' status of many young Bissau-Guineans, prisoners in age-and-learning systems in which they are no longer children but not yet adults, by promising that anyone can be learned and empowered, even if they are a young man or woman.

According to these interviewees, thus, one of the elements that makes these new religious movements so fascinating for Bissau-Guinean youths is that they address the main problem that youth face in Africa today, namely how to become an elder and to be responsible for their own agency. They offer, to put

---

[13] The clash between different modes of Islamic training is the object of an insightful article by Eduardo Costa Dias (2005), astutely avoiding a facile divide between 'Black Islam' and 'orthodox Islam'.

it this way, a right-now and ready-made modern adulthood. But this view is contested by some other interviewees. Some of our more 'traditional' young Muslim respondents insisted that newer forms of Islam, such as Shi'a and Tablighi Jama'at, are not really addressing young people's problems. Rather, they are successful at manipulating youths' desires and expectations. These interviewees argue that the relationship between youths and elders (and between men and women) is very fluid in traditional forms of Islam, and abusive gerontocracy does not really exist: all Muslims are equal before God, irrespective of their age or gender. Youths of today, insist holders of this view, are being manipulated by external agents willing to create division in Guinea-Bissau by playing on youths' aspirations.

This may be true at some level (depending on how we define 'manipulation'), but it should not mean that youths have no agency whatsoever in their conversion. They may be 'manipulated' at some point, but they may also be 'manipulating' the situation to their advantage. Perhaps the success of some forms of religion depends on their becoming an all-win equation, in which everybody is happy with what they are getting out of the global situation...

In any case, the diversity of forms of Islam is striking and is a constant topic of theological discussion among Muslims and of social views about Islam in general. While this is probably the case for any Muslim context, it is rather extreme in Guinea-Bissau. The Islamic community is today so strongly divided that it boasts two Islamic councils: the National Islamic Council and the Superior Islamic Council, divided along ethnic and political lines (the former being composed mainly of Mandingas and the second of Fulas, increasingly incorporating exiles from Guinea-Conakry). The division is so acute that last year the two councils celebrated the *tabaski* (the West African name for the annual *Eid-al-Ahda* feast) on different days, following different readings of the liturgical calendar.

Religion, modernity and connection

Perhaps because Guinea-Bissau has been such a marginal, out-of-the-way place where for too long modernity has been beyond the reach of many of its citizens, it has been the object of some of the most innovative works on the fascination with modernity among young Africans (Gable 1990; Bordonaro 2010). In this final part of our chapter, we seek to show that many of the religious transformations the country has experienced in the last thirty years can be seen as indigenous ways to appropriate what people perceive as a modernity from which they feel excluded and to make alliances with broader worlds, an 'extroversive' attitude that has characterized the local worlds of Guinea-Bissau since their early days.

Perhaps the most paradigmatic example of this religious appropriation of modernity is the prophetic movement Kyang-yang (Cardoso 1992; Caellewart 2000; Temudo 2008; de Jong and Reis 2010). The Kyang-yang (a word meaning 'shadows' in Balanta) is a religious movement that affected almost exclusively the rural Balanta. It emerged in 1984 when a woman called Ntombikte (later known as Maria) claimed to have received commandments by God. She had thousands of followers, who under her initial guidance (later under the guidance of other Kyang-yang prophets, including Ntombikte's brother) abandoned traditional religion and converted to what, from an external point of view, was a syncretistic form of monotheism. They mixed Muslim and Christian symbols and rituals and gave a centrality to idioms of 'prayer'. They also materialized their religion and beliefs through sculptures and drawings. It is striking, when analysing this imaginative material culture, to notice how important modernity was for those who adopted Kyang-yang. It was as though Balanta farmers, aware of their marginalization from the Bissau-Guinean public and political spheres (particularly acute in the early years of the 1980s, after Vieira's *coup d'état*), attempted, through conversion, to join the modern world from which they were explicitly expelled. Through their exuberant religious imagination, they built or designed hospitals, schools, modern homes and religious buildings similar to either a mosque or a Christian temple. The movement was highly mimetic, but it had real effects on people's lives.

The Kyang-yang gradually died out. Today there are just isolated individuals living in Balanta villages who sometimes gather in small groups to pray, but less and less often. There have been few or no conversions over the last decade. Its gradual disappearance has been replaced, as far as young Balanta people are concerned, by two new religious arrivals in the villages: Pentecostalism and Islam, even in regions previously known for their fierce opposition to Islam. These two religions are seen today (and, unlike Kyang-yang, not only for Balanta) as local mechanisms to reach modernity and to be connected to a wider world, effecting, probably, a much more real and less imaginative connection than that earlier expressed by Kyang-yang prophets. In March 2011 one single man, Maulama, a Balanta Nhakra who had studied in Morocco where he converted to Islam, brought Islam into his village (in the region of Oio) and converted hundreds (some say thousands) of young people to Islam. Several villages decided collectively to convert, so as to have access to 'hospitals, wells, and schools', to cite verbatim the three things their dwellers mentioned in interviews as the main advantages of conversion (in the hope that development agencies from other Muslim countries would help them obtain them).

The rise of new forms of Evangelism and Pentecostalism in Guinea-Bissau is a recent boom (linked to the expansion of Brazilian churches), but it builds upon a deeply established Protestant community which, although very small till recently, should not be neglected (for its history, see Brierley 1955; Gonçalves 1961, 1966; Santos 1968; Wallis 1996; Costa Dias 1999; Lima 2007). Neo-Pentecostalism often serves to promote forms of 'development' and to provide an anchorage for young people to feel that they belong to wide networks and possibilities, being very efficient at combining religious with other social services.[14] In the Bijagó island of Formosa, for instance, the Evangelical headquarters includes a pharmacy. Evangelists also rely on the power of the radio, and in particular it may be worth singling out 'Radio Luz'. This station was born in the 1998–9 civil war environment. It was during the war that the Brazilian pastor Cláudio Silva (from the Assembly of God), then in Cape Verde, had a dream in which God commanded him to go to war-torn Guinea-Bissau to undertake evangelical work there. TV channels, especially 'Record TV' (belonging to the Universal Church of the Kingdom of God), also form a prominent element of evangelical action. Evangelist churches arriving from Brazil have in their favour the fascination that Bissau-Guineans feel towards things Brazilian: the culture, the people, the music, the tastes, and even the characteristic Brazilian accent and way of speaking Portuguese. Brazil, a country Africans perceive as being much more developed than their own, is in itself a symbolic mediator that allows for Christianity to arrive in ex-Portuguese Africa without any colonialist connotation. Brazilian religious expansion is not only a 'south–south' phenomenon, but one that gives hopes to Africans that they can find their own way of being on the 'developed' side of the world.

These waves of modernization through religion (the semi-extinct Kyang-yang, Islam and Pentecostalism) have some common trends. First of all, they all share the notion that religion brings connection. Non-Muslim and non-Chris-

---

[14] The huge literature on (neo-)Pentecostalism in Africa is often based on a clear-cut distinction between Pentecostal and non-Pentecostal forms of evangelical Christianity. However, in the field the line gets very blurred. Many Bissau-Guineans we interviewed did not even know whether their church was Pentecostal, Evangelical or mainstream Protestant.

tian people know that their world-religious neighbours belong to complex networks linking them to each other and to wider international circuits. Being modern is being connected to this network and, through this connection, able to gain access to development, wealth and improvement in quality of life. Secondly, we find in these religious dynamics reconfigurations of age and gender. Young people may find it easier to express and effect revolt against their elders if they feel God is on their side. The three religious examples have produced breaks with tradition and with kin obligations. Women, too, may find in religion ways to organize themselves against traditionalist male hegemony. Since its arrival in 2010, the Brazilian-initiated Evangelist organization Filhas da Sara ('Sarah's daughters') is rooting itself in Bissau-Guinean society and providing women with a relatively autonomous sphere within Christian religious culture.[15] Last but not least, religion is part and parcel of the reconfiguration of alliance and relatedness we witness in Guinea-Bissau today. New idioms of love, of individual autonomy and of the nuclear family are emerging, and religion plays a very important role in encouraging young people to look for their partners and break with traditional structures of kinship and alliance.

This discussion on new trends in religious dynamics and new discourses and practices may give the impression that religious change is uni-directional. But this is not the case. Guinea-Bissau is today also an ideal context for the study of what we could call religious reconversion. In the largely animist Papel and Bijagó regions, for instance, when people convert to Christianity but their move is later felt unsuccessful, they may perform some very expensive rituals to ask for forgiveness from the ancestors and local spirits and be reincorporated into their religious communities. These cases of reconversion have so far been poorly studied by specialized scholars. In any event, they show how multi-directional the plural condition of religious life in Guinea-Bissau really is and how far away we still are from understanding its full complexity. It is a field mined with ambiguities. The person who converts to a neo-Pentecostal religion today and affirms that tradition is evil may reconvert to her traditional religion a few years later and consider that neo-Pentecostal pastors or Muslim proselytizers are liars. It is this constant navigation from one belief to another that we encourage scholars to research in order to understand the place of religion in the making of the nation and its future.

---

[15] http://ministeriofilhasdesara.blogspot.pt/p/guine-bissau.html, accessed 10 April 2014.

Conclusion

Guinea-Bissau is a small country at the edge of a big continent and of an even bigger ocean, but boasts many different religious traditions and many different compromises. Sociologists are often puzzled to find that when people are asked about their religion in questionnaires, they do not write down 'Muslim', 'Christian' or 'animist', but rather 'mixed'.[16] What might a 'mixed religion' be like? What do people really mean? This must be ethnographically studied, but the use of the concept, in itself, tells us a lot about the lived-world of contemporary Bissau-Guineans. Their spiritual landscape offers a rich variety of discourses and practices, and history has taught them that it is best to keep options open. Their success, as individuals and as groups, depends on tapping into different sources and making simultaneous alliances (in some parts of Guinea-Bissau it is very common to find people who send one child to the mosque and another to the Catholic church, thus maximizing their own and their group's alliances).

Managing multiple identities and mastering the arts of ambiguity have long been part and parcel of being a person on the often turbulent frontiers of the Upper Guinea Coast. Historical work is still necessary to analyse the depth of the different traditions, the connotations some groups have inherited, the representations different religions have had in different times, and the compromises made at specific moments. Sociological and anthropological work is equally necessary to improve our understanding of how this historical legacy is incorporated, what are the cultural logics of religious change and mixture, and how the cunning ability of actors to negotiate and find resourceful mediations works, especially in the highly uncertain days in which Guinea-Bissau is living today.

In the conclusion of *O Mestiço e o Poder*, Tcherno Djaló warns against the potential polarization between a luso-ized elite and a Muslim one, and reminds us that only a properly democratic institutional setting will prevent this from becoming a political problem for the country (Djaló 2013: 273–4). Democracy is indeed necessary, but in any case Bissau-Guineans have sufficiently demonstrated that they do not sit well in strict polarities, be they racial, political or religious: they are very good at managing ambiguity and

---

[16] Bissau-Guinean sociologists with whom we have informally discussed the 'mixed religion' common answer include Mamadu Jao, whose critical insights and support to the FCT project we thank here.

mediation and at offering imaginative solutions in the middle ground. In the making of the modern global world, Bissau-Guineans are better regarded as actors than as outcomes. Their own willingness to remain actors is what lies beneath their skilful management of alliances and extraversions and what gives rise to the religious inventiveness of this apparently marginal, but in reality very central, part of the Atlantic world.

6

GENDERED PATTERNS OF MIGRATION AND CHANGING GENDER RELATIONS IN GUINEA-BISSAU

Aliou Ly

During my 2013 field trip in Bissau, I was having a casual conversation with one of my Bissau-Guinean friends: 'How are things going in Bissau these days?' I asked. My last visit had been in 2010. My friend flatly responded, 'Man, since the 1998 civil war, the country has been governed by militaro-political gangs involved in drugs and arms trafficking. The United Nations should replicate what they did in [East] Timor in the past. The UN should have full control of the country for at least ten years.'

Suddenly my friend asked me if I had seen the guy in the white car that had just passed by. He said, 'This guy was one of the ministers in the previous government and now he is one of the secretaries of state. He was accused of drug trafficking in the 1980s in an Asian country.' I asked how someone like him could be performing any function at state level. My friend laughed at me and answered, 'Do you know that one of the frontrunners for the PAIGC party's presidency was accused of drug trafficking in Europe? Having top officials involved in dirty activities is now a standard phenomenon in this country. If you look at the city since your last visit, you can see a lot of new buildings and businesses; and most of them are from dirty money.' This answer made me ask some deeper questions. Whatever the truth of these specific comments, Western governments had led the accusations regarding Guinea-Bissau and the narcotics trade. But how could the country arrive at this extreme of disruption and desolation? And why and how has Guinea-Bissau become so widely seen as a 'narco-state'?

As a specialist in gender relations, I understand that in order to explore these questions we need to ask another set of questions. How has the marginalization of women in the political, social and economic structures contributed to the growth of narco-trafficking in Guinea-Bissau and the failure of the state? More precisely, what roles have gender inequalities played as Guinea-Bissau has become a 'narco-state', and how have these roles changed as a result of the situation in the country?

In order to explore these questions, I have analysed my field interviews, field notes and archival materials, gathered in Guinea-Bissau from 2008 to 2013, in light of scholarly texts on gender and politics, statecraft and state failure, and narco-trafficking in West Africa. My focus concerns gendered power relations as they affect state political operations.

My findings lead me to argue the following. Disregarding the desire for concrete economic and social change as a core concern of women participants in the national liberation war, the male leadership in independent Guinea-Bissau weakened the state and contributed to its failure. Women fighters participated for concrete goals (Urdang 1979: 21). They wanted to improve the social and economic life of their families, within a more egalitarian society (Urdang 1979: 32 and all). Most male fighters participated in the struggle for more abstract motivations. They saw freedom in terms of abstract political independence, while they also sought individual opportunities to become decision-makers. When the country became independent, male leaders consolidated their political and economic positions as groups and individuals. This in turn contributed to the consolidation of a formalized masculine political realm of both personal and state power. The male leaders forsook the work of trying to build the progressive, egalitarian and prosperous society that Amílcar Cabral and most of the former women fighters had envisioned. Their rush to consolidate gendered decision-making and male self-interest for a small group of men became a crucial factor in the emergence of a 'failed state'. That failure opened the floodgates to narco-trafficking in the twenty-first century.

The demise of women's roles in post-independent Guinea-Bissau and its impact on society

Women of Guinea-Bissau faced socio-cultural and economic challenges from pre-colonial times through the Portuguese colonial period. Both traditional socio-cultural structures and also colonial systems kept them under the supervision of men. In order to change these inequalities and burdens, they fought on the side of the PAIGC during the national liberation war from 1963 to 1974. By 1980, it became clear that women's socio-cultural and economic position had not changed since independence. As participants in decision-making, they have been under-represented in all paramount components of the newly independent state structure. As community members, workers and mothers, their interests have not been represented at all.

The underrepresentation of women in systems of education, administration and politics

Despite new sets of laws for gender equality between the sexes in employment and political positions, women of Guinea-Bissau have very few employment opportunities. Among the forty-two former women liberation fighters I interviewed, only three of them are fully employed. Binetou Nankin Seydi[1] said, 'We as women have never been respected or included in the country's policies after independence' (Binetou Nankin Seydi 2008 and O Militante).

When the newly independent country allocated stipends to all former fighters, former women fighters had to go through a series of obstacles before even being registered as former freedom fighters. They needed to produce two male former fighters as witnesses to their participation in the fight. This policy is itself symptomatic of the political mentality that led to a failed state. On a more concrete level, many of the women former fighters received no compensation for their war participation (Quinta Da Costa interview 2010).

Despite the clear disregard for women's rights, Maloba argues that the PAIGC commitment to women was 'consistent and genuine'. She does point

[1] Binetou Nankin Seydi was aged twelve when she witnessed the PAIGC organizing what is known as the CASSACA conference in her village Cassaca (south region). She learned about the assassination of Amílcar Cabral when she was in Havana, Cuba where she had gone for secretarial training. She worked in different ministries as a typist and is now one of the executive members of the women's organization Udemu.

out that there are 'interpretations and speculations' to the contrary (Maloba 2008: 96). She bases her argument on the fact that most women were peasants living off the land and that land was granted to all men and all women. This, she says, was exceptional in Africa at the time (Maloba 2008: 97). But from all the women I interviewed, I learned that after the war they all moved to Bissau. They had not in fact been living off the land. During the war they had been constantly on the move because of their PAIGC war assignments and the need to be with their husbands. The population of Bissau increased after the war by 90,000 (Galli and Jones 1987: 73), a large proportion being women.

The education policy set in place after independence did not help support women's participation in the workforce (Galli and Jones 1987: 161–76; J. M. Pereira 1986: 78; Rudebeck 1974: 206). It was clear that Bissau-Guineans were holding to their traditional belief that women's main task was to learn how to take care of their husband and family. Even Carmen Pereira,[2] one of the very few women who achieved a public role after independence, recalls this traditional belief from her own childhood. Her father, the first Bissau-Guinean lawyer, took her out of school when he felt she had learned enough to read and write. He thought it was time for her to learn 'how to be a woman' (Pereira 2008).

Impact of female marginalization in post-independent Guinea-Bissau

After Nino Vieira's *coup d'état* in 1980, women's conditions deteriorated further, because the normal rules of gendered government and administration became increasingly based on individualism, corruption and personal interest. The lack of responsible leadership led to political turmoil as rivalries heated up between different groups of leaders, and the army became involved in politics. The internal conflicts seriously dislocated the economic tissue of people's daily lives. Hunger and famine become the norm. According to interviewees, those who suffer most as a consequence are women and children (Joanita Da Silva Rosa interview 2010).

[2] Carmen Pereira joined the PAIGC accidentally in 1962 as she was following her husband Umaro Djalo, one of the early PAIGC members. She lived in Senegal before going to the Soviet Union for medical training in 1963. She was deputy president of Guinea-Bissau National Assembly, then Minister of Health and Social Services, before later becoming a member of the Council of State. As President of the National Assembly, she was Acting President of Guinea-Bissau from 14 to 16 May 1984.

In 2002, 65.7 per cent of the population were defined as poor (Barry and Creppy 2007: 59). In the context of Sub-Saharan Africa, poverty means that a woman has less than a 30% chance of seeing all her children survive to age five. It also means that the average life expectancy is forty-eight years and that the average person eats 30% fewer calories per day than Latin American or East Asian people (Easterly and Levine 1997: 1203–4).

Most of the women I interviewed talked about their very difficult living conditions. For example, Fatoumata Diallo,[3] a Fula woman, joined the PAIGC almost as a by-product of ensuring that her only son, a PAIGC fighter, was well fed. Despite becoming a liberation fighter herself, she receives no compensation and must live off the care of the Abelhas, a middle-class Bissau-Guinean family living in the Bairro neighbourhood of Luanda in Bissau. She receives regular offerings or gifts from that family and others. Another example is Joanita Da Silva Rosa, who lost her husband during the war. A liberation fighter herself, she also lost her right eye. Today she lives without any financial or economic support. At the age of 85, she would be homeless without the help of her church. She says that the amount she received as a veteran of the war helped her to live for just one week (Joanita Da Silva Rosa and Fatoumata Diallo interviews 2010). Meanwhile, Binetou N. Seydi was sent to Cuba for training as a typist during the war. When she came back to Guinea-Bissau in 1973, she managed to hold jobs in several structures of the state, but since the 1998 civil war she has been unemployed. With the three exceptions mentioned above, the former women fighters I interviewed had had no employment, although most of them had participated in the national struggle in the hope of a better concrete future for themselves and their children.

What are the causes of this deterioration? The women and a few of the male PAIGC leaders, including Amílcar Cabral, did seek the emancipation of

---

[3] Fatoumata Diallo, a Fula woman from the Cacheu region, joined the PAIGC by accident in her eighties, in 1964. Her son, Alpha Dabo, was one of the fighters on the northern and eastern fronts. Her son and other fighters often used to stop by her house looking for something to eat or to rest after long journeys of marches and fighting. Her son Alpha was a PAIGC sympathizer before he became fully involved in the party in 1962. She decided to become fully involved because the Portuguese police pursued her son and others in Cacheu. It was a sad moment because Alpha was her only son. She worried about her son's health and well-being. To make sure her son had food, she started taking food to the maquis on a weekly basis. She walked through the forest for hours to do so. One day she asked herself, 'Why not live with them and cook for them and save myself from the risk of being arrested by the Portuguese army or police?' After that, she stayed in the maquis.

women as an integral part of the national liberation struggle. But most male PAIGC members and freedom fighters never entertained the idea of liberating women from traditional socio-cultural and economic exploitation as part of the national liberation struggle.

This situation was, of course, far from anomalous. In refusing to change traditional and colonial gender inequalities after independence, the Bissau-Guinean leaders did not differ from leaders of other African nationalist movements and independent countries. Before 1944, none of the nationalist groups in West Africa had thought out or articulated economic and social programmes besides stating in general terms the need to seek economic and social development for all groups of the population (Schmidt 2002: 283–5). The integration of women's emancipation into nationalist programmes resulted from Western-educated West African women joining the nationalist groups, and from the women's capacity for mobilization for national struggles in southern Africa (Isaacman and Isaacman 1984: 166; PAIGC 1973: 52). As recompense for women's ability to mobilize, male-dominated African nationalist movements started to integrate women's emancipation agendas into their stated goals (Schmidt 2002: 283–5). In several African nationalist movements, many male participants soon realized that independence must mean not only political freedom, but also socio-cultural and economic opportunities for women with full rights of citizenship. In Guinea-Bissau, Amílcar Cabral and a few members of his initially all-male party really believed in the true need for women to have opportunities to emancipate themselves and be proactive agents rather than passive recipients of development.

In this view, independence was only the beginning. The PAIGC would build a new state on the foundation of a better life for families and communities. Cabral advocated a practice that would be founded on local socio-economic realities and would encourage all groups in the communities to participate fully in building the country's independence. In this way, Cabral developed policies grounded in an analysis of the local realities, and guided by neo-Marxist theory.

By and large, however, the men saw themselves as fighting against colonialism. They understood the main fight as being against the Portuguese and for political independence and personal freedom. Their main issue was the opportunity to decide for themselves and for their country. When Bissau-Guinean males referred to personal freedom and political independence, they referred to male personal independence and to males replacing the Portuguese at political and decision-making levels. They did not see feeding the family as an important political issue.

130

Most male fighters believed that by becoming politically free and independent, all other socio-economic issues would be automatically resolved. They would be able to develop their country without working for changes in traditional gender relations.

Thus, although fighting for women's equality was an explicit goal of the party agenda, most PAIGC males did not see changing the traditional socio-cultural inequalities that held women back as part of the fight (Cornwall 1972: 50; Davidson 1969: 78–80). In fact, this male view denied any traditional socio-cultural and political changes with regard to gender relations (Urdang 1979: 17, 107, 125–8). Indeed, although women had been on the front lines of the PAIGC mobilization and fight for independence, male fighters as well as historians of the liberation war have always put them in the background and presented them as followers (Urdang 1979: 115). Despite the fact that women fought heroically, some male fighters continued to believe that women were not suited to participating in direct combat operations. For example, Barnaté Sahna[4] believed that 'Women slowed down the marches of the fighters when carrying heavy loads and were not suited for military operations' (Barnaté Sahna interviews 2010). Urdang reports the same attitude (Urdang 1979: 228).

In order to reconcile fact with belief, men considered the women who participated in combat operations as exceptional heroines or singular super-women. But when we look closely we see that almost all the women participants in the liberation war engaged in direct combat operations from 1963 to 1965 and after 1972. Even between 1965 and 1972, during the period when they had been ordered to stay out of combat, many of them refused and insisted on continuing. Both maintaining the form of this male myth and contesting its content, Francisca Pereira said, 'Titina symbolized the kind of woman that the PAIGC was trying to produce and she refused to lay down her arms when women were asked to stay behind' (Pereira 2008, 2010).[5]

---

[4] Barnaté Sahna joined the PAIGC in January 1963 at the age of eighteen. After periods of military and political training under Osvaldo Vieira's orders, in 1965 he became a fighter on the northern front. In Mores he met Amílcar Cabral and Titina Silla. In 1968 he lost his right eye during a combat operation and was hospitalized in Dakar, Senegal.

[5] Francisca Pereira was born in 1942. She joined the PAIGC in 1959 in Conakry, Republic of Guinea at the age of seventeen. She represented the PAIGC at the Pan-African Women's Organization, and was also president of the Udemu in 1977. She is still active in Guinea-Bissau politics.

However, her symbolic status as exceptional actually represents the many women who acted as she did.

Who was Titina? Ernestina ('Titina') Silla was born in Cadique Betna, Tombali region, in April 1943. She was first contacted in 1961 by two mobilizers, Nino Vieira and Umaro Djalo. From the first time they approached her, she threw all her energies into the struggle. Her initial task was to distribute clandestine literature, which she hid in a can in her backyard. Later she acted as liaison between the mobilizers living in the forest and the peasants (Urdang 1979: 195). In the end she ran away from her mother to join the PAIGC in Conakry and was sent to the USSR with other young women. She returned in 1964 before finishing her military and political training, but 'her revolutionary fervor was not dampened, and she continued her political work among the people as a "responsavel"' (Urdang 1979: 195). Titina ended up as one of the three political mobilizers of the PAIGC and was in charge of the northern region. She was a fierce political and military leader, but was killed while going to Conakry for Amílcar Cabral's funeral on 31 January 1973. That day is celebrated in Guinea-Bissau as Women's Day.

Although Titina Silla and Fatmata Sibili represented women's participation in combat operations, they were only the tip of the proverbial iceberg. As presented by Stephanie Urdang, Fatmata was a young Fula woman who joined the PAIGC guerrilla groups. She trained with male fighters and went through all the physical sessions with them (Urdang 1979: 228). Many other women, especially from the southern region, participated in direct fighting between 1963 and 1967 (Urdang 1979: 115). Theresa NQuamé,[6] a Balanta woman, is just one example of the many women in combat. She joined the PAIGC in 1963, and the PAIGC trained her as a *sapadura*, someone who set mines in water and on land to destroy Portuguese naval embarkations, bridges and roads. After training in the PAIGC's facilities around Boé, the PAIGC military commanders sent her to the northern front. NQuamé said that two other women also specialized in mine-setting in the north.

Theresa NQuamé mentioned Titina Silla as one of the many military and political trainers on the northern front. But she spoke about Titina with more personal emotion. They had worked together and Theresa talked about how she was personally affected when Titina drowned after jumping out of the

---

[6] Theresa NQuamé was a *sapadura* (someone who set mines in water and on land to destroy Portuguese naval embarkations, bridges and roads) during the liberation war. She affirms that in her section in the north region two women were in the specialized groups of men working on those tasks.

boat that was transporting some PAIGC members to Amílcar Cabral's funeral. She jumped to avoid being arrested by a Portuguese naval patroller, even though she did not know how to swim (Theresa NQuamé 2010).

Maintaining gender inequalities after independence

After having resisted the participation of women during the independence struggle, Bissau-Guinean men continued to resist gender changes after independence. But the law nevertheless introduced reform.

New laws in favour of women's independence

The newly independent country implemented new socio-cultural and economic laws that protected women from traditional male abuses and also granted women the same economic and political rights as their male counterparts. The country's constitution advocated total equality and equal opportunities for all citizens of the country. It also declared monogamy as the law of the land. Thus, the National Assembly passed laws that facilitated divorce, legalized common law marriages and abolished the concept of 'illegitimate' children. One of the most important laws decreed that all children must be seen as legitimate whether they were born in or out of formal marriage.

Before independence, divorce was prohibited because of both Portuguese laws influenced by Catholicism and customary law (Urdang 1979: 277). The new National Assembly guaranteed women the right to divorce, but set a waiting time for any tentative reconciliation. Whereas colonial law declared children born in these marriages as 'illegitimate', the new constitution declared them 'legitimate'. Where colonial law prevented women and children from inheriting from the deceased father of informal marriage, the constitution recognized the right to inheritance in such cases of customary marriage (Urdang 1979: 277).

Other laws were designed to protect women who married PAIGC combatants in the maquis during wartime. After the war, many wartime husbands abandoned them for younger urban women. New laws declared that all marriages contracted in marriage ceremonies had the status of common law marriages if they existed for at least three years with or without the consent of one of the couples. These unions could be dissolved only through a legal divorce process, in which case the husband would have to pay financial support (Maloba 2007: 95). Also, wife-beating became illegal.

In 1974, after the departure of the Portuguese administration, the Republic of Guinea-Bissau created a constitution and new laws meant to protect women and give them social and economic opportunities to participate in the construction of the newly independent state. Because of the new laws, the women I interviewed said that Bissau-Guinean women felt that they would be protected and that the country they fought to liberate was giving them opportunities to be agents of development outside the shadow of men. For the women of Guinea-Bissau, 1974 was a period of hope.

The new constitution and new laws were not only intended to protect women, but also to change the traditional socio-cultural structures of the country. Guinea-Bissau might have been one of the earliest among the very few African countries that soon after becoming independent decided to transform gender relations and to lift women's burdens. Establishing laws are one thing, but implementing them is another matter altogether, especially if the change requires people to transform their own socio-cultural behaviour, and if the law-makers themselves would be the ones who would have to release their actual and traditional power over women.

How then did the Bissau-Guinean men feel about the new laws? They felt them as a loss of their long-time power and control over Bissau-Guinean women. Most Bissau-Guinean males found ways to bypass these socio-cultural and economic laws. They continued to practise polygyny and arranged marriage. In order to circumvent the new requirement of monogamy, they married through traditional regimes instead of conducting legal civil marriage (Tertilt 2006; Urdang 1979: 111; Urdang 1989: 202; Einarsdóttir 2004: 179; and my group conversations in Bissau 2010). Monogamous males also snubbed the new laws by having mistresses. Many condemned the idea of a monogamous society by claiming that the idea came from outside and was not part of their customs and beliefs.

Men's resistance to post-independence changes in gender relations

The difficulty of eliminating polygyny and arranged marriage presents a problem in other parts of Africa (Tertilt 2006). 'It was, and remains, a tough nut to crack' (Urdang 1989: 202). In my interviews, the people most likely to attach ideological importance to marriage were men. Some men claimed that polygyny is part of the 'African heritage' in contrast to monogamy. Aliu Fadia,[7] who followed the path of avoiding civil marriage in order to avoid

[7] Aliu Fadia was born in 1933 in Bulama. A polygamous Fula man, he was the father

monogamy, is an old Muslim man married to a Balanta woman. He claimed that polygyny was an ancient tradition and part of the African way of life. He claimed that monogamy was a new way of thinking that modern governments were forcing on their citizens: 'Even when men were allowed to be polygynous, men rarely contracted a civil marriage because it is not part of our culture and belief. Now, with the constraint of having only one wife, do you think it will encourage us to get a civil marriage certificate with all the laws that may come with it? No, I do not think so' (Aliu Fadia interviews 2010).

Many men condemned the government's decision to impose monogamy as the only civil marriage recognized by the state. Diabira Gassama[8] claimed that he saw the imposition of monogamy as an institution imported from European culture in an attempt to make women equal to men, which he claimed was foreign to Africa. For Diabira, the idea of contracting a civil marriage is not 'African': 'Why should we copy the Europeans? You know, our leaders were brainwashed by the Europeans and they want to impose on us a European way of life. If at least they were helping the population to live a decent life and respect the institutions, we can follow them. They do nothing for us and want to impose on us a way of living, [but] it is not going to work. Look, most of the married men I know never contract a civil marriage because nothing comes with this contract. No help' (Diabira Gassama interviews 2010). In essence he argued that the law did not reflect public opinion. For him, it was not unusual for men to resist legal reforms that undermined their authority over matters of marriage (Diabira Gassama interviews 2010). In arguments against civil marriage, men refer to the refusal to be limited to one wife, even though some of those who make these arguments are not polygynists, but see the law as something from outside their country imposed by their government, a government that does not respect tradition or fulfil its duties.

By and large, the newly independent country's men also opposed the economic laws in favour of women's emancipation and rights. They saw the laws as encouraging women to leave their customary and traditional familial work and status. Worse, they saw the laws as encouraging competition for jobs that

---

of my host in Bulama. During the liberation war in Guinea-Bissau he and his family migrated to Ziguinchor, Senegal. They went back to Guinea-Bissau in 1974 after the declaration of independence. During his adult years he was a trader but also a seasonal cashew nut collector during the cashew collecting campaign. He passed away on 21 May 2012.

[8] Diabira Gassama is a young Mandinka from the region of Gabú.

they considered men's jobs. They were especially wary about jobs in the administrative and economic sectors. In Hutna Yalla's interview, he says that some men were frustrated by the idea of allowing women to have the same job opportunities because men already had a hard time finding jobs. 'So why allow women to get into the job market?' (Hutna Yalla interview 2010). As a response to such complaints, some male job recruiters did not hesitate to make the hiring process difficult for women.

Treatment by the military was similar. In addition to the obstacles women faced in receiving their military stipends as mentioned above, they were excluded from the new national army, whereas most of the male veterans of the liberation war were accepted into the new military structure. Because of this post-war exclusion, the veterans' affairs department did not help many former women fighters. Therefore, although many of these women came out of the liberation war with illnesses and injuries, they received no treatment (Theresa NQuamé, Ndalla Mané, NDo Mané and Na NDati interviews 2010). Compounding this, the reformulation of the village committees for better women's participation faced refusal in many villages (F. Pereira 2008; A. Cabral 1969a: 12; Chaliand 1969: 47).

Most men refused to accept the new civil laws intended to liberate Bissau-Guinean women from their control not by directly challenging the laws, but by defining new ways to force women to accept them as the decision-makers (Biaye interview, 2010). In this case, even law-makers and representatives broke the law because they knew that nothing would happen to them in terms of judiciary sanctions. In addition, most women did not act to implement the new laws because they could not face social disapproval should they raise their voices. And in the final analysis, some women were not really interested in making changes (Einarsdóttir 2004: 27, 31–2, 179; Cira Diallo interviews 2009; Dianké Mballo interview 2010).

Male resistance creates an independent political state, but not a socially equal state

I would argue that gender inequality and ethnic/class inequality arise out of the same foundations, namely traditional socio-cultural structures and colonialism. Those factors that cause gender inequality also lead to ethnic and class inequalities within the male group in Guinea-Bissau. I will borrow the definition of ethnicity as presented by Peter Arthur from his reading of Crawford Young's book *Ethnicity and Politics in Africa*. 'Ethnicity is an "imaged community," a social and historical construction and a product of human activity and agency—a social construction, in which such commonalities and shared values as speech, language, and political organization and activities are woven into the psyche and consciousness of people who believe they share the same identity' (Arthur 2009: 48). Gender power also acted as compensation for indigenous men who suffered from class and ethnic inequality, as most of them were polygynists and refused any gender structure change: in effect, the historical consequences of local and global economic inequalities were 'cashed out' in Guinea-Bissau through gender inequalities. Finally, the quest for privileges within the male group has taken the place of developing the country; this has led to internal conflicts and opened doors for personal and group interests rather than allowing reformers to pose a serious challenge to established interests.

Ethnic and class inequalities: privileged vs. unprivileged

The external phenomena that created gender inequality also created ethnic and class inequalities within the male group. Traditional socio-cultural structures imposed gender inequality, while the colonial system set ethnic and class inequalities within the male group. In post-independent Guinea-Bissau, Luís Cabral was one of the beneficiaries of ethnic inequality; he could act equally to all ethnic groups, but he preferred to preserve Cape Verdean privileges by limiting power to their ethnic group. The result of Luís Cabral's policy replaced 'nation-making' with 'state-breaking' (Heredia 1997: 1010; see also Forrest and Green, this volume).

Luís Cabral kept most of the 'colonial bourgeoisie' workers in place (Lopes 1982/1987: 155–81; Davidson 1981: 101–7; Galli and Jones1987: 78, 94, 97, 99) and permitted Cape Verdeans and Cape Verdean descendants to maintain and develop social and political dominance (Forrest 1992: 138; A. Cabral 1969b: 31; De Sena and Lambert 1977: 103; *Tercero Plano de Fomento Para, 1968–1973*). Indigenous soldiers, though more numerous and more experienced than the Cape Verdeans, were often overlooked for leadership positions by Cabral's government. In fact, in 1979 Balanta male officers voiced their frustration when Luís Cabral exercised his desire to modernize the national armed forces by nominating officers only from the Cape Verdean ethnic group to leading positions (Uwazurike 1996: 2).

It was this which ignited the military coup of 1980, and thereafter the country was plunged into a permanent struggle between different privileged groups interested in keeping their privilege and increasing their political and economic positions (Forrest 1987: 101–7). As the struggle between the privileged and unprivileged kept growing, conditions that created gender, ethnic, military and political inequalities kept increasing these inequalities. The growth of inequalities and class privileges led to the 1998 civil war, in which military officers who were isolated by the presidential structure decided to fight back and regain their privileges. The 1998 civil war was not the result of a people's uprising, but rather of different politico-military factions, with power and political interest as privileged groups, fighting to keep their socio-politico-economic interests (Collier and Hoefflert 2004: 563–4; Rudebeck 1998: 486; Temudo 2008: 245–63). For Lars Rudebeck, the main reason for the politico-military struggle was a completely corrupt presidential power structure and harsh conditions existing in the country at privileged and under-privileged levels (Rudebeck 1998: 486).

The consequences of the 1998 conflict are still visible across the country: a weak public sector, insecurity, political instability and crime. The explosive situation led to increasing politicization of ethnicity by self-serving leaders seeking to increase their legitimacy and power (Barry and Creppy 2007: 27–30; see Green and Kohl, this volume). What then followed was the rapid emigration of skilled workers, leading to a deterioration of the environment. In the end, the economy was completely damaged (Collier 1999: 168–9). The conditions led those with privilege to hang on to what they had and be readier to take risks. Some of them would not mind developing alliances, such as with military officers and politicians, politicians using the ethnic card, and struggles between different militaro-political factions (Boubacar-Sid and Creppy 2007: 27–30). Hence, inequality had been institutionalized along political and ethnic lines by the early twenty-first century.

Gender power as compensation for males who suffered from ethnic and class inequalities (indigenes as a majority of the polygynists)

Gender power in contemporary Guinea-Bissau therefore functioned as compensation for males who suffered from ethnic and class oppression and inequality. Protecting their gender power soon became more important to them than fighting the widening ethnic and class division. They protected their gender power by refusing any laws that advocated gender equality and women's rights and opposed polygyny.

Women are the group that suffered the most from such gender, ethnic and class-based inequality. Indigenous men, meanwhile, defended their gender power as a way to compensate them for ethnic and class inequalities. All the indigenous men I interviewed attested their refusal to accept these post-independence civil laws granting women the same rights as men (Aliu Fadia 2010; Barnaté Sahna 2010; Mario Cissokho 2008).[9] Most indigenous men are still polygynists and refuse to complete civil union documents, embodying their refusal to move away from their traditional socio-cultural organizations and structures. They do not have powers or dominance over other ethnic groups or indigenous militaro-political groups, but they still control their own household and they refuse any outside or state involvement in their family matters. The dislocation of the political and economic tissue of the country reinforced indigenous male desire to keep their gendered society as it was. Thus their domination and control over women was more necessary because this acted as compensation for their suffering of ethnic and class-based inequalities. The consequence of progressive crises of state and society in post-colonial Guinea-Bissau has therefore been manifested in the contemporary crisis of gender relations. As these crises reinforced the dislocation of the state, laws and women's rights became obsolete as no social authority sought to enforce them. The 1974 gender and social laws were mostly ignored because they became the least concerns of a society in the midst of disruption. Seeking official marriage documents, or recognizing children born outside official or traditional marriages, became the least concerns of men in power. The shame of women seeking divorce or leaving their husband's house led married women to avoid court trials or other legal actions.

Conclusion: Quests for privileges instead of concentrating on national development

As Galli and Jones say, 'Guinea-Bissau was seen to be a model for both political and economic development in the African context. But Guinea turned out to be neither' (Galli and Jones 1987: 1). During the early stage of independence, the PAIGC executive bureau showed its incapacity to face the challenges its male members threw up with regard to women's emancipation and rights. As shown above, men's intransigence against women's emancipation and refusal to recognize women's concerns for improving family and community were directly linked to a strong investment in masculine identity. A major element of this identity was male rivalry. Therefore, their acquiescence to

[9] Mario Romalho Cissokho was a member of the PAIGC after 1961 and former Director of INEP (Guinea-Bissau's National Institute of Research).

misogyny constituted one of the early signs that the political leadership was moving away from its early decentralized decision-making to a more centralized type of governance based on crushing its rivals, and therefore increasing the spiral of rivalries between male factions. These rivalries led to Malam Sanha's attempted coup in 1978. This attempt, in turn, made Luís Cabral tighten internal and external security mechanisms, giving power to small groups and creating a pervasive sentiment of fear in the country (Jones and Galli 1987: 1–2). Thus continued a vicious circle that suppressed even further the once key agenda of the PAIGC and nationalist movement to liberate women from traditional socio-structures, and thereby revolutionize those structures themselves.

In addition to reinforcing gender inequality, Luís Cabral's tight group, composed mostly of Cape Verdeans and men of Cape Verdean descent, also increased ethnic and class inequalities (Mario R. Cissokho interviews 2008). This vicious circle of gender inequality, male rivalry, quest for privilege and the spread of civil fear sowed the seeds for a future failing state (Piazza 2008: 470; Zartman 1995; Rotberg 2002). As also shown above, when a newly independent state thus builds itself on the rejection of women's rights and concrete concerns, it also reinforces discrepancies between traditional and modern, as well as rural versus urban (Forrest 2003). Its institutions do not respond to the public interest in terms of effectiveness, fairness or efficiency ((Boubacar-Sid and Creppy 2007: 25). The struggle for personal wealth and power suppresses all other governing concerns. Political and military instability ensue, and state failure and corruption are the inevitable results. A failing state, consumed by its own internal conflicts, poses a potential threat to its own society. Thus we see that Guinea-Bissau's situation as it emerged in the 2000s as a hub for transnational terrorism and narco-trafficking has deep roots in both global and local inequalities, and the failure of the early independence governments to address these issues (Piazza 2008).

During my summer 2013 trip to Bissau, when I asked how drug trafficking affected the country's life and gender inequality, I always received bold responses. For a small number, the country has been wrongly accused of hosting drug traffickers. 'The story about drug trafficking is completely made up,' said a private Bissau businessman whom I had known since my early visits to Guinea-Bissau, when I mentioned to him several drug trafficking-related scandals.[10] On

---

[10] A South American pilot landed with a large amount of cocaine but was released by a local judge in 2008. Charles Parkinson affirms in *Media Magazine* of 29 August 2013 that the pilot was Carmelo Vasquez Guerra who was later arrested in

the other hand, a large number of my interlocutors acknowledged the importance of drug trafficking in Guinea-Bissau. Most of them trace the drug trafficking to the 1998 civil war and the 2003 military coup. They link the traffic to yet another downward turn of the spiralling political instability, economic hardship and increased corruption (see also Hoffman and Lane 2013). Another Bissau-Guinean friend whom I will call 'Nanthio' said to me, 'You see how Bissau has changed since your last trip [summer of 2010]: all these new or restored buildings flourishing around Bissau. Who are the owners? Where they got their money?' He continued his argument. 'You know one of the PAIGC frontrunners for the party presidency and potential presidential candidate in the next country's elections was supposedly accused of drug trafficking in Portugal [under the Portuguese judiciary system, this is very difficult to verify as criminal records have a limited time span]. He was elected as PAIGC deputy in 2008 and was adviser to PAIGC leadership since the mid-2000s.' When I asked how the dislocation of the country and drug trafficking affected gender relations, most of the time my interlocutors laughed at me. 'This is not about men or women, we all suffered from the situation of the country, only the drug traffickers and their local partners profited from the situation,' said Angelina Gomis, a 38-year-old woman who has lived in Dakar since 1998. 'You see all the ones who can migrate to other countries did it, even the ones who are still here hope to do so, men and women.'

But she continued: 'Yes, if you want, we can say women suffered more because they are in charge of feeding their children. In many cases their husbands left seeking better lives in Senegal or somewhere else, but ended by completely disappearing while the women could not' (Angelina Gomis 2013). In this seemingly incidental afterthought, Gomis brings up precisely the issues of women's daily concerns that motivated their participation in the PAIGC struggle; and that Amílcar Cabral saw this as the basis for national regeneration (Urdang 1979: 106). Here we see how even a woman devalues its importance as a key issue in state-building.

Venezuela in 2011. According to some studies of international organizations, the '2009 assassination of military chief Batista Tagme Na' Wei and President Vieira was the result of a dispute over drug trafficking' and the military coups that disrupted the country in 2010 and 2012 came from drug-related issues (Parkinson 2013; Johansen 2008; Hoffman and Lane 2013). This pattern was confirmed by the capture of the former head of Guinea-Bissau's navy, José Américo Bubu NaTchuto, by the USA navy in April 2013 (for more detail see Reitano and Shaw 2013).

During my several fieldwork visits to Guinea-Bissau, I received a lot of help from these Bissau-Guinean women who migrated to Senegal looking for domestic work. Most of them went there because of political instability, economic turmoil, lack of payment to state workers, or botched agricultural campaigns in their home country. Unlike the men, they must constantly travel between Senegal and Guinea-Bissau, spending six to eight months in foreign domestic work and then returning with their meagre savings, getting ready to farm during the rainy season. They are contending with gender conditions that have dramatically worsened since the 1998 civil war. But just as the masculine narrative hid the importance of women's concrete concerns for family and community in building a new egalitarian, masculine discourse, it also hides the dramatic widening of gender inequality in the 'narco-state'.

Amílcar Cabral understood that the main challenges Africa would face lay not in colonialism but in traditional socio-cultural inequalities (Urdang 1979: 277 and 1981: 124–7; Forrest 1992: 127–8; Maloba 2008: 94–5). He also understood that in order to build an independent and socially egalitarian society, the state would need strong institutions that guarantee people rights and freedom. As NDo Mane said, 'Amílcar Cabral promised to build a country with equality and better life for all and we believed in him. Sadly, his followers destroyed the country by keeping or deepening the inequalities or reinforcing men's power. God will make them pay for what they did to Amílcar Cabral's country. I am sure that wherever he is, he is not happy at all' (NDo Mane interviews 2010). She at least holds on to a discourse that reminds us of the gendered roots of the current 'narco-state'.

7

THE GUINEAN DIASPORA AFTER 1998

José Lingna Nafafé

The changing shape of the diaspora since the civil war: transnationalism beyond the lusophone sphere

This chapter sets out to examine the changing shape of the Bissau-Guinean diaspora since the civil war of 1998–9. The civil war had a major impact in propelling people from Guinea-Bissau into migration, and the subsequent instability and gathering poverty (see Introduction by Green, this volume) have accelerated this trend. The chapter will therefore examine the concept of transnationalism in relation to Bissau-Guinean movement beyond its traditional lusophone sphere into other European member state countries, such as the UK and Spain. It will argue that the Bissau-Guinean diaspora has continued to play a major role in the political sphere of the country, and shows how any lasting political settlement there will have to take the needs and patterns of the diaspora into account. Moreover, if international actors wish to alter this pattern and reduce migration in the long term, the root causes of this inequality, instability, and underemployment at home will have to be addressed.

The context of migration from Guinea-Bissau has changed radically in the past two decades. In the immediate post-colonial phase, the traditional pattern of migration was of movement from father to mother countries, namely from the former colonies to their old colonial masters' countries. In the case of Britain, the migrant communities used to come from their former colonies: for instance, Pakistanis, Indians and Ghanaians could be found in much larger numbers in the UK than in Portugal. A similar pattern was found in mainland Europe, in Portugal, Spain and France, so many more Angolan migrants went to Portugal than France. In cases of African migration into the EU, to Britain, France, Germany, Spain, Portugal and Belgium, all retained links with their ex-colonial countries in Africa, while the former colonial powers continued to employ significant numbers of migrant workers in their national economies. These trajectories reflected the preferences of migrants who were familiar with the culture and identity that shaped them. However, this pattern has shifted in recent times. Migrants are choosing other destinations amongst the European countries, depending on the push factors in their countries of origin and the pull factors from the European economies. This new trend is driven not by similarity of culture, identity and history, but rather by labour and market forces within the EU.

Here, it is important to be aware of some deep-rooted historical patterns. Although, in the initial post-colonial phase, patterns of migration tended to be directed from African nations towards the former colonial powers, in fact the changing patterns of the Bissau-Guinean diaspora in the EU represent a very old configuration. Since the early contact that the region had with Portugal, Spain, Germany and England in the period of European expansion in the fifteenth century, the Bissau-Guinean diaspora has suffered some considerable transformation (Nafafé 2007; Pélissier 1989; Sangreman et al. 2012; Green 2012; Hawthorne 2010; Havik 2004). The first establishment of the Guinea-Bissau diaspora on European soil in fact occurred in the fifteenth century, when many Africans from the Senegambia region (to which Guinea-Bissau belonged) were taken to Europe and then to the Americas as slaves (Walter 2010; Green 2012; Wadstrom 1794; Rodney 1970). However, in the nineteenth century there began the flow of migrants from the northern part of country, in the region of Canchungo, Calequisse, Caio and the island of Pecixe, specifically from the Manjako ethnic group, who traditionally were boat rowers from earlier days of the Portuguese settlement in Cacheu and Bissau (Machado 1998, 2002, see Beaver). They were hired by the Europeans in the region carrying out similar jobs (Beaver 1805). Some of them were employed in these seafaring jobs which operated in Senegalese coastal areas, and from there they found their way to France (Diop, 1996: 47, Sangreman et al. 2012: 36). They were '*grumets*' from Guinea-Bissau who were trading and providing labour for Europeans in Bissau, Cacheu, etc. (Beaver 1805). There were also a small number of Mankanhe people from the northern part of Guinea-Bissau who migrated to France (Machado 2002; Hochet 1983; Galli and Jones 1987).

Later, during the colonial period, a small number of Bissau-Guineans migrated to Portugal for health and educational reasons. There were also a significant number of migrants who went to Portugal and remained there, among them professionals and those with Portuguese nationality whom Machado calls the 'luso-guineense' (Machado 1998: 11). Nevertheless, it was only a small number that remained there until the period of independence of Guinea-Bissau and the Portuguese 'Carnation Revolution' of 1974.

In the second half of the 1970s there began the second wave of Bissau-Guinean migration, soon after independence from Portugal. The composition of this diaspora began with soldiers who had fought alongside the Portuguese armed force, in the country, in particular the 'comando' (Machado 2002). The 'comando' were the specialized Portuguese armed forces, highly trained men who had fought against the national army of Guinea-Bissau. However, in the early 1970s they were mainly composed of Bissau-Guinean soldiers loyal to the Portuguese cause. When the war ended, they could not stay in Guinea-Bissau. They went to Portugal and were given protection and Portuguese nationality (Machado 2002). Their presence is important to understanding the pattern of Bissau-Guinean migration to Portugal; however, it falls outside the remit of this chapter. Nevertheless, they played their part in opening up a debate about Portuguese national identity, national space and what it means to be Portuguese: or, simply put, who is Portuguese?

In the 1980s, there was a student population of Bissau-Guineans in Portugal that constituted what Machado calls the 'qualified' migrants, different from those registers of the early days mentioned above (Machado 1991: 88–100). In this period there then followed labour force migrants who travelled to Portugal for work, in particular to the building industry, railways and hotels of the Algarve, termed the 'Algarve migrants'. They came to the tourist coast because their service was required for these specific jobs, and most of their recruitment came directly from Bissau-Guinean building contractors living in Portugal at the time. Indeed, migration from Guinea-Bissau to Portugal appeared to be encouraged in order to help building contractors to take on work.

Among these workers were qualified teachers from Guinea-Bissau, some of whom went to Cape Verde to teach and stayed there for a couple of years. This group was able to enter Portugal in the wake of the Algarve boom. Alongside this was another well-qualified strand of the labour force that came via Eastern Europe to Portugal. These were Bissau-Guinean students who had gone to study in the former USSR and East Germany; among them were engineers, medical doctors, agrarians, economists and historians, some of whom ended up working on the building sites in Lisbon and the Algarve. They were an invisible or unrecognized diaspora in terms of their potential for contributing to the Portuguese economy. Portugal did not openly recognize this well-qualified diaspora until the arrival of the East Europeans in Portugal in the latter part of the 1990s. Indeed, this diaspora continues to be largely invisible in Portugal, despite its expertise.

Given this historical survey of the Bissau-Guinean diaspora, we can now return to its progress after 1998, which is the core concern of this chapter. The war of 1998–9 which took place mainly in the capital, Bissau, saw many people exposed to heavy shelling between the two forces loyal to President Vieira and those that composed the bulk of the national army. The war lasted for nine months, and in the end Vieira fled the country and was exiled to Portugal (see also chapters by Kohl and Temudo and Abrantes this volume). The vast majority of the population fled the city of Bissau; some took refuge in other cities outside the capital. Gomes et al. state that 'by the end of 1999, 265,000 internally displaced persons (IDPs) had returned and out of 7,100 refugees who left the country, 5,300 had returned. Camps never became a prominent feature of the war in Bissau; displaced people moved in with relatives, friends, or strangers in the rural areas' (1999: 878). There were also other refugees who were brought by Portuguese warships to Portugal. Among them were both a highly qualified labour force and also unskilled workers who were shipped to Portugal. They came under the label of war refugees, and when the war was over the majority of them did not return to Guinea-Bissau. Most of them stayed and worked in Lisbon. They were later afforded Portuguese citizenship. Those migrants of the 1980s were able to request family reunion with their relatives who had been left in Guinea-Bissau. However, unlike in the immediate post-colonial era, most of these emigrants did not remain in Portugal: the majority are no longer living there, but have migrated to other European countries as citizens of Europe with Portuguese passports or dual nationalities, Bissau-Guinean and Portuguese.

The Bissau-Guinean diaspora's dispersal through Europe after the 1998–9 civil war can best be gauged by analysing migration statistics of the relevant EU nation states. The Borders, Immigration and Asylum reports published by SEF

(Serviço de Estrangeiros e Fronteiras, or Foreigners and Borders Service) show that in 2008 there were around 440,000 foreigners legally residing in Portugal: 'Ukraine is the country with the second highest number of foreign migrants in Portugal, reaching 52,494 residents, whilst Cape Verde has 51,352 residents. Afterwards there is Angola and Guinea-Bissau, with 27,619 and 24,391 residents' (SEF website). The High Commission for Immigration and Ethnic Minorities (ACIME: Alto Comissariado para a Imigração e Minorias Étnicas) states that in 2004 there were 25,148 Bissau-Guineans with residence and permanence status in Portugal, and they are the fifth biggest foreign community in Portugal; Brazilian representation is highest, followed by Ukraine, Cape Verde and Angola (SEF website).[1] By 2014 these statistics had changed, the numbers having decreased: Angolans, 20,000; Cape Verdeans 42,000 and Bissau-Guineans 20,336 (SEF, Relatório de Imigração, Fronteiras e Asilo).

The situation in other European countries differs. In the UK, there remains a small Bissau-Guinean population in the census; in general, the African population remains low. London, the south of England, Yorkshire and the north tend to have the greatest number of lusophone African migrants. In Spain, according to the Padrón Municipal of 2008, Madrid has 3,890 Luso-Africans: of which Angola represents 973 (563 men, 410 women); Cape Verde 1,258 (453 men, 805 women); Guinea-Bissau 1,659 (1,398 men, 261 women). In Spain as a whole, Guinea-Bissau represents 5,500 migrants, Cape Verde 2,500 and Angola just over 1,000 migrants to the country (see Figure 1). Thus, Guinea-Bissau sends the largest number of migrants to Spain of the three countries. Meanwhile, according to the Global Migrant Database (Sussex Centre for Migration Research), there are 8,125 Bissau-Guineans in France, and 5,701 in Germany (Sangreman et al. 2012).

These data demonstrate the scale of the Bissau-Guinean diaspora across the European Union, indicating the impact of Guinea-Bissau migrants on European space. They exercise their civic rights there, thus contributing to European decision-making (Hanson 1997). Their increasing spread across the EU is facilitated by their access to dual-nationality and Portuguese passports, and the freedom of movement enshrined within the EU. Meanwhile, their incentive to migrate has been increased by the instability in Guinea-Bissau since 1998, which is clearly apparent.

These figures are important and need to be contextualized. It should be borne in mind that Guinea-Bissau's population is significantly lower than that

---

[1] ACIME (Alto Comissariado para a Imigração e Minorias Étnicas) has now changed its name to ACM (Alto Comissariado para as Migrações).

of Angola (UN data[2] estimated that in 2011 Angola's population was 19,618,000, Cape Verde 501,000, and Guinea-Bissau 1,547,000), and so their presence in Portugal, Spain and the UK is significantly disproportionate to their size as a country. While the Bissau-Guineans were seen as a small diasporic community in Europe in the 1970s soon after independence (Machado 2002), this began to change. A large number of them settled in France, as stated above, especially those from the Manjako ethnic group (Abreu 2012). Now this diasporic community can be found outside its traditional country of destination, especially in France, Spain, Germany, Italy and the United Kingdom. The increase in the Bissau-Guinean diaspora is due to two factors: first, the civil war of 1998, and second, the economic crises in Western Europe. The push factors from Guinea-Bissau have certainly exacerbated the trend of migration, in comparison for instance to Angola, and thus questions of Bissau-Guinean equality, labour and political stability will have to be addressed before this process begins to change. Otherwise, with instability increasing in the Sahel and Sahara regions in general, following the recent events in Libya and Mali, migrants will continue to seek to take advantage of new routes opening up towards North Africa and the Mediterranean as a result of political changes and the rise of new people-trafficking routes that have followed them, to great public concern in the last year: it is not tighter border controls which will resolve this, but the equitable development of the country of origin.

This brings us to the question of whether, given their wide dispersal, we can really talk about Bissau-Guineans as a diasporic community. Without going into greater detail concerning the term 'diaspora', Bissau-Guineans certainly can be thought of as a diasporic community. The use of the term appeared first in the Bible, referring to the Jewish community exiled in Babylon who were similarly yearning for return to their homeland. The term was used in the 'Septuagint' (Deuteronomy 28:25), the Jewish Bible that was translated into the Greek language for the Greek-speaking community outside Israel. 'Diaspora', from the Greek διασπείρω, carries the meaning of spreading out and scattering. It referred to scattering the children of Israel throughout the face of the earth. Safran defines 'diaspora' as a 'memory, vision, or myth about [the] original homeland' (1991: 83–99). For Bissau-Guineans, memory is about their place of origin, their region—be it Catio, Nhakra—and this is often defined by comparison with their new location, such as Lisbon or France. It is

---

[2] Figures taken from http://data.un.org/

an attempt to link their diasporic experience with memories of their birth-place. This link with homeland is associated with their ancestors. They retain the desire to assist the place to which they belong, but this does not necessary lead to a desire for return; thus the spiritual connection of Bissau-Guineans to their homeland is a key aspect of honouring the links between diaspora and homeland (see also the chapter by Sarró and de Barros, this volume).

When using the term 'diaspora' to refer to Bissau-Guineans, therefore, one is using it to refer to those people displaced for reasons of war, employment, marriage, education, political persecution, religious motives, citizenship and retirement, who find themselves living away from their national jurisdiction but still maintaining strong ties with it (Clifford 1994: 306). This includes those Bissau-Guinean soldiers who fought alongside the Portuguese army in Guinea-Bissau or worked loyally as civil servants in Guinea-Bissau but are now living in Portugal. They are what Anderson terms 'long-distance nationalists' (1992: 12–14). They continue to engage with their country of origin. This is evident too in the setting up of internet communities with the aim of debating issues relating to Guinea-Bissau, such as *Didinho*, *Doka Internacional* and *Intelectuais Balantas na Diáspora*. We will return to these later in the chapter. However, the term diaspora still causes debate in different quarters. Weinar has recently questioned the narrow use of the term, and has argued that it does not necessarily imply a yearning for return, but could suggest a movement of people 'no longer referring to the specific context of their existence' (Weinar 2010: 75).

As part of this complex process of identity formation, the Bissau-Guinean diaspora continues to be involved in activities linking them with their original country, through remittances, political activities and the transference of skills: they are agents of transnationalism (Cohen 1995: 5–10; Bamyeh 1993: 81–95). Defining transnationalism is, however, an impossible task, as there is no obvious consensus about how it might be constituted. Despite the varying perceptions, 'transnationalism' could broadly refer to varieties of social, cul-tural and economic ties, exchange and interactions that connect the diasporic community to their nation or home (Cohen 1996: 507–10). Bissau-Guineans in Europe maintain these activities through family ties, friends and colleagues, by sending money and organizing activities that have direct effects in Guinea-Bissau, such as their involvement in elections, staging debates and demonstra-tions against the government of Guinea-Bissau in many cities of Europe, such as in Lisbon and Paris (Hannerz 1996; Kriesberg 1997: 3–10).

Thus, the Bissau-Guinean diaspora is certainly set to stay in Europe for the time being, and it has a significant effect on its country of origin through its ongoing engagements with it. Ties of birth and memory make for affective connections, as do the financial impact of remittances, and their political involvement. Hence, any long-term peace solution is likely to involve consultation with this community.

The impact of the diaspora on Guinea-Bissau: the brain drain, lack of tertiary-educated professionals, impact on the civil infrastructure, and remittances

From 1980 to 1998 many of the Bissau-Guinean students who gained their degrees abroad, in countries such as the former USSR, were expected to return home. These universities sent many people with graduate diplomas back to their country of origin. It was a coordinated strategy by the Bissau-Guinean government at the time to curb the 'brain drain'. But this did not deter the qualified labour force of Guinea-Bissau from leaving the country. This process then accelerated quickly in the period of civil war in Guinea-Bissau (1998–9).

Even before the civil war, however, few graduates from countries such as Portugal, France, the USA and Italy returned to Guinea-Bissau by comparison with those from Cuba and the USSR. Soon after independence, formal education was the key objective of the national party, the PAIGC. Many students were sent to Cuba and Soviet countries to study, and few were sent to Western countries. Those who were educated in the West were relatives of those in power in the country, such as ministers and directors, etc. There was no university in Guinea-Bissau directly after independence; Portugal had not established university education in Guinea-Bissau as it had in Angola and Mozambique. Most of the graduates in Guinea-Bissau now came through the educational system introduced by the PAIGC. They also introduced adult literacy classes in all regions of the country, in order to improve literacy rates. Those who finished high school at the time, before leaving for their tertiary education abroad, needed to give a contribution to the country. The programme was for three years, during which students had to teach in secondary school or *lycée*, depending on their grades. If they failed to participate in this programme, students were faced with a long wait to get a scholarship to study abroad for their first degree.

To curb the problem of the brain drain from the country, the first cohort of graduates from the USSR, Cuba and East Germany were not given their diplomas in those universities from which they had graduated, but were sent back home to Guinea-Bissau to await them. This programme lasted until 1990; but after the fall of the Berlin Wall and the collapse of communism in the Eastern Bloc, from 1992 many if not all graduates were allowed to receive their certificates from their universities. This process has continued, and according to my recent conversation in Lisbon with the state secretary for education in Guinea-Bissau, the education system is still following some of these same rules. Nevertheless, these measures could not stop the country from experiencing a brain drain. The civil war of 1998 saw an exodus of highly qualified labour leaving the country, seeking destinations in many EU countries, particularly Portugal, where many educated Bissau-Guineans end up doing manual labour, especially in construction (Cardoso 2002).

The situation has been exacerbated by there being fewer scholarships available in the former USSR than there used to be, and this has made the situation in Guinea-Bissau worse. There are now many students from Guinea-Bissau studying for degrees at universities in countries such as Morocco, Algeria, Nigeria, Russia, Macau, China, Senegal and Brazil. But this number is still smaller than those who went to Soviet countries in the 1970s and 1980s. Thus there is a serious shortfall in capacity-building in comparison to former times. Moreover, Guinea-Bissau is also faced by the challenges posed when these students do not return home.

These issues become especially clear when examining the case of remittances. Bissau-Guinean transnational communities have shown themselves very active in the transfer of capital—sending monetary 'remittances'—and also in the transfer of ideas, or 'social remittances'. There are no statistics from Western Union or Money Gram in Guinea-Bissau to reveal the amount of money being sent home each year, unlike in Cape Verde, where the government releases these figures every six months or yearly. Attempts have been made to get such figures for Guinea-Bissau, but there appears to be uneasiness in Bissau about releasing them. Western Union and Money Gram are not the only systems used for transfer of capital to Guinea-Bissau. Other people prefer to send money back home through friends and relatives, and this will not of course be noted in the statistics (Abreu 2012).

From the 1980s to the mid 1990s, Bissau-Guinean migrants living in Portugal kept strong ties with their relatives back home, with the idea of investing back in Guinea-Bissau. There were some migrants prepared to live in shanty towns (*barracas* in Bissau-Guinean Kriol) in suburbs of Lisbon such as Burraca, Damia, São Filomena, (Amadora) Marianos [Carcavelo], Fim do Mundo [Estoril], Prior Velho e Quinta de Mucho, Quinta da Bolonha [Póvoa de Santa Iria], Forte da Casa, Arsena [Alverca], Bairro Jamaica [Cruz de Pao]. Others meanwhile lodged in small rooms and shared accommodation in order to save money to send home. Others were prepared to live separate lives from their wives and children for years in an attempt to invest in land purchase and house-building in Guinea-Bissau. Few were prepared or able to invest in properties in Portugal. From 1998 the war changed people's perspective on remittances and investing in Portugal. People are now prepared to bring their family to Portugal, and many Bissau-Guineans have taken out mortgages in Portugal. It has become an 'inward diaspora'. This is not to say that these people are not also contributing back home; however, the focus has become family reunion in the diaspora.

Some concrete examples demonstrate how the nature of the Bissau-Guinean diaspora has changed over time in terms of its contacts with the country of origin. In the 1980s, the Bissau-Guinean diaspora in France made some concrete proposals to the government of Guinea-Bissau about their investment in towns such as Canchungo. The majority of these migrants were Manjako people, but their plan was rebuffed by the PAIGC government of the time, who accused the Manjakos of tribalism and regionalism. They were even dissuaded from putting their investment in the capital Bissau. As a result, many of the Manjako migrants moved their capital investment to Dakar, Senegal (Abreu 2012).

Relations between the diaspora and the homeland

Abreu's PhD thesis (2012) traced the development of migration in two villages: Caiomete and Braima Sori, exploring how migration could act as an exogeneous force for development in contemporary Guinea-Bissau. He addressed the relations between diaspora and homeland, looking in particular at Portugal and how these migrants are having a positive impact on the development of the country. Although seminal in its inception, the research has not spawned an extensive study of the Bissau-Guinean diaspora in Europe. However, recent research on the 'Potential Evaluation of Development of the Guinea-Bissau Diaspora in Portugal and France' has brought attempts to address this broader question (Sangreman et al. 2012).[3] Abreu also argued in his thesis that migration has the potential both to foster and to hinder development in contemporary Guinea-Bissau. R. B. Có et al., in their working paper, appear to have taken a similar view and suggest that contrary to what has happened in some African countries, the creation of different diaspora

---

[3] The current section of this chapter is indebted to this work.

associations in Portugal has failed to make a direct impact on the development of Guinea-Bissau. They state that 'a qualified Bissau-Guinean diaspora [labour force] due to the enactment and negative reproduction of social and symbolic capital have shown some inability to organize themselves and to make their country of origin benefit from their know-how and migratory opportunities' (Có 2009: 7).

Nevertheless, the Bissau-Guinean diaspora has maintained strong ties with its country of origin. However, recent political crises in the country have strained this relationship. Some quarters of the diaspora in Europe appear to harbour the feeling that Guinea-Bissau has not made an effort to encourage policies that facilitate transfer of knowledge and capital to the country. The policy of dual nationalities that Guinea-Bissau has adopted has failed to live up to expectations. Visas are still required for those who have dual citizenship. There appears to be no effective policy encouraging direct investment in the country. Customs laws penalize diaspora communities, and actually deter them from making contributions to the country of origin. These are some of the issues that definitely hamper the relationship. From Guinea-Bissau's point of view, there is also uneasiness about the diaspora being seen as a threat to the country through its disproportionate financial weight. Moreover, the fragility of the political system makes it difficult for the diaspora to trust the country's intentions, another homeland damaging the relationship, to the long-term detriment of both homeland and diaspora. This is reflected in recent research carried out by Sangreman et al.

Nevertheless, there are some important changes taking place. Politically, a more formalized relationship between the diaspora and Guinea-Bissau is being sought on the ground. There are now two Deputies or MPs for the Diaspora who were appointed in the recent elections, one for Europe and one for Africa. Most of the diaspora who took part in the decision-making via the electoral process came from Portugal, France and Spain. These are the three countries in Europe that have the largest number of Bissau-Guinean migrants. The UK still represents too small a number to warrant votes.

The Bissau-Guinean community in the diaspora is also making strong connections with the country via social media, as will be discussed below. Diasporic social networking has made a substantial contribution to building relationships between migrant communities and Guinea-Bissau. They bring news about the home country, fostering debate about politics, legal systems and issues of general reform back home. The issues most often discussed between diaspora and the country include: reconciliation, reform of all sectors, and deconstruction of the foundational myths about inter-ethnic conflicts in the country, or at least calling them into question (see chapters by Green and Kohl, this volume). We shall now return to the question of diaspora and internet space and its influence on Guinea-Bissau politics.

Bissau-Guinean diasporic engagement with political space in Guinea-Bissau via the internet is a recent phenomon. This came about in the last ten years with the increased distribution of social media in the country and the creation of internet blogs in Guinea-Bissau such as *Ditadura do Consenso* (http://ditaduradoconsenso.blogspot.co.uk/) and *Progresso Nacional* (http://progressonacional.blogspot.co.uk/). In the diaspora there are *Didinho* (http://www.didinho.org/), *Doka Internacional* (http://dokainternacional-denunciante.blogspot.co.uk/) and *Intelectuais Balantas na Diáspora* (http://tchogue.blogspot.co.uk/), listed here in their chronological order of emergence. The writing in these diasporic cyberspaces is revising the normative ways in which politics is played out in Guinea-Bissau and provoking a rethink of democracy in the country. The postings aim to challenge issues in modern Guinea-Bissau such as the internal mismanagement of resources, employment, education, governance and judicial systems. These have been reflected in the articles published on all the blogs. They are attempts to represent disillusioned voices from the diaspora in terms of influencing the national project of development. These blogs question the politics of development, participation, corruption, the transformative role of the state, and narratives of the nation (see *Intelectuais Balantas na Diáspora*, 11 May 2013, the revelation of two former prime ministers' mismanagement of state funds; and see also *Doka Internacional*). These blogs also constitute sites for information for the Bissau-Guinean diaspora during the elections and concerning everyday news in the country. In the presidential elections of 2014, they announced the winner prior to the National Election Commission making it public (see *Intelectuais Balantas na Diáspora*, *Doka Internacional* and *Ditadura do Consenso*). Their intention is to make public the world of politics in Guinea-Bissau to the wider diasporic community, in terms of circulation of information, ideas and simultaneous debate (on the use of internet and political communication, see Dalhgren 2005; Habermas 1989).

The operation of these blogs from the diaspora constitutes a media outlet unregulated by state control in terms of ownership, regulation, financing and any legal framework that might censor freedom of communication. The government has shown itself increasingly concerned about the impact of these blogs, as was recently demonstrated by the arrest of the founder of *Doka Internacional* on his arrival on Guinea-Bissau soil. He was imprisoned for two weeks and had his passport confiscated by the authorities without charge, accusing him of defamation (see *Doka Internacional*, http://dokainternacionaldenunciante.blogspot.co.uk/2015/09/carmelita-pires-e-sua-dg-da-pj-tentam.html, last accessed 3 February 2016).

Diaspora blogs have been designed with the aim of engaging Bissau-Guinean migrants in discussing issues concerning the country. They are also sites of contestation between those blogs created at home and those from the diaspora (Keane 2003). Those from the diaspora appear to be critical of government policy, while those from the country appear to be pro government; for instance, *Progresso nacional* suggests that it has been created by political authorities as a counter-blog to that of the diaspora (for that debate see *Doka Internacional*). Thus social media foster debate on and contestation of the relationship between the diaspora and the homeland, and different strands of power and discourse are shaped.

Increasingly the diaspora blogs claim that they are defending the people and victims of political violence in the country since independence (*Doka Internacional*). This violence has included the death penalty being given to former soldiers who served alongside the Portuguese armed forces, the '*comando*', who by the mid-1960s and early 1970s were predominantly Bissau-Guinean solders fighting against the PAIGC. Some of these victims were political descendants of the main national party, the PAIGC, who challenged the centrality of the party. *Doka Internacional* has recently changed its name to *Doka Internacional Denúnciante* (or whistleblower) in an attempt to challenge the authors of violence in the country, who are still at large because of an 'immunity law' passed by the People's National Assembly, the legislative body in the country (equivalent to the House of Commons in Westminster). Meanwhile, the philosophical blog *Intelectuais Balanta na Diáspora* aims to demythologize some of the opinions held about different ethnic groups and their composition in the country (http://tchogue.blogspot.co.uk/2013/04/resposta-critica-de-dr-carmelita-pires.html, accessed 3 February 2016). The presence in the site name of the adjective 'Balanta' has little to do with its ethnic configuration, but rather is an invitation from the site to engage in the debate about the alleged inter-ethnic conflict and the problem of social division in the country, which politicians from all sides have attempted to play on to woo voters (https://www.facebook.com/Grupo-de-Intelectuais-de-Binhan-Brassa-Na-Di%C3%A1spora-387493841306425/timeline/, accessed 3 February 2016). Both these sites are investigative in nature, but it is *Doka Internacional* that brings the ghost of the past back to the foreground in its attempt to give a voice to those who lost their loved ones through violence, including *Doka Internacional* himself. Both blogs are claiming a return to the basic politics that are inclusive through the nation, regardless of ethnic compositions.

The ways in which the Bissau-Guinean diaspora is using these blogs to influence politics in the country are having an effect. S. Wayland's work has pointed out the importance of the diaspora in shaping national politics. She states that 'the diasporas can play a major role because the resources they provide can upset the existing balance of economic, political and military power in the homeland' (2004: 426). These blogs have been unsettling political actors in some quarters in Guinea-Bissau. Take for example *Doka International*, whose founder has claimed to have received death threats in Guinea-Bissau and has claimed that pictures of mutilated bodies have been sent to his daughter in England via Facebook. It is interesting to see how the blogs and Facebook posts have been used by both sites to inhabit the Bissau-Guinean space, which otherwise would have been impossible to occupy with a physical presence (http://dokainternacionaldenunciante.blogspot.co.uk/2015/10/imagens-que-enviaram-no-facebook-da.html, accessed 3 February 2016).

This could lend support to the view taken in this chapter that the Bissau-Guinean diaspora could be an important agent in shaping the future destiny of the country. The diasporians are mobilizing themselves through various blogs created in Europe and the USA. We have seen a proliferation of these sites, in which news and information are shared rapidly around the world; to name a few: Guinea-Bissau Community Association in USA, https://www.facebook.com/pages/Guinea-Bissau-Community-Association-in-USA/142403942497872?sk=wall; G.Bissau.com http://www.gbissau.com/; Conosaba, http://conosaba.blogspot.co.uk/; and Corrupção na Guiné-Bissau http://www.portugues.rfi.fr/africa/20150106-justica-na-guine-bissau-sofre-da-corrupcao-e-impunidade, etc.

In spite of this proliferation, however, there may be some who would question the significance of these blogs in the politics of the country, since many of the posts remain anonymous. However, this need not mean that their engagement is less effective. Letters sent to the president of the republic about his recent policy on military ethnic quarters in the presidential palace have received widespread condemnation from the diaspora, but these were anonymous letters or signed with pseudonyms (http://tchogue.blogspot.co.uk/2014/08/conselho-sobre-intencao-da-sua-ex-sr.html) with the exception of *Doka Internacional* (http://dokainternacionaldenunciante.blogspot.co.

uk/2015/06/opiniao-dr.html#comment-form). Anonymity is used as a stratregy to question state policies without being implicated, and can raise issues which the government has to respond to without prejudicing the safety of any of the contributors.

A vital additional point is that the use of blogs and social media also contributes to and reinforces the diaspora network in Europe and in the Americas via Guinea-Bissau's different regional constituencies, such as Bafatá, Oio, Nhakra, Bissau, Catio, Canchungo, Bulama, etc. There are diasporic associations that reflect these varied experiences of diasporic actors vis-à-vis their own histories, the struggles in their host regions, their level of engagement with politics in Guinea-Bissau, their networks and activities on the internet, and their future aspirations. Many are organized to supply goods to the regions or cities from which they originate in Guinea-Bissau. There are also collective efforts to arrange funeral ceremonies, so that bodies of citizens who died in Europe can be sent back to Guinea-Bissau to be buried there. All these examples are key to maintaining the diaspora network and reinforcing diasporic ties to Guinea-Bissau. Communications around the diaspora are also maintained via Facebook, enabling members of the same region to communicate across countries in Europe. There are internet radio set-ups to provide information, chats about Guinea-Bissau or occasional discussion on national issues, such as GumbeRadio and GFM Radio.

What is the future of the Bissau-Guinean diaspora?

As this chapter has shown, the future of Guinea-Bissau cannot be addressed without considering the role of the diaspora. Prospects may in large part be said to rely upon addressing the vacuum created by political instability, with a fairly comprehensive overview of the various national Bissau-Guinean diasporic communities. These diaspora organizations must impact positively on the rechannelling of human resources to end internal conflict.

It is not possible for long-term peace, stability and reconciliation to occur without Bissau-Guinean transnational actors engaging with issues that are affecting the country. Transnational communities could provide solutions to preventing ethno-political tensions being incited in the country. The diaspora can also play a major role in providing resources that could rebalance the existing economic, political and military insecurity in the country. The diaspora must lend support to the country, and it need not think of itself as representing dislocated victims and as politically voiceless, but rather as agents who can provide resources to support progress. The future diaspora must provide solutions on the ground to problems of expertise, research and development, and viable politics.

From the perspective of the country itself, the Bissau-Guinean leaders too must work in tandem with present and future diasporas to ease the tensions and mistrust that currently exist. The future diaspora must therefore resist the temptation of getting caught up in inter-ethnic politics. It must draw on the new technologies now available to mobilize all Bissau-Guinean diasporic constituencies to engage in activities and issues in the home country. It must draw on conciliatory and positive elements for the country. The Bissau-Guinean diaspora needs to create a forum for managing knowledge towards projects designed to help Guinea-Bissau promote development and build peace. It must actively lobby host-country governments, be they African, Asian, American or European, to devise policies that support initiatives by diasporic members wishing to create knowledge networks across ethnic boundaries for the development of Guinea-Bissau.

PART THREE

POLITICAL CONSEQUENCES OF THE CRISIS

8

ETHNICITY AND THE POLITICAL SYSTEM POST-1998

Christoph Kohl

Introduction

The end of the civil war of 1998–9—widely known as the 'Military Conflict'—did not mean a turn for the better for Guinea-Bissau. Quite the contrary: since then the country has experienced increased political instability. This development has found expression in frequently alternating governments, a growing number of military coups, interference of armed forces in politics, and the mutual manipulation of some politicians and army officials. Continuous socio-economic problems, low education and training levels, an ailing public infrastructure, widespread corruption and the involvement of political and military personalities in illicit practices such as, most prominently, narco-trafficking have reinforced the negative image of Guinea-Bissau. Simultaneously, ethnic discourses have intensified, tying in with developments since the late 1970s, and demands to legally (re-)recognize chieftaincies have ultimately strengthened. At the same time, politicians and army officials have repeatedly attempted to manipulate ethnicity for political ends. Given all these difficulties, outside observers have therefore often regarded Guinea-Bissau as a 'fragile', 'weak' or 'failed' state (see Bethke 2012; Huria 2012). Meanwhile, political conflicts are often seen through an ethnic lens, as a few ethno-political entrepreneurs have indeed tried to exploit ethnicity for their power aspirations. In this regard, it was the notably power-hungry former president, the late Kumba Yalá, who turned out to be the most notorious trouble-maker after the end of the Military Conflict, relying on allies and kin from within the military.

Recent developments have reaffirmed the trend towards political instability. The assumption of a new, democratically legitimated executive in mid-2014 ended more than two years of unconstitutional transitional government rule after the coup of 2012; it gave rise to hope, both domestically and internationally, that Guinea-Bissau might sail into calmer waters. However, in mid-2015 political crisis returned to Guinea-Bissau, due to political actors' and their networks' personal animosities and competing self-serving interests and ambitions. This was all the more surprising given that there had been a good deal of optimism both inside and outside Guinea-Bissau that the 2014 elections would prove to be a turning point.

Certainly, the peaceful, free and orderly elections of 2014 were very promising. The general elections that took place on 13 April 2014 showed once again that the PRS (Partido da Renovação Social) was not able to mobilize sufficient voter support, even under favourable conditions, to win elections: general chief of staff António Indjai and former PRS chairman Kumba Yalá had tried to push 'their' independent candidate Nuno NaBian, and rumours said that attempts were made to influence the voter census in favour of the PRS's and NaBian's anticipated Balanta electorate. Nevertheless, these strategies backfired. NaBian's candidacy—supported by former PRS leader Yalá who had unexpectedly died shortly before the elections on 4 April—was to the detriment of the official PRS candidate, Abel Incada, who came in fourth, indicating the divisions within the PRS, and paving the way for defeat.

Instead, the PAIGC presidential candidate, former finance minister José Mario Vaz ('Jomav'), won the first round of the elections (41%). The second round of the presidential elections took place on 18 May and was won by Vaz (62%) against runner-up NaBian (38%). The PAIGC (Partido Africano da Independência da Guiné e Cabo Verde) under the leadership of Domingos Simões Pereira ('DSP') won the parliamentary elections with a clear majority, achieving fifty-seven seats, the PRS fory-one, and three minor parties together four seats. The PRS did not only perform well in regions populated in their majority by Balanta (particularly in Oio), but also achieved good results in the eastern regions of Gabú and Bafatá as well as in Bolama–Bijagós with respective Fula–Mandinga and Bijagó majorities. By contrast, the PAIGC scored very well in Bissau and in neighbouring Biombo, thus underlining its urban character (Instituto Nacional de Estatística 2009; election results released by the Comissão Nacional de Eleições). Nevertheless, a closer look at the data reveals a different picture. The PAIGC's victory was not as clear-cut as it seems, as it smoothes over growing differences within the party. About fifteen of its parliamentarians belong to a faction dissatisfied with the fact that the eastern, Muslim-dominated regions were not considered when selecting the PAIGC chairman and presidential candidate (both Vaz and party leader Pereira are nominally Christian and originate from the country's western part).

Nevertheless, the results were clear and led to the formation of a government composed of all parties of parliamentary representation, brokered by the international community to prevent political discord over decisive issues, such as the reform of the security sector. The strong popular support for coup-rejecting parties strengthened the position of those political forces in favour of an end to military interference in politics and administration. The government led by Domingos Simões Pereira took office on 4 July 2014, while state-president José Mario Vaz had been already sworn in on 23 June. Guinea-Bissau's relationship to the international community soon started to normalize, and sanctions imposed after the coup were lifted. A resumption of international cooperation followed, including new attempts to reform the country's security sector. The new government enjoyed much popular support, and Bissau-Guineans were in an optimistic mood, evoked by many improvements that the new government managed to achieve with strong international financial support, such as the regular payment of state employees' salaries and many salaries in arrears, the rehabilitation of the public infrastructure (roads, electricity and water supply) and a reduction in corruption. An important step towards the subordination of the military under civilian control was the dismissal of general chief of staff António Indjai by state-president Vaz on 15 September 2014. He was replaced by Biague NaNtam who used to be head of the presidential guard and is regarded as an ally of Vaz.

Yet, in the course of time, pre-existing differences between President Vaz and Prime Minister Pereira began to worsen, culminating in Pereira's and his government's dismissal on 12 August 2015. President Vaz was much criticized for provoking a government crisis despite the fact that the government had enjoyed parliamentary support. Vaz subsequently installed a government by 'presidential initiative' without the consent of the majoritarian PAIGC. Vaz nominated former minister Baciro Djá as prime minister on 20 August 2015. This step led to a constitutional and government crisis, and Djá's appointment was ultimately declared unconstitutional by the High Court, leaving the president's image damaged. The political and PAIGC veteran Carlos Correia was nominated by its party as a compromise prime minister candidate on 17 September, but he had not succeeded in forming an all-party coalition by early October 2015. However, the new government was not only confronted by the now oppositional PRS but also by aggravating internal divisions. Simultaneously, state-president and PAIGC member Vaz added fuel to the fire when he refused Correia's candidates for the interior and natural resources portfolios. He also made common cause with the PRS, supplying its party members with the posts of attorney-general and the head of the court of audit in November. A motion of no confidence in the new government held on 23 December 2015 was not only supported by the PRS but also by fifteen PAIGC parliamentarians of largely Muslim, Eastern Bissau-Guinean origin. They were headed by the businessman and Pereira adversary Braima Camará, whose followers had been largely sidelined, and thus excluded from access to resources and positions, by the Pereira and Correia administrations. They were expelled from the PAIGC in January 2016, as had been Baciro Djá in November 2015.

Another motion of no confidence was then scheduled to take place in mid-January 2016. However, the fifteen dissenters refused to accept a decision by the speaker of parliament, Cipriano Cassamá (PAIGC) to revoke their parliamentary mandates, replacing them by loyal PAIGC parliamentarians. The dissenters refused to leave the parliament and aligned with the PRS. Although some lawyers declared Cassamá's decision constitutional, others did not, supporting the fifteen's claim and pointing to constitutional and legal ambiguities. Thus, in spite of the apparent turn for the better that appeared to have been heralded by the 2014 elections, as this book goes to press a return to the pattern of recurring political instability and crisis that characterized the entire period from 1998 to 2014 seems possible.

This chapter aims at reviewing Guinea-Bissau's political landscape and intends to examine the role of ethnicity in the political system since the Military Conflict. Indeed, there is evidence that the past fifteen years have seen an increase in the ethnicization of Guinea-Bissau's politics. However, I argue that the ethnic discourse remains largely relegated to the political sphere, partly buttressed by international organizations and external observers, whereas in the informal sphere other ties (familial, professional, ancestral, neighbourly, etc.) remain more important. In fact, the majority of the population continue to reject the politically motivated exploitation of ethnic ties in a country marked by high degrees of cultural and ethnic diversity.

The chapter starts by taking a brief look at Guinea-Bissau's politics and the role of ethnicity after independence. The following section will analyse the Military Conflict of 1998–9 and subsequent developments up to 2004, this period of time being characterized by the dominance of President Kumbá Yalá and his party, the PRS. The fourth section sheds light on the period until 2009, which brought the PAIGC back to power and was marked by political antagonism between the re-elected President Vieira and Prime Minister Carlos Gomes Júnior. The fifth section is dedicated to developments in the run-up to the military coup of April 2012. The subsequent section analyses the aftermath of the seizure of power by the military and the instalment of the so-called transitional government, in power until mid-2014. The final section will encompass a review and outlook of politics and ethnicity and a brief assessment of popular perceptions of governance and ethnic relations.[1]

A brief glance at the past

For a better understanding of the connectedness between politics and ethnicity since 1998, we need to take a brief look back. When Guinea-Bissau gained independence in 1973–4, the victorious independence movement PAIGC installed an authoritarian one-party system, aligned, *inter alia*, with many socialist-communist countries (cf. Fistein 2011: 445). The party- and state-leadership was composed of Bissau-Guineans of diverse ethnic origins. Creoles of Kriston (literally 'Christian') origin and Cape Verdeans were over-represented in the leadership. Some of the latter (like the co-founder of the PAIGC, Amílcar Cabral, and his half-brother, subsequent Bissau-Guinean president Luís Cabral) were born in Guinea-Bissau or had labour-migrated to the continent (like the subsequent Cape Verdean state-president Aristides Pereira, for instance). This disproportionality and the desired unity of Guinea-Bissau and Cape Verde, skillfully exploited by Portuguese propaganda, had already caused differences during the independence war (Keese 2007; see also Green's chapter, this volume). When, in the late 1970s, Guinea-Bissau faced a

---

[1] Findings are based on existing literature as well as on ethnographic fieldwork conducted in 2006–7, 2013 and 2014.

serious economic crisis, growing authoritarianism and a controversial constitutional reform—that Cape Verdeans should be allowed to hold political posts in Guinea-Bissau whilst Bissau-Guineans were not permitted to hold offices in the archipelago—this then paved the way for the country's first successful coup in November 1980. The Guinea-Bissau-born Cape Verdean Luís Cabral was replaced by Nino Vieira, himself of Creole (Kriston de Geba and Pepel) background, and a respected war commander. Some observers interpreted this as an ethnic conflict between Cape Verdeans and Bissau-Guineans. Yet there was little evidence to support claims of ethnic conflict, the coup being motivated rather by economic and political imbalances (Chabal 1983: 202; cf. McCulloch 1983: 33–4; Duarte Silva 2011: 192–3). The Cape Verdean issue then resurfaced before the first multi-party elections in 1994, when Vieira was confronted with allegations that his true father had in fact been a Cape Verdean and not a Pepel, as claimed by him. If these claims had been recognized, Vieira might not have run for the presidency, as there were discussions of refusing eligibility to non-'pure' Bissau-Guineans (Schiefer 2002: 160).

Thus, since independence, the question of Cape Verdean ethnicity has often arisen in the political context, but its importance remains contested. Cape Verdeans have often been equated with phenotypical ascriptions like *burmedju wak* ('very red' in Kriol, Guinea-Bissau's lingua franca), in contrast to *pretu nok* ('very black') often associated with 'indigenous' Bissau-Guineans. However, social reality proves much more complicated, as supposedly 'indigenous' Bissau-Guineans may also be of lighter skin colour (as in the case of the Fulas, for instance), whereas there are also many dark-skinned Cape Verdeans. Moreover, many Cape Verdean families have resided in the country for generations and therefore can hardly be regarded as immigrants. Much more important than this purported ethnic division in the political context has in fact been the difference between urbanites on the one hand (among them many Cape Verdeans and Creoles), with access to education, political and civil society, economic elite networks and Western lifestyles, and on the other hand largely excluded rural residents.

Much more far-reaching for the question of ethnicity in the politics of Guinea-Bissau has been the emergence of the Balanta question since the 1980s. During the 1960s and early 1970s, disproportionally high numbers of young men of the Balanta ethnic group, one of the largest in Guinea-Bissau, had joined the PAIGC's anti-colonial struggle. This prevalence was due to the war's initial impact on many remote, poor areas populated by Balanta; the

Balantas' decentralized political structures; and their extensive suffering under colonialism (cf. Chabal 1983: 74–6; Handem 2008: 153–4; Temudo 2008). After independence, many of these individuals remained in the armed forces or changed to other sectors of the state bureaucracy, notably the police and related security forces, although they were often among the least able and skilled. Soon, many of these former fighters felt deprived of their peace dividend, given the fact that their rural home areas remained underdeveloped, depriving their families of any advancement (cf. Temudo 2008).

Tensions simmered, and in 1985 the high-ranking politician and military Paulo Correia, a Balanta, was arrested. He was accused of spearheading a growing Balanta 'tribalism'. Correia and his alleged co-conspirators—of whom eleven were Balanta—were charged with planning to overthrow President Vieira. Many of them were subsequently sentenced to death and executed (Rudebeck 1990a: 46; Forrest 1992: 60; Delfim da Silva 2003: 147–63; Temudo 2008: 248). Some external observers who followed the official version interpreted the case as a presidential manoeuvre to deprive the Balanta of power and influence (Forrest 1987: 111–12; 1992: 59–60; Schiefer 2002: 171). Both party and army were reportedly 'cleansed' of Balanta, thus contributing to their marginalization (Zamora Induta 2001: 27–32; Temudo 2008: 246, 248). Evidence suggests, however, that the affair was more a personal conflict between two warlords and their respective factions than an act of defence against an ethnically motivated coup attempt (Temudo 2008: 259; Delfim da Silva 2003: 162).

Following the Correia affair, economic and political liberalization took place from the mid-1980s on. This led to the introduction of a multi-party system and the country's first free general elections in 1994, won by the PAIGC and acting president Vieira. This economic and political context is therefore vital to understanding how the 'ethnicization' of politics and the rise of the 'Balanta question' have emerged over the past three decades.

The Military Conflict and its aftermath

The Military Conflict broke out on 7 June 1998, ravaging predominantly the area of greater Bissau (hence the local alternative name 'War of Bissau'). On this day, Ansumane Mané launched a *coup d'état* against the democratically elected government headed by president Vieira. Mané had been an ally of Vieira, serving as general chief of staff until he was dismissed by Vieira earlier that year. Mané's dismissal resulted from the fact that both he and Vieira had accused each other of supplying the rebels in the Casamance with weapons. On the basis of existing treaties, Vieira called for military assistance from the governments of Senegal and Guinea-Conakry. The Senegalese and Conakry–Guinean army troops that subsequently entered Guinea-Bissau were regarded as invaders by most of the population. This and the fact that many held Vieira responsible for bad governance and corruption led most people to side with Mané, who was backed by a junta that encompassed most regular soldiers. Eleven months of violent conflict followed, interrupted by ceasefires until peace was officially restored on 11 May 1999. Nevertheless, Guinea-Bissau's interior was indirectly affected by the armed conflict, notably due to the heavy influx of displaced persons who fled greater Bissau and the general breakdown of public administration and infrastructure (van der Drift 2000; Ostheimer 2001; Rudebeck 2001b; Rodrigues Zeverino 2005; Vigh 2006).

Peace talks brokered by ECOWAS (Economic Community of West African States) had resulted on 1 November 1998 in the Abuja Accord, providing, *inter alia*, for a ceasefire, the appointment of a government of national unity, the withdrawal of Senegalese and Conakry–Guinean forces and the deployment of an ECOWAS peace force. Nonetheless, Mané ousted Vieira on 7–8 May 1999. Beforehand, in April 1999, UNOGBIS (United Nations Peace-Building Support Office in Guinea-Bissau) had been created to help prepare for elections and the return to peace. A caretaker government, headed by the veteran PAIGC politician and acting speaker of parliament Malam Bacai Sanha as interim president, took office, while Francisco Fadul of the PUSD (Partido Unido Social Democrático) headed the national unity government after December 1998. Sanha's expanded mandate and extraordinary competences violated the constitution, and the same holds true for the fact that crucial political decisions were only to be taken in consensus with the military leaders, i.e. the junta and its supreme leader Mané. Thus, the junta secured numerous special rights for themselves, and Mané did not shrink from warning his PAIGC comrades against re-electing the acting party leader, Vieira. Meanwhile, plans were laid to tighten the constitution, from demanding that the parents of the president had to be born in Guinea-Bissau to a requirement that the grandparents of aspirants for high political office had to be Bissau-Guineans; but these plans were not realized. Similarly, attempts to institutionalize the junta as some kind of overseeing body for ten years failed (Ministério da Administração Interna 1995: 27/§ 63(2); Rudebeck 2001b: 28–33; Duarte Silva 2010: 208, 213–21).

Meanwhile, the armed forces grew quickly, as the personnel strength more than doubled to about 11,000, or even about 17,000 during the conflict, according to different sources (Herbert 2003: 22; United Nations Office on Drugs and Crime 2007: 14; Handem 2008: 153–4).[2] Among the forces were many veterans of the independence war and young Balanta men from the countryside—alongside Casamance rebel fighters—who joined the junta (Vigh 2006: 70), feeling sidelined and excluded by the Vieira regime and possibly joining the military on the basis of familial and friendship ties. Other observers (Garcia 2000: 224) identified Islam as a crucial factor, given the facts that Ansumane Mané was a Mandinga born in The Gambia and that Libya supported the insurgents (see chapter by Ceesay, this volume). By contrast, Vieira was reportedly supported by young fighters of predominantly Pepel origin (known as Anguentas), one of the president's own ethnic groups (Vigh 2006: 54–5; Costa Dias 2013: 19). As a consequence, many Bissau-Guineans with the necessary means left Guinea-Bissau for Portugal and Cape Verde during wartime, and many never returned (cf. Machado 2002: 3, 6, 79, 87). Among them were apparently many Bissau-Guinean Cape Verdeans and citizens with Creole ethnic backgrounds, from the middle and upper classes. Another difficult legacy of the violent conflict was a substantial loss of confidence between the military and the police, the former mostly siding with Mané, the latter rather with Vieira.

General elections took place on 28 November 1999 and 16 January 2000. For the first time since independence, the PAIGC, which had built the state, was ousted from power, winning only twenty-four seats (out of 102). The PRS (thirty-eight seats) and RGB/MB (Resistência da Guiné-Bissau/Movimento Bafatá) (twenty-nine seats) formed a coalition government and PRS leader Kumba Yalá, of the Balanta ethnic group, was elected president in the second round (69%), relegating Malam Bacai Sanha to second place (27%). Since the PRS has a predominantly Balanta electorate, it continues to be seen largely as a Balanta party. Yalá was well-received by Balantas for his populist disparagement of rival politicians, his accusations against the urban political establishment as being corrupt and alienated from the rural grassroots, and his exploitation of ethnic ties by explicitly referring to Balanta cultural symbols (Rudebeck 2001b; Nóbrega 2003a: 24–9; 2003b: 294; Temudo 2008: 249, 252–3).

[2] However, owing to demobilization efforts, the military's personnel strength decreased to about 5,100 in 2005 (United Nations Office on Drugs and Crime 2007: 14), and 4,500 in 2008, according to a census (Girão de Sousa 2013: 58–60), while the World Bank (2015) indicated a personnel strength of about 6,450 for the period 2010–13. Thus, '[t]he ratio of troops to population between 1999 and 2004 was 10 times the ECOWAS average ratio of the region' (United Nations Office on Drugs and Crime 2007: 14).

The coalition government collapsed in January 2001 as a consequence of Yalá's erratic and authoritarian rule, violating human rights and eroding the separation of powers. Yalá was quickly internationally isolated. Human rights violations increased (against journalists, amongst others); a socio-economic downturn accelerated due to mismanagement and corruption; while Yalá intimidated the judiciary and rejected signing the revised constitution that would have limited presidential powers. Mané and the army pretended to act as a counterweight and intermediary to Yalá's fragile presidency, Mané considering himself not only as supreme junta leader but also as 'co-president'. In November the tense co-habitation culminated in what was regarded as a coup attempt instigated by Mané after he had first declared himself general chief of staff and, some days later, supreme commander of the armed forces, a position actually fulfilled constitutionally by the president of the country. Shortly thereafter, Mané was killed in fighting with troops loyal to Yalá (Ostheimer 2001; Duarte Silva 2010: 224–6). During Yalá's rule, he provided Balanta supporters in many cases with ministerial and other posts and favoured the army (Costa Dias 2000; Ostheimer 2001; Davidson 2003: 38; Magalhães Ferreira 2004: 47–9; 2005: 3). Yalá was connected through ties of family and friendship to some army leaders. Indeed, he reportedly granted the army control over Bissau's port authority, to import goods by bypassing customs. Therefore external observers quickly detected a distinct balantization (or *balantização* in Portuguese) of Bissau-Guinean politics (see e.g. Ostheimer 2001: 6; Nóbrega 2003b: 293; Magalhães Ferreira 2004: 48).[3]

The tense political situation was exacerbated even further after Yalá dissolved the parliament and dismissed the government in November 2002. New parliamentary elections were repeatedly postponed, so the newly appointed government depended on Yalá (Duarte Silve 2010: 226). Despite the backing from the army that Yalá had bought, he was finally overthrown in a military coup on 14 September 2003, which was widely welcomed both at home and internationally. The putsch was staged under the leadership of the general chief of staff Veríssimo Correia Seabra, of the Pepel ethnic group, in the name of a Military Committee. This demonstrated also the fractionalization of the military, and moreover challenges the idea that the balantization thesis alone explains political struggles since the 1998 conflict, since Yalá, a Balanta, was ousted by the Balanta-dominated army. Thus despite continued talk about

---

[3] The term *balantização* apparently first appeared in a newspaper article by Eduardo Costa Dias (2000).

balantization, factors other than ethnicity have to be considered in the realities of political conflicts in contemporary Guinea-Bissau. Socioeconomic conditions are also of crucial importance in assessing relative political popularity. For instance, my fieldwork observations were that a great many economically and socially vulnerable individuals felt attracted by Yalá and his PRS. Moreover, election results suggest that Yalá gained major support from Muslim voters in the run-off presidential elections of 2000, even in the stronghold of his rival Sanhá, himself a Muslim of the Beafada ethnic group (Rudebeck 2001b: 71; Nóbrega 2003a: 71).

Following Yalá's dismissal, a caretaker government was installed, and a Political Transition Bill was signed by the committee and almost all registered political parties. The independent Henrique Rosa, a widely respected Bissau-based businessman and devout Catholic of part-Portuguese and Creole ancestry, was nominated president as part of a National Transitional Council, with the task of preparing parliamentary and presidential elections (Vaz/Rotzoll 2005; Duarte Silva 2010: 233–8). After numerous government reshuffles under Yalá—including, *inter alia*, four prime ministers—relative stability returned under Rosa, with Artur Sanha (PRS) serving as prime minister until the parliamentary elections in May 2004. However, the country did not settle down: General Seabra was killed in a mutiny on 6 October 2004 when soldiers returning from a UN peace-keeping mission in Liberia demanded their unpaid salaries.

The situation was at this point widely seen to be tipping the country towards a lasting political crisis. Systemic failure and symptoms of state collapse were to be found in these repeated coups and coup attempts, several failed disarmament, demobilization and reintegration programmes for Military Conflict veterans, lasting problems in the security sector and the judiciary, and the upcoming involvement of army figures in narco-trafficking. In the light of this bleak picture, the international community was prompted to prepare for a security sector reform (see Massey, this volume).

Return of the PAIGC to power

Parliamentary elections took place on 28 March 2004. The PAIGC recovered from its defeat in 1999, gaining forty-tive out of 100 seats, the PRS gaining thirty-five and the PUSD 17. Rosa nominated PAIGC leader Carlos Gomes Júnior (also known widely as Cadogo) prime minister, to negotiate a coalition with the PRS. Unlike other political parties, the PAIGC could benefit from its lasting image as the least 'ethnic' party, revealing the extent to which there had been a definite rise in ethnic-related themes in Bissau-Guinean politics under Yalá. The two rounds of the presidential elections were held on 19 June and 24 July 2005, the election process being accompanied by minor protests resulting in about five deaths. Nino Vieira returned to power, with a narrow majority (52%). Vieira had returned from Portuguese exile and ran as an independent against the PAIGC candidate Sanha (48%), attracting also many of Yalá's voters who had come third in the first round (Vaz and Rotzoll 2005; Duarte Silva 2010: 235–6). At the time the country was awash with rumours that Vieira had distributed a great number of election gifts to voters, including, in a few cases, even cars; many suggested that he had unknown wealthy sponsors. Indeed, rumours circulated that made Vieira responsible for establishing links to Colombian drug-dealers (interview with an employee of an international organization, Bissau, March 2013).

Once again, renewed attempts to exploit ethnic ties could be observed as politicians' electoral strategies included negative ethnic campaigning. During the presidential election process, for instance, according to my informants, Vieira attempted to fuel fears of his Muslim rival candidate Sanha's coming to power, warning people to resist an impending Islamization of Guinea-Bissau (discussions with Bissau-Guineans, Bissau, July 2006). Indeed, Vieira was able to win a clear majority of votes in areas characterized by non-Muslim populations, such as Biombo (as homeland of the Pepel ethnic group, often regarded as Vieira's stronghold) and Bolama (see the results in Vaz and Rotzoll 2005: 540). Vieira and his network tried to represent Sanhá as a Mandinga, even though Sanhá regarded himself as a Beafada. This was part of a deliberate strategy to discredit Sanhá in the eyes of the Fula voters, since many Bissau-Guineans think of Fulas as historical slaves to the Mandingas. However, the application of a simple ethnic arithmetic is not easily feasible in the case of Guinea-Bissau. For example, in the run-off election, Sanhá and Vieira ran neck-and-neck in the eastern region of Gabú, an area where the majority of inhabitants are Fula (about 80%), followed by Mandinga (14%) and Balanta (2%) (Instituto Nacional de Estatística 2009: 70; own calculations), thus proving that Vieira's strategy was not in the least successful.

With Vieira, a rival to Prime Minister Gomes was sworn in as president. Vieira's and Gomes' rivalry dated back to the 1990s: initially, Vieira had supported Gomes's rise but, according to narratives circulating in Bissau, after Gomes was tasked to manage formerly state-owned estate and property for Vieira, he eventually appropriated parts of these assets for himself (interviews,

Bissau, February–March 2013 and September 2014).[4] Tensions were therefore high, and within a short period of time Vieira managed to divide the PAIGC parliamentary group into pro-Vieira and pro-Gomes factions: Vieira dismissed Carlos Gomes Júnior and unilaterally appointed as prime minister Aristides Gomes (they are not related), a PAIGC-dissenter, in November 2005.

This 'presidentialism' has been domestically criticized, as various politicians and lawyers argued that the president was not allowed to nominate a prime minister by 'presidential initiative', that is, without consultation with the executives of those parties represented in the parliament—a situation that repeated itself in 2015 under José Mario Vaz; however, the constitution is not entirely clear on this point. The government headed by Aristides Gomes was supported by a 'Convergence Forum for Development', composed of pro-Vieira PAIGC dissenters, PRS and PUSD (Duarte Silva 2010: 239). Thus the political atmosphere was poisoned by Vieira's struggle for dominance and revenge. While Carlos Gomes Júnior was regarded by many Bissau-Guineans as an efficient leader who implemented many reforms, he was also power-hungry and had conflictual personal traits. The assassination of the former army chief of staff and Mané ally Lamine Sanhá, and the asylum-seeking of Gomes Júnior in early 2007, as well as reports of increased drug trafficking, all underlined the country's precarious socio-economic situation under his tenure.

In March 2007 the PAIGC, PRS and PUSD agreed to form a new government and to replace Aristides Gomes. They elected PAIGC vice president Martinho N'Dafa Cabi as prime minister. This signalled the parliament's victory over Vieira's 'presidentialism'. However, political conflicts continued. To safeguard parliamentary seats and secure power, the parliament approved a law in April 2008 which sought to extend its legislative period after the elections for an unspecified length of time. This step was declared unconstitutional by the supreme court in July. Simultaneously, relations deteriorated between the PAIGC and PRS and within the PAIGC, and also between N'Dafa Cabi and Carlos Gomes Júnior supporters. The PAIGC eventually withdrew its confidence in N'Dafa Cabi in February 2008. All these developments resulted in the withdrawal of parts of the PAIGC from agreement with the other parties, letting Vieira appoint the seasoned PAIGC veteran Carlos Correia as caretaker prime minister in August 2008. The atmosphere remained tense. In

---

[4] In that aspect, Carlos Gomes Júnior's biography is said in some quarters of the Bissau rumour mill to resemble that of current president José Mario Vaz, though there is no hard evidence for this.

August and November two coup attempts against Vieira failed, the first reportedly planned by former navy chief of staff José Américo Bubu NaTchuto, known as a drug kingpin; the second was reportedly masterminded by a nephew of Yalá. Possibly, circles close to Yalá were involved in these struggles for power and influence. The elections that were finally held in November 2008 brought a landslide victory to the PAIGC of 67 seats of 100, while the PRS won 28 seats (Kohl 2008, 2009b; Duarte Silva 2010: 240–47).

The same year, 2008, saw the beginning of the security sector reform mission by the EU (known as EU SSR), which further inflamed what was already a politically tense situation. Apart from a lack of communication with both government institutions and other donors, such as UNOGBIS and UNIOGBIS (United Nations Integrated Peace-Building Office in Guinea-Bissau, the 2010 successor of UNOGBIS), UNDP (United Nations Development Program), and the UNODC (United Nations Office on Drugs and Crime) amongst others, it was apparently EU SSR's hasty and insensitive top-down reform implementation that prompted the mission's failure in 2010 (Kohl 2014; see Massey, this volume). The EU SSR brought the Balanta question back on the agenda. Apart from revising police-, military- and justice-related legislation, reorganizing and training police and military and their infrastructure, it was the intended downsizing of the military that caused mistrust and fears among the security forces. Some army officials felt alienated by the EU SSR's reported intention to introduce ethnic quotas in the military, aiming at reducing the Balanta bias. Even more fundamentally, some military factions feared for their lucrative illicit businesses, power and prestige. Although General Chief of Staff Batista Tagme Na' Waie could be convinced to support the reform, his tense relationship with President Vieira would be a heavy burden for the upcoming developments.

After the elections, there initially seemed to be a normalization of political affairs when Carlos Gomes Júnior was again appointed prime minister in December 2008. But as early as January 2009, signs of a storm brewing appeared again: Na' Waie ordered the disarmament of the presidential guard (the Anguentas), carried out the same day after he had been attacked by some of its members. This signalled the weakening of the power of Na' Waie's adversary Vieira. On 1 March Na' Waie was killed in a bomb blast in Bissau's general staff building. Some hours later, Vieira was assassinated in revenge by soldiers loyal to Na' Waie and reportedly close to António Indjai, the military's man of the future. Raimundo Pereira, speaker of parliament, PAIGC member, and ally of Gomes Júnior, was appointed interim president, and he nominated José Zamora Induta (also loyal to Gomes Júnior) as new general chief of staff.

Thus the most important political posts were now occupied by individuals allied with Prime Minister Gomes Júnior, who together supported the reform of the security sector. The international community regarded Gomes Júnior as its partner, a leader who was supposed to share fundamental values and interests, taking forward Guinea-Bissau's economy and the security sector reform. However, Gomes' 'dark', power-hungry side and his own commercial interests were largely left out of this picture. The politically tense situation deteriorated further when the politicians Baciro Dabó and Helder Proença, allies of Vieira and PAIGC dissenters, were assassinated in June 2009. Hence, the spiral of violence and revenge, of coups and army interference in politics, accelerated visibly (Kohl 2009b, 2010).

Precursors to the 2012 coup

The early presidential elections were scheduled for 28 June 2009. In the run-off round on 26 July, Malam Bacai Sanhá—a PAIGC internal adversary of Carlos Gomes Júnior—beat Kumba Yalá by a clear majority (63% vs. 37%). Once again experts were wrong, as they had not expected former interim president Henrique Rosa to win third place in the first round. Because he was said to have no strong ethnic basis, as an urban resident and independent candidate, Rosa was not supposed to achieve a good result. Yet, the country did not calm down. Tensions rose again in December when Bubu NaTchuto returned from exile in The Gambia and, after his homecoming had become public, had to seek refuge in Bissau's UN headquarters. NaTchuto only left the compound on 1 April 2010 when a military insurgency took place: Prime Minister Gomes was arrested but released the following day, whereas General Chief of Staff José Zamora Induta was detained until December the same year. The insurgents were backed by the deputy general chief of staff, António Indjai, who had reportedly been involved in the assassination of President Vieira the year before (Duarte Silva 2010: 251; Kohl 2011).

There were several possible reasons for this abortive coup. Some politicians and army figures felt threatened by the ongoing security sector reform. They feared losing influence, status and illegal sources of income from the arms trade and the intensifying drug trafficking. Moreover, plans to restructure the various police forces as part of the security sector reform were regarded by parts of the military as a potential threat. It became clear that Gomes was the main image of the enemy when Indjai—following the 1 April 2010 incidents—threatened him with death if protesters in his favour did not withdraw. Possibly, as in other such events, Yalá may have been involved in this power struggle, using his personal relationships. This occurrence refutes the simple thesis of an ethnic Balanta conspiracy—both Indjai and Induta are Balantas—and rather underlines the factionalization of the military, irrespective of ethnic affiliation. Thus not ethnicity but common interests appear to have been paramount within the armed forces. It appears that ethnicity was subsumed in other factors, such as ancestral, cultural, geographic and buddy ties, rather than being the overriding factor. The military has thus been marked by an increasing informal–formal 'privatization' (Costa Dias 2013: 18–19) in favour of its leaders and their entourage, ethnicity playing only a subordinate role.

This abortive coup demonstrated that the military leaders—in particular Indjai—increasingly regarded themselves as a parallel power detached from political control. Despite widespread national and international rejection of their acts, Indjai nonetheless managed to survive the removal of his superior, General Chief of Staff Induta. Following problems with implementing the security sector reform, the EU SSR used Indjai's interference to terminate its mission. Indjai was promoted to general chief of staff, reluctantly appointed by President Sanhá, whereas NaTchuto—who was accused of being a drug kingpin by the US prosecution (United States Attorney's Office, Southern District of New York, 2013)—was reinstated as naval chief of staff.

It was in this tense situation that a new and important player emerged on the Bissau-Guinean scene. In early 2011 Angola deployed a peace mission, called MISSANG (Angolan Technical Military and Security Mission in Guinea-Bissau), to continue with the security sector reform. Since mid-July the PRS and allied extra-parliamentarian parties had organized protest rallies in Bissau, making Carlos Gomes Júnior's PAIGC-led government responsible for high living costs and the inability to solve the 2009 assassinations. Over the past decade, military leaders had repeatedly sought to influence and thwart judicial investigations and proceedings in cases with armed forces involvement, intimidating judges, lawyers and attorneys. Although the government succeeded in achieving debt relief and in implementing reforms, prominent problems such as increased drug trafficking, energy and water supply shortages in the capital and the inability to pay civil servants' salaries (particularly teachers and health workers) remained on the agenda. On 26 December 2011 there was another coup attempt, probably masterminded by José Américo Bubu NaTchuto. The fact that MISSANG brought Gomes Júnior to safety fuelled further criticism from the opposition, accusing him of selling Guinea-Bissau to Angola. After NaTchuto was detained following the coup attempt, he and Indjai accused each other of being involved in narco-trafficking (Kohl 2012b). And indeed, two weeks before the abortive coup in late December, a plane charged with Latin American cocaine had landed close to Indjai's newly constructed residence in Mansôa in central Guinea-Bissau (Kohl 2012b); there was widespread talk in high circles in Guinea-Bissau that the real source of the coup attempt had been a falling-out following the 'disappearance' of the drugs after landing, with some very high-ranking members of the military allegedly cut out of the deal.

During this continuous discord and instability, President Sanhá died on 9 January 2012. With Sanhá gone, politics lost an important stabilizing individual who had attempted to settle differences between politics and the military. Again, Speaker of Parliament Raimundo Pereira became interim president. The crisis increased further when Prime Minister Gomes announced his candidacy for president without formally resigning. This was grist to the mill of the PRS-led opposition movement, which intensified its campaign against Gomes, accusing him of election fraud and demanding the withdrawal of MISSANG, depicted as a 'foreign intervention force' (Kohl 2013a, 2013b)—demonstrating the proximity between the PRS and the military. MISSANG was accused of safeguarding Angola's economic interests (notably in bauxite resources in eastern Guinea-Bissau) and her supposed protégé Gomes. The PRS presidential candidate, Kumba Yalá, tried again to play the ethnic card (International Crisis Group 2012: 6). During the electoral campaign he reportedly made populist attempts to exploit existing reservations against *burmedjus* by portraying presidential candidate Gomes as an elite urbanite detached from rural social reality, and as not being ethnically affiliated to any of the ethnic groups: 'Everybody knows who Carlos Gomes Júnior is. Me, I am a Balanta; this one here, he is a Mandinga; and that one there, he is a Fula. ... But him [Gomes Júnior], so, who is he? What ethnic group? What region?' (Grands Dossiers 2012; my own translation from French). Moreover, Yalá had converted to Islam in 2008 (Duarte Silva 2010: 245, 254), obviously aiming at Muslim voters. This was how he apparently tried to impress his potential electorate. By contrast, many Bissauans indeed ascribed Gomes an ethnic affiliation, assuming that he belonged to the Pepel ethnic group, while also pointing out his family's Creole origins. Ethnicity was also an issue with other candidates. For instance, rumours mentioned a Fula network with a further candidate, Manuel Serifo Nhamadjo, a PAIGC dissenter and deputy speaker of parliament, at its centre.

The first round of the elections took place on 18 March 2012. Yet, they were ill-fated: after an ally of deposed general chief of staff Induta was assassinated on the eve of the first round, rumours of a pending coup circulated. According to the official, contested results, Yalá's strategy of shoring up the Balanta vote through ethnicizing strategies and appealing to Muslim voters through his conversion did not prove very successful. Without achieving an absolute majority, Gomes produced a sizable advantage over Yalá (49% vs. 23%) and Nhamadjo came third (16%). Yalá only won Tombalí province (a Balanta–Fula stronghold) but failed in both the Balanta stronghold of Oio province and the predominantly Muslim eastern provinces of Bafatá and Gabu. Importantly, therefore, in spite of the manipulations of ethnicity by the political class, there was no strong correlation between perceived ethno-religious interests and political success. However, after the elections, tensions rose even further: several presidential candidates led by Yalá contested the official election results. Yalá, as runner-up candidate, rejected any international mediation. The run-off round was eventually scheduled to take place on 29 April, but this was not to be: continuous criticism from both the PRS opposition and the military leadership prompted Angola to announce the withdrawal of MISSANG on 9 April. Shortly after, during the night of 12–13 April, army factions rose up again, detaining the acting president Pereira and presidential candidate Gomes.

The 2012 coup and its aftermath

The armed intervention was apparently poorly organized and—at least in retro-spect—authorized by António Indjai. As the putsch was seemingly not centrally planned but rather initiated by military secondary figures with Indjai jumping on board, this points to a multi-polar structure within the armed forces. The coup plotters justified their overthrow with a pending international intervention allegedly approved by Gomes and Pereira. From the beginning, the PRS was prepared to take part in a transitional government. However, the coup plotters, the PRS and presidential candidate Nhamadjo, seemed to be surprised by the popular, national and international condemnation of the coup, and conse-quently temporarily shelved the plan to assume power.

The ECOWAS members—particularly its most powerful member state Nigeria, as well as Ivory Coast and Senegal—had been very critical of Angola's political and economic involvement in Guinea-Bissau, regarding the south-western African country as a rival. Ultimately, ECOWAS broke the interna-tional anti-coup consensus and sided with the coup supporters. In so doing, ECOWAS remained the only body that recognized the transitional government that took office in May 2012. By contrast, all other major international players, such as the UN, AU, EU, CPLP and USA, rejected recognition and imposed sanctions. ECOWAS deployed a largely ineffective peace force, called ECOMIB, to replace MISSANG. The transitional government consisted of members of the PRS and its extra-parliamentarian allies, whereas the interior (supervising the police) and defence ministries were controlled by the military. From the beginning, it was clear that Indjai and his entourage acted as strong men, while Yalá could be considered as the *éminence grise*. Rui de Barros—a former finance secretary during Yalá's presidency—was appointed transitional prime minister, and PAIGC dissenter Nhamadjo became transitional president. The PAIGC rejected any participation (Kohl 2013a, 2013b). Hence the government was effectively controlled by a tacit PRS–military alliance, strongly—though not exclusively—grounded in personal Balanta ties, and the new alliances which Yalá had more latterly achieved with members of Guinea-Bissau's Islamic communities.

From the outset, the transitional government was plagued by international financial sanctions. ECOWAS was unable to compensate for the loss of international financial aid. Rumours circulating in Bissau said that the government even paid its civil servants with drug money. More than ever before, the political and social atmosphere in Guinea-Bissau was poisoned by suspicion and mutual accusations of involvement in drug trafficking. In the aftermath of the coup, petty and grand corruption apparently grew considerably. The transport police, for example, strengthened controls to demand bribes. Many newly nominated government officials were said to use their short time in office to enrich themselves. Accordingly, it was in their interest to drag out the transition period originally set for one year. New elections were first postponed until November 2013 and finally scheduled to take place on 16 March 2014, lack of money cited at the official reason. The human rights situation after the coup deteriorated as the military prohibited demonstrations. Intimidation and beatings, supposedly carried out by the military and some PRS figures, of 'undesirable' persons (in the eyes of influential political and military figures) indicated the growing tensions.

Several flare-ups epitomized these tensions. An attack on an air force base in Bissau on 21 October 2012 was ascribed to army captain Pansau Ntchama, known for his good relationship with Indjai, former bodyguard of Induta, and reportedly involved in killing President Vieira in 2009. Military and political circles tried to ethnicize the incident, indicating that the alleged raid headed by Ntchama, a Balanta, had been jointly planned by some Floup conspirators, about six of whom died. In the days following the attack, a hunt for Floup reportedly started within the military, the soldiers involved possibly spurred on by a rumour circulating at the time in Bissau. Several Balanta had accordingly arrived in a Floup village to steal cows, as part of their initiation test of courage. Following that (allegedly 'urban legend' style) narrative, a combat had taken place, leaving some people dead or wounded. The air force attack was logically framed by some as a revenge campaign against presumed Balanta involvement in the imaginary attempted theft. Possibly, some circles had an interest in staging a conflict between Balanta and Floup within the army, either to tighten ranks or to weaken the position of general chief of staff Indjai.

Thus, most importantly, a closer look at the events suggests that ethnicity was again used as a scapegoat for power struggles within the armed forces, rather than being the cause of the tensions. An interlocutor from within the security forces confirmed that it was not ethnicity but instead the willingness to fraternize with high-ranking officials and their entourage, often connected by family ties, to join their networks and take part in illicit acts.[5] However, once the ethnic designator becomes a scapegoat, very real 'ethnic' tensions can ensue.

Pressured by the international community, the PAIGC joined the transitional government, rebranded as an 'inclusive government', in May 2013. But the party remained internally divided. Divisions within the PAIGC separated not only proponents and opponents of government participation, but reportedly also Muslims and Christians/Creoles in the preparations for election of a new party leader (Silva 2013), thus again being linked to ethnic designations. However, it is unclear how serious such divisions really were. It is conceivable that such discourses were mere election bluster accompanying internal party competition. Public perceptions of the minor PRID (Partido Republicano da Independência e Desenvolvimento)—once founded by PAIGC dissenter Aristides Gomes—as a Pepel party can be attributed to the fact that politicians often surround themselves with individuals who share cultural, social and geographic proximity. Consequently, the image of 'ethnic' parties and networks emerges, although ethnicity is in fact only a secondary phenomenon. More fundamental under the transitional government was the evidence of armed 'party militias' of young people maintained by some political parties (according to local information, notably the PRS), serving to bring people into line (cf. Kohl 2014).

Meanwhile Guinea-Bissau's global reputation as a drug hotspot grew. The detention of NaTchuto on 2 April 2013 on a ship off the Bissau-Guinean coast

---

[5] Interview, Bissau, 15 February 2013.

by US security agents, impersonating narco-traffickers intending to arrange a drug deal, demonstrated to what extent corruption and drug trafficking permeated even the highest political levels. US prosecutors' investigations cast a negative light on both de Barros and Nhamadjo, as evidence suggested that both of them may have been involved in or at least informed about NaTchuto's (and possibly Indjai's) narco-trafficking plans (cf. Lewis and Valdmanis 2013). In late 2013 it became apparent that Bissau-Guinean officials may have profited from counterfeit passports (Kohl 2014), pointing even more to a progressive 'privatization' of the state (Bayart, Ellis and Hibou 1999). These developments accompany an ever-increasing military interference in civilian political affairs. Ostensibly to fight increased corruption, Indjai announced in October 2013 the delegation of military 'executors' in almost all public institutions to collect taxes and hand them over to the treasury. Meanwhile, even ECOWAS seemed to grow tired of Guinea-Bissau (Kohl 2014), due to the costly transitional process and the inefficiency and corruption of those in power. ECOWAS eventually played a positive role and, together with the rest of the international community, supported the general elections in 2014. Given the stalemate situation, the elections were by many regarded as a new political beginning.

Ethnicity and politics: review and outlook

Guinea-Bissau's recent government crisis has underlined again a number of basic structural problems that have characterized the past fifteen years and continue to persist. These include politicians and their loose networks, guided by self-interest with a tendency to corruption, the differences between police forces on the one hand and the military on the other, as well as friction within the armed forces. Yet in spite of the ongoing political tensions in Bissau, there have been some signs of positive change. Although the disrespect for state legal and humanitarian norms remains an issue, since 2014 the intimidation of 'undesirable' individuals (among them journalists, politicians and judicial personnel), which peaked during the transitional government rule, has declined considerably. In addition, the manipulation of military leaders by politicians (and vice versa) in their struggle for power and resources, practised in the past particularly by the late Kumba Yalá, appears to have declined substantially—although it cannot be ensured that this remains the case.

Nevertheless, many challenges remain in the country, especially in the informal links that connect economic and political interests. Members of the political class have important economic interests, and hence the ongoing presence of illicit businesses causes political problems. These include narco-trafficking, illegal logging, arms trade, and support of illegal fishing, all of which are sometimes committed by high-ranking army officials and are covered by cooperating politicians, in conjunction with an appropriation and 'privatization' of state institutions that have been (to varying degrees) repressed recently, but which may quickly regain their strength in a more favourable political environment.

In this context, discourses concerning the ethnicization of politics are most important. Ethnicity has been repeatedly used for political purposes. Yet ordinary citizens largely maintain a critical, deprecatory stance on manipulating ethnic ties for political ends—in contrast to some external observers—as the election results of the past fifteen years have shown repeatedly. As early as the mid-1990s, Patrick Chabal had already identified ethnicity as one of the major recurring explanations to interpret conflicts in Africa. According to him, the 'tribal imperative', as he called it, had often been 'represented as *ultima ratio* of African politics' (Chabal 1996: 48, italics in the original), just as, for instance, in the case of the 'balantization' discourse.

A closer analysis of Guinea-Bissau reveals, however, that politicians as political entrepreneurs have so far failed to instrumentalize ethnicity as part of their moral ethnic strategies to such an extent as to result in political tribalism (Temudo 2008: 260; cf. Berman 1998). This means that horizontal competitions of various extensive ethnic networks—which may cause third parties to believe that ethnic groups form a unified monolithic bloc—have not yet come into existence in Guinea-Bissau. So far, external observers are actually taken in by some political leaders' groupist rhetoric (Brubaker 2004) and concur with the prevailing 'ethnic' coding practices and traditions in both scholarly and popular literature (including developmental and civil society-related publications). So far, (ethno-)political entrepreneurs have not yet succeeded in manipulating ethnicity for their purposes (Tambiah 1990: 750) as much as in Rwanda or Burundi, for example. In fact, the manipulation of ethnicity on political grounds is rejected by much of the population. This is illustrated by the case of Braima Camará who ran for PAIGC chairmanship in February 2014. Camará played the ethnic/eastern Bissau-Guinean/Muslim card in his campaign, but was defeated by Domingos Simões Pereira at the party's convention. Many citizens I talked to in Guinea-Bissau, even in the eastern part, vehemently rejected Camará's attempts and disapproved of 'tribal' rhetoric. Hence, ethnicity in Guinea-Bissau is not (yet) repeatedly

invoked in popular day-to-day discourses, ascribing ethnicity such an importance that it leads to strict separation of 'ethnic spheres' and ethnicized patterns of interpretation. National cohesion remains very strong among
Bissau-Guineans, relying on shared historical events, the trans-ethnicization
of cultural features, and common suffering (Kohl 2009a; Kohl and Schroven
2014; cf. also Havik 2012).

Of course, as in any society, mutual ethnic stereotypes and animosities
against the generalized other exist, as becomes clear in conversations with
Bissau-Guineans. Among these stereotypes are images of the cattle-raiding but
physically hard-working Balanta, the streetwise Senegalese and Conakry–
Guinean trader, the man-eating but close-mouthed and serious Floup, or the
hypocritical Fula. Although such stereotypes can, under certain circumstances, contribute to an escalation of conflict, the population nonetheless
lives together peacefully as long as they are not manipulated in a negative way.

Indeed, in spite of attempts by some in the political class to capitalize on
ethnic differences, ethnicity often continues to be officially downplayed,
owing to a state ideology based on the writings of Amílcar Cabral, the PAIGC
co-founder and long-term party leader. The tendency to downplay ethnic ties
can also be observed among the population, where ethnicity is often relegated
to the political sphere, portraying the population not only as victims of bad
governance and neglect but also of ethnic manipulation attempts by politicians. Ethnic mixing prevails in daily life as many villages and neighbourhoods
are multi-ethnic. As I have shown elsewhere, multi-ethnic associations, known
as *manjuandadis*, can even contribute to inter-ethnic integration (Kohl 2009a,
2012a), reinforcing—together with collective victimization discourses—the
already strong national consciousness. These victimization discourses refer to
colonial exploitation (and its complement, the victorious liberation struggle),
post-colonial bad governance, the betrayal of potential 'redeemers' (like
Amílcar Cabral) and the purported interest of neighbouring Senegal and
Guinea-Conakry in perpetuating Guinea-Bissau's plight. Hence, people imag-
ine Bissau-Guineans as a 'community of fate' (Kohl and Schroven 2014).
Focusing on 'bottom-up' processes of inter-ethnic, national integration in
Guinea-Bissau, I was able to observe and experience during my ethnographic
field research how Bissau-Guineans of various ethnic backgrounds identify
themselves with cultural representations such as *manjuandadis* and carnival.
These institutions not only satisfy general human needs for sociability, solidarity and pleasure; they also promote the integration of multifaceted cultural
forms that stem from different ethno-cultural and religious groups. Thus there

are many institutions in the country that serve to 'perform' the multicultural nation at grassroots levels in daily life. In addition, Kriol has played an important role in this regard, for it has contributed (given its weak ethnic reference) to connecting people of different ethnic backgrounds (Kohl 2009, 2012a).

However, recent international intervention may contribute to an advancement of ethnicization not only of politics, but also of people's perceptions. As part of its justice sector reform projects, the UNDP—in collaboration with the EU and the Bissau Law Faculty—initiated in 2009 a project to collect and codify the customary law of six ethnic groups (Loureiro Bastos n.d.). Tacitly, the project departed from the culturalist assumption that each of the selected ethnic groups would possess a clearly delineated cultural repertoire, including specific legal norms. This was not the case, as became clear during a fact-finding mission. Individuals belonging to the same ethnic group contradicted each other when asked about 'their' typical, ethnic-specific conflict-resolving norms. This is because legal cases are traditionally solved flexibly on a case-to-case basis, as such formalized ethnic legal frameworks do not exist. A report encompassing detailed results on legal customary norms among the six ethnic groups was nevertheless released in November 2014 (Faculdade de Direito de Bissau/Instituto Nacional de Estudos e Pesquisas n.d.). It is more than likely, then, that should Guinea-Bissau's government transform these allegedly 'traditional' norms into state law, this may indeed result in an ethnicization of political and everyday affairs. This would confirm the analysis that suggests that the instrumentalization of ethnicity in Bissau-Guinean institutions is most often derived from institutions with an externalized authority, although it is the people of Guinea-Bissau itself who then have to manage the consequences (Green, this volume).

9

GLOBAL GEOPOLITICS AND THE FAILURE
OF SECURITIZATION IN GUINEA-BISSAU

Simon Massey

Guinea-Bissau is a country seemingly in permanent transition. Gaining independence following a bitter war of liberation against Portugal initially inculcated a sense of national unity, which arguably still broadly persists, but it also established the primacy of the soldier over the politician, laying the foundations for decades of *coups d'état*, assassinations and a period of outright civil war. Although Guinea-Bissau held its first multi-party election in 1994, no elected government has completed its full mandated term, each administration being curtailed by the intervention of the military (although in each case the military intervened with the support of political rivals of the incumbent). Each coup has ushered in a further period of transition as a new interim government attempts to rebuild a form of constitutionality acceptable to the military and its leadership.

The international community's support for reform, including reform of the police and armed forces, has to date foundered on determined opposition from senior military officers ready to mobilize their troops should they perceive a threat to their predominance and personal wealth. Yet, despite growing frustration with the intractability of the country's dysfunctional politics, the list of international organizations and countries willing to seek solutions to Guinea-Bissau's problems is as long as the list of their tangible accomplishments is short. The United Nations (UN) and its agencies have had a permanent presence in the country since the civil war of 1998–9, and the UN Peace-Building Commission (PBC) takes the lead in acting as a hub for international efforts in the country. Following a coup in 2012 in which the predicted victor in the second round of voting in the presidential election, Carlos Gomes Júnior, was arrested by the military and the polls were cancelled, the international community split between the few organizations that recognized the transitional government of interim president Manuel Serifo Nhamadjo, and the majority that did not. The most prominent member of the former camp was the Economic Community of West African States (ECOWAS), which has for the last three and a half years been the international organization with the most visible on-the-ground presence, through the 600 peacekeepers of the ECOWAS Mission in Bissau (ECOMIB). Organizations that suspended membership or assistance include the African Union (AU), which nonetheless appointed a special representative for Guinea-Bissau and maintains an office in the capital; the European Union (EU), which until 2012 was a major donor and a provider of technical expertise; and the CPLP (Comunidade dos Países de Língua Portuguesa), the global lusophone organization that is expanding its involvement in conflict resolution. Lusophone states usually seek to act in concert as members of the CPLP, but are also amongst the most engaged of bilateral partners, notably former colonial power Portugal, emerging global power Brazil and incipient continental power Angola. Other states with an interest include neighbours and near neighbours Senegal, Guinea-Conakry and The Gambia, as well as France, China and the US, following a spectacular law enforcement intervention by its Drug Enforcement Administration (DEA) in April 2013. Despite this impressive catalogue of stakeholders, the level of involvement has been manifestly insufficient to make any lasting difference to political stability, military reform or the life chances of the vast majority of Bissau-Guineans. Paradoxically, for most of its history Guinea-Bissau has been almost invisible in the international arena, and arguably the extent of international involvement and the failure to secure a peaceful resolution confirm the need for change to come from within.

Policies towards Guinea-Bissau adopted by almost the entirety of the international community in the country provide a textbook example of a consensus to prioritize security over development. This strategy has been implemented despite extreme poverty, and the failure is there for all to see: development and security, as Guinea-Bissau shows, are fundamentally connected. Outside the capital, for example, there is no access to electricity or clean water, and in Bissau, despite some recent improvement, mains electricity is extremely limited and sporadic. Chronically unstable, but without a major and visible humanitarian crisis, Guinea-Bissau has, however, attracted a higher international profile since about 2005, based on its sudden emergence as a trans-shipment hub for South American cocaine. Reliable evidence is beginning to emerge, notably since the arrest by DEA in April 2013 of the former chief of the Bissau-Guinean navy, Rear Admiral José Américo Bubu NaTchuto, of the extent of the cocaine trafficking syndicates' penetration of military and political elites. The claim that Guinea-Bissau presents a serious transnational threat, not only as a result of cocaine trans-shipment, but also as a result of related activities including arms smuggling, the illicit sale of timber, trafficking in human beings and terrorist funding, has led to 'developmental' policies being formulated through a security prism.

This chapter outlines the status of the relationship between the international community (and its component parts) and Guinea-Bissau, specifically in the area of Security Sector Reform (SSR). It will investigate how the arrival of South American drug syndicates in the country has impacted on the political balance, notably by reshaping political–military elite bargains; it further explores the intrinsic challenges to reform of the police and armed forces, and assesses the securitization of policies ostensibly designed to develop Guinea-Bissau, and how these might be improved through a renewed understanding of the links between equitable economic development and security. It concludes by exploring the implications of the DEA's sting operation on the relationship between the political and military elites, and assesses the potential for substantive reform of the security sector.

Many actors, little reform

In order to grasp the divergent interests that have attempted to take a stake in Guinea-Bissau, it is necessary to understand something of the conflicting and overlapping positions which organizations as diverse as the UN, AU, ECOWAS and EU have adopted.

The UN became active in peace-building in Guinea-Bissau in 1999 following the end of the civil war (see chapters by Ceesay and Kohl, this volume). The ousting of Nino Vieira then and the establishment of a government of national unity led to the creation of one of the UN's first explicit forays into peace-building, UNOGBIS (the UN Peace-Building Support Office in Guinea-Bissau), in March 1999. On 1 January 2010 UNOGBIS was replaced by UNIOGBIS (the UN Integrated Peace-Building Office in Guinea-Bissau).

Wide and arguably over-ambitious, UNIOGBIS's mandate has two main strands: to address insecurity in the country directly through SSR; and to combat organized crime, notably the drug trade, whilst also engaging with Guinea-Bissau's fundamental peace-building needs; strengthening national institutions; supporting the criminal justice system; and encouraging political dialogue and reconciliation. A succession of special representatives of the UN Secretary General have been posted to Bissau. The current holder of the post is Miguel Trovoada, former prime minister and president of São Tomé and Principe, who was appointed in July 2014. He replaced the most high-profile international personality to have served as special representative, José Ramos Horta, Nobel Peace Laureate and former president of East Timor. Ramos Horta's working methods involved actively seeking dialogue with all stake-holders—political, military and civil society—and seeking to avoid isolating any of the protagonists, including senior military officers and their factions.

Ramos Horta also advised that the subsidiarity prefigured by Chapter Eight of the UN Charter would be the most likely mechanism to break the recurrent crises that stem from the 'deep mistrust within the politico-military elite' (Chatham House 2013; Embaló 2012: 278). However, the inter-governmental organizations that historically have been involved in Guinea-Bissau's political crises—the AU, ECOWAS, EU and CPLP—have a record of only intermittent engagement with the reform process, as well as a deep underlying rivalry. ECOWAS and the CPLP, for example, championed different sides in the 1998–9 civil war, with ECOWAS supporting Vieira and the CPLP backing the majority of the armed forces rallied behind the army chief of staff Ansumane Mané (Massey 2001). These divergent agendas were once more apparent in the crisis following the 2012 coup, with the CPLP promoting a broadly lusophone position supporting the predicted victor in the presidential poll, the exiled Gomes Júnior, and ECOWAS offering tacit moral support to the transitional government, but also material support in the form of peace-keepers.

The AU asserted its normative policy of zero tolerance for unconstitutional changes of government, as it has in other similar recent cases including Madagascar, Niger, Mali and Burkina Faso (Souaré 2014). As with these coups, the AU suspended Guinea-Bissau pending the restoration of constitutionality through credible elections. Nonetheless, by backing the diplomatic initiatives of ECOWAS, led by an unlikely alliance of Nigeria, Côte d'Ivoire and Senegal, the AU has adopted an ambiguous position, reaffirming its norm of outlawing coups, whilst tacitly supporting as the primary external actor in the position of mediator and intervenor the inter-governmental actor of ECOWAS, which recognizes the transitional government, a position described by Eduardo Costa Dias as 'irresponsible' (Dias 2013). The AU has tended to act as a mediation multiplier, throwing its support behind regional organizations as the lead crisis managers, yet intervening directly at key junctures in the mediation, or constitutional, process. During the 2012 elections in Guinea-Bissau, the AU special representative Ovidio Manuel Barbosa Pequeno and—adding even greater moral weight—former President of Mozambique Joaquim Chissano, as head of the AU election observer mission, were present at the first and second polls, appealing to the electorate to participate in a peaceful electoral process that would rehabilitate their country.

The EU member states were formerly key multilateral donors, but they suspended aid to Guinea-Bissau in 2011 after an army mutiny in April 2010 which resulted in the temporary arrest of the prime minister, Gomes Júnior, and President Malam Bacai Sanhá's replacement of the existing commanders of the army and navy, under apparent duress, by General António Indjai and Admiral NaTchuto. These two figures had already been officially designated by the US as 'drug kingpins'. The suspension of aid was compounded by the EU severing formal development assistance after the 2012 coup. Following the 1998–9 civil war, the EU had established what Marie Gibert describes as 'traditional economic development programmes and budgetary aid' (Gibert 2009: 630). This funding survived the coup that ousted President Kumba Yalá in September 2003, and was instrumental in ensuring successful elections in March 2004. Yet it was shortly after these elections, as evidence emerged of the growing scale of the drug trade in the country, that the EU's attention shifted towards explicit security policies rather than traditional development goals. For Anderson and Williams, the Cotonou Agreement that guides development policy fails 'to distinguish between security and development goals' (2011: 10). The role of the EU in shaping the securitization of development policy in Guinea-Bissau is analysed in more detail below.

In contrast to the EU's response to the 2003 coup, in 2012 it withdrew budgetary aid and redirected aid for humanitarian projects to the non-governmental sector. The EU delegation chief, Joaquin Gonzalez-Ducay, was explicit in his analysis: 'We cannot continue to give institutional assistance, more so budgetary aid, to people who are not [legitimately elected], who cannot manage the state budget and who are infiltrated by drug traffickers' (IRIN 2012). As with other recent unconstitutional changes of government, the EU collaborated with the AU to reinforce financially what the latter organization has sought to achieve through political pressure, in particular the suspension of Guinea-Bissau from the AU.

Understanding the variety of international actors with a stake in the country also requires something of a historical context. Since before independence, Guinea-Bissau had adopted a non-aligned posture, encouraging investment and development assistance from Cuba, China and the former Soviet Union, whilst also accepting aid from Sweden and the US. However, the traditional point of contact with the rest of the world has been with former colonial power Portugal, which has been Guinea-Bissau's most important bilateral development partner and an informal advocate for the country in international fora. This relationship has survived repeated strains. For example, prior to the civil war, Vieira moved the country towards France's sphere of influence in West Africa, joining the CFA zone and prompting frosty relations between the two EU member states. Having backed the victors in the civil war and reasserted its influence, the profound impact of the global economic crisis on Portugal has, more recently, limited the resources available to maintain the relationship, leading to suggestions that it is strategically content to share influence with other CPLP members, notably Angola and Brazil.

Angola rivals Nigeria as Africa's largest oil producer, and has attempted over the past decade to build itself into a power commensurate with its booming economy. Angola has enjoyed a close working relationship with China in the oil sector, but also particularly in construction, and this has underpinned a close relationship in Guinea-Bissau where the two countries have become significant investors and providers of aid, filling the budgetary gap left when European donors withdrew in 2012. However, in an ambitious departure from traditional development assistance, Angola agreed to work with the government of the then prime minister Gomes Júnior, with the backing of the CPLP, to send a military mission, alongside a smaller mission from Brazil tasked with reconstructing the army headquarters, to continue with the reform of the armed forces originally undertaken by the EU. As will be discussed later in the chapter, this initiative came to a premature end two days before the 2012 coup when, faced with increasingly fraught relations with the Bissau-Guinean army on the streets of Bissau, Angola was given little option but to withdraw. Highly dependent on oil revenue, Angola's economy has been hit hard by the fall in oil prices since 2014, placing a question mark, at least temporarily, over its ambitions as a regional power and its future substantive involvement in Guinea-Bissau.

For the United States, Guinea-Bissau has been amongst the lowest priorities, being one of the few countries where it does not maintain a full mission, but rather a liaison office in Bissau staffed by locals, with the non-resident ambassador located in Dakar, and a virtual 'presence post' on the internet (US Department of State). Conducting its diplomacy at arm's length, the US has, according to the International Crisis Group (ICG), been offering its 'discreet support' to the policy of inclusive dialogue (ICG 2014: 4). So the decision, apparently taken at the highest level, to authorize the DEA to implement a daring sting operation against the top traffickers was a shock not only to the arrested NaTchuto, but equally to his fellow target Indjai, and the wider Bissau-Guinean and international community. At least in the short term, this single action has changed the political calculations of the country's elites, although whether this will positively or negatively shape the security environment is currently uncertain.

In counterpoint to the securitization policies adopted by organizations and countries within the broader international community is the stance taken by Brazil. If its overarching goal in Africa is to source new markets for its manufactured goods, in the case of Guinea-Bissau this is currently only an aspiration. Brazil's engagement with the country, nonetheless, supports its developmental efforts on the continent as part of its ambition to be seen as a major power. This type of south–south cooperation is a fundamental element of its strategy to win a permanent seat on the UN Security Council (Stolte 2012). In preference to defining (in)security in Guinea-Bissau in terms of the threat posed by an unreformed military, and the concomitant drug trafficking and related criminal activities, Brazil gives concrete expression to the rhetoric of state-building and social development through substantially increased development cooperation. Increasingly taking the lead within the CPLP and supplying the Chair of the Guinea-Bissau Configuration of the PBC, Brazil has been essentially unique in its conceptualization of a development policy for the country that is not explicitly security-focused. Describing Guinea-Bissau as 'a litmus test for Brazil's democracy and human rights promotion in Africa', Abdenur and de Souza Neto commend Brazil's optimism whilst cautioning that 'pure' development requires 'other approaches' if it is to succeed (Abdenur and de Souza Neto 2013: 115). Nevertheless, Brazil's approach is a reminder of the importance of ensuring the adequate distribution of resources as a prerequisite for all security.

Cocaine trafficking: the core driver of instability or merely a distraction?

The UN Office on Drugs and Crime (UNODC) suggests 2005 as the year when the scale of the illicit export of narcotics from West Africa—a trade that has existed since at least the first half of the twentieth century—accelerated markedly (Akyeampong, 2005; Ellis, 2009). In the case of Guinea-Bissau, it was around this time that the impact of cocaine trafficking on the fabric of Bissau city became increasingly conspicuous.

Formerly devoid of international standard hotels, the small capital now boasts several up-market and boutique establishments with designer restaurants, as well as some stylish bars and Western-style coffee shops. This despite Guinea-Bissau having no tourist industry to speak of, and a truncated economy dependent on the vagaries of the international cashew market and development aid. It is no secret to the local population that the occupants of the several new hacienda-type residences constructed on the edge of the city hail from South America, and that these occupants are also the owners of the top-of-the-range German saloon cars and US-manufactured armoured Humvees that have appeared on Bissau's potholed streets. At the same time, at the consumer end of the supply chain, there is visible evidence that drug dependency is becoming a problem in Bissau city, as some young men and women become addicted to strong, cheap *pedra*, a locally made version of crack cocaine.

By 2010, North American and European governments and international law enforcement organizations such as the UNODC and INTERPOL had concluded that the amount of cocaine being trafficked through Guinea-Bissau was increasing precipitous, as a result both of the incapacity of the country's law enforcement agencies to prevent the trade and of the compliance of military and political elites with the traffickers. This assessment has been the main driver behind the international community's securitization policies discussed above. Yet, despite an increasing number of international stakeholder meetings seeking 'solutions' to Guinea-Bissau's woes, the causative role of the drug trade remains undecided: entire conferences are predicated on the threat from the trade, matched by conferences where trafficking does not feature at all on the programme.

The term 'narco-state' is often applied to Guinea-Bissau (cf. Introduction by Green, this volume). The term has obvious resonance for journalists (cf. Vulliamy 2008), but also has a scholarly provenance (Jordan 1999; West 2006; Kohnert 2010; Paoli, Rabkov, Greenfield, Reuter 2007). Jordan defines the process of narco-statization as:

the corruption of the political regime as a result of narcotics trafficking; the crimi-nalization of the state. Narcostatization undermines the democratic check on the abuses of power by insulating elected officials from accountability and transforms the authoritarian state into a criminal one (Jordan 1999).

Arguably, accountability in Guinea-Bissau was in short supply prior to the onset of the 'bulk trade' in drugs through the country, the variable being the peculiar characteristics of cocaine trafficking and the international attention that such trans-border criminality attracts. Dirk Kohnert contends that the notion of the 'narco-state' as a sub-set of the category of 'failed states' is intrin-sically 'biased' and based on an audit of a state's perceived threat or utility to Western interests (Kohnert 2010: 12–14). Questioning the logic that state failure enables international organized crime, and maintaining that the activi-ties of organized criminals are more simply a likely consequence of feeble constitutionality, Carrier and Klantschnig argue that 'ironically, political instability, rather than the emerging drug control efforts of the state, might be the best guarantee for the decline of Guinea-Bissau's status as a 'narco-state' (2012: 114). During Ramos Horta's tenure as special representative, he consistently refuted the validity of the label, arguing that the drugs trade 'is serious enough, but not to the extent of calling a country a narco-state ... Guinea-Bissau has the chance to not be completely taken hostage by organ-ized crime' (IRIN, 10 June 2013). However, his denial of the 'narco-state' label became less forceful following the DEA sting operation.

Guinea-Bissau's unique geography, and the insecurity and corruption that social, economic and political collapse breed, are the pull factors attracting traffickers (see also chapter by Ceesay, this volume). Major seizures in 2006 and 2007 indicated that the amounts of cocaine transiting Guinea-Bissau were very significant. However, the direct involvement of political and military elites in the cocaine trade meant a steep fall-off in seizures by law enforcement agencies, which in turn has made accurate estimates of the size of the trade problematic. The UNODC has tentatively signalled a decline in cocaine flows through the West Africa region from an estimated high of 47 tonnes in 2007 to 18 tonnes in 2011 (UNODC 2013: 18). However, seizure reports and estimates from West Africa are notoriously patchy and inaccurate. Reports gathered by Davin O'Regan and Peter Thompson of suspect aircraft continu-ing to land at strips in Guinea-Bissau indicate that the flow of cocaine has not abated following the indictment of NaTchuto and the dismissal of Indjai (2013). By 2011, according to interviews conducted by Mark Shaw, 'money from drug trafficking appeared to have seeped across much of the Bissau elite, with increasingly the military, and Indjai at the apex, controlling the tap' (Shaw 2015: 355). In November 2012, the UN Secretary General reported that hundreds of kilograms of cocaine with an estimated street value in Europe of at least $10–20m were being brought into Guinea-Bissau each week (O'Regan and Thompson 2013: 17; United Nations, Report of the Secretary General, 27 November 2012).

Tuesday Reitano and Mark Shaw mapped the increasing rate of coups and assassinations and graphically demonstrate the 'accelerating cycle of violence and political instability following the introduction of cocaine into the country' (2013: 2). For O'Regan and Thompson, 'the drug trade has amplified the level of instability in the country and refutes the common assumption that transhipment of drugs ... has a benign effect on the transited country' (2013: 18–21). A further recent study examining the record of the international community in addressing the drug trade in Guinea-Bissau is unambiguous in its conclusion that 'the influence of drugs in the political process is becoming stronger not weaker' (Kemp, Shaw and Boutellis 2013: 24).

A need for security sector reform?

If there has been a long-standing consensus within the international community that Guinea-Bissau's security sector stands in need of reform, the conception of a post-reform security sector has differed greatly according to the desired outcomes of those international organizations that have become involved in SSR delivery. This varies between the EU perceiving SSR as a means of stemming the flow of drugs before they are moved on to Europe; Angola's idea of SSR influenced by their own experience as a rising regional power; and ECOWAS, whose representatives according to staff from international organizations working on the ground 'are hardly even familiar with the concept of security sector reform' (Kohl 2014: 11).

The major obstacle faced by any team tasked with bringing about sustainable reform is the exceptionally entrenched structures and practices across the security sector and the deep mistrust of change, seen as a threat to status and income, amongst Guinea-Bissau's police officers and soldiers. The policing sector suffers from a multiplicity of overlapping agencies—public order police (POP), judicial police (PJ), the rapid intervention police (PIR), border guards, immigration services, financial oversight services and state intelligence services—with ill-defined jurisdictions, weak levels of training and low and irregular pay. Despite its numbers, the POP, comprising 2,000 officers of whom 5% are women, plays a negligible role in combating crime. As in the military, there is a reversed hierarchical pyramid, with over 70% of the force ranking as senior officers. There is a lack of equipment, including buildings, vehicles and communications equipment, but also personal equipment and uniforms. Although currently under the authority of the Ministry of the Interior, the formation of the POP following the civil war of 1998–9 was ad hoc: initially the force had no legal existence, an evolution that has resulted in no organizational cohesion, administrative policy or annual budget. There is no police training facility, no access to criminal information and no overarching crime policy, including any strategic plan to confront drug trafficking. The only unit within POP to have received training is the PIR, a rapid response unit of 80 members which has received training in Angola. Given the POP's impediments, the onus for addressing serious crime, including drug trafficking, falls on the PJ, which falls under the authority of the Ministry of Justice. Its remit is criminal investigation throughout Guinea-Bissau's territory, although personnel and equipment shortages effectively restrict operations to the greater Bissau area. Equipment shortages in the PJ reflect those of the POP, made more serious by the investigative nature of its role. There is, at present, no surveillance, communications or forensic equipment or expertise and only limited training in investigative techniques or in addressing the transnational complexities of organized crime.

The military, comprising the army, navy, air force and gendarmerie, are over-staffed and its hierarchies are inverted, with a disproportionate number of high-ranking officers. There is a lack of relevant training, a persistent legal vacuum, low and irregular pay and deteriorating working and living conditions. Veterans of the war of independence, or their descendants, either swell the ranks or are treated as de facto members of the military. Nonetheless, given the impotence of the police, the military constitutes the only entity within Guinea-Bissau potentially capable of preventing the landing of cocaine and the activities of the traffickers. As such, it is the armed forces, rather than the police, the political elite or judiciary, who determine the price to be paid by the traffickers for renting Guinea-Bissau's sovereign territory for their activities. Moreover, as Ashley Bybee argues, in the effective absence of functioning state law enforcement and criminal justice apparatus, 'rather than grand corruption, simple non-enforcement of the law is sufficient for drug trafficking organisations to operate with impunity' (Bybee 2012: 78). The potential importance of the military in combating the trafficking may highlight not only collusion of some elements in the narco-trade, but also the fact that solutions may involve working with the army (see Green, Introduction to this volume).

Nevertheless, this is at present more easily said than done. Skimming a facilitator's percentage from the profits of cocaine trafficking proved a rent-seeking opportunity too easy and too lucrative for some senior military officers to refuse. In so doing, since about 2005 successive military leaders and their factions have undermined the concept of a tacit elite bargain that has for much of Guinea-Bissau's independent history acted as the mechanism for maintaining fundamental, if temporary, political stability (Stoleroff 2013). Influential personalities from the elite and their supporters, within both the military and political spheres, have been excluded from the proceeds of cocaine trafficking, provoking intensified blood-letting within the elites, coups and assassinations.

The 2013 arrest of one of Guinea-Bissau's two most senior military officers, both designated by the US as 'drug kingpins' that year, had an immediate impact on the movement of cocaine in the country. Admiral NaTchuto was arrested by the DEA in what was claimed to be international waters between Guinea-Bissau and Cape Verde. The sting operation, based on evidence gathered by 'confidential sources' working for the DEA, rather than DEA operatives, also targeted, but failed to lure, General Indjai. The formal indictment charge was that in the wake of the 2012 coup, NaTchuto took advantage of a weak government to ship 'ton-quantities' of cocaine from South America to Guinea-Bissau. The cocaine would then be reshipped mainly to Europe through Portugal with a smaller percentage being reshipped to the US. NaTchuto's fee is alleged to have been $1m per tonne of cocaine (US District Court 2013a). Indjai's indictment is still more detailed, alleging direct negotiations with FARC (Fuezas Armadas Revolucionarias de Colombia), a group proscribed as a terrorist organization for the supply of surface-to-air missiles in exchange for cocaine with the explicit collusion of the interim president Nhamadjo (US District Court 2013b). Indjai, however, is charged with negotiating with the 'confidential sources' posing as representatives of FARC, whilst Nhamadjo denies any involvement in cocaine trafficking. The mechanics and deficiencies of plea bargains notwithstanding, the accuracy of the case against NaTchuto has been seemingly corroborated by the guilty pleas of the two co-conspirators in the case and their incrimination of 'the Admiral'.

Does the interception of NaTchuto and the indictment of Indjai signal, as the EU Ambassador to Guinea-Bissau declared at the time of the arrest, that 'the era of impunity is over' (*New York Times*, 15 April 2013: A4)? Reitano and Shaw concur, noting that 'the DEA intervention is significant because it has ended impunity in a dramatic way', but cautioning that 'without the proper follow-up Guinea-Bissau will become a flashpoint for further instability and conflict' (Reitano and Shaw 2013: 1). By 'proper follow-up', Reitano and Shaw mean a serious step change in the intensity of international support for state-building, notably in the areas of law enforcement and criminal justice. Yet, whilst seen in some quarters as a game-changer, the decisive action by the US could further polarize the disjunction between the military and the politicians. As a senior US official has stated, 'there is a sense in some circles that we have commandos lurking offshore ready to pounce... I don't think this will become a regular occurrence in Guinea-Bissau, but if they think it is, no harm done there' (Reuters, 24 July 2013).

However, by failing to capture Indjai, the US created a situation in which the country's most powerful individual's options were limited. Within the military, and especially amongst the Balanta, the ethnic group that has traditionally dominated the ranks of the armed forces, there was deep unease with the charges against an honoured 'patriot' of the war of independence. However, this same constituency also recognized a need to weigh the risks of giving unconditional support to a 'marked man'. The sense that the DEA's actions might have opened an opportunity to break the hold of military strongmen on the governance of the country was evidenced by the more frequent visits of the US non-resident ambassador, including a face-to-face encounter with Indjai prior to the 2014 elections, when his options from a US perspective were, no doubt, made plain. The outcome of this confrontation will be assessed at the end of the chapter.

Security first; development after

The idea of 'securitization' draws on the influential reconceptualization of 'security' for a post-Cold War world proposed by Barry Buzan, Ole Waever and Jaap de Wilde (1997). Since this reconceptualization, the goal of establishing a 'secure' environment, even if this involves using extreme measures, has crystallized within international organizations and amongst bilateral partners. In the context of drug trafficking, Emily Crick notes a dichotomy in some quarters whereby drug traffickers pose an existential threat to those not involved in the drugs trade, concluding that 'the international community continues to be hooked on the "drugs as a threat" discourse (2012: 414). Robin Luckham and Tom Kirk contend that 'interventions by members of the international community are characterised by their own forms of hybrid politics, which warrant similar analytical lenses to those turned upon national and local actors' (2013: 15). Whilst international agencies often claim that their policies and actions are to protect and safeguard the poor and vulnerable, 'the welfare and security of end-users all too often take second place to geopolitical concerns, inter-agency rivalries and patron-client relationships' (Luckham and Kirk 2013: 15).

For the international community, a fundamental lesson following the civil war in Guinea-Bissau was the need for wholesale reform of the armed forces, to down-size its numbers and thin out its top-heavy structure, but mainly to persuade its senior officers of the long-term benefits of accepting civilian control (cf. also the Introduction by Green, this volume, on the problems of this strategy). Yet, fifteen years after the war, the Chair of the PBC's Guinea-Bissau Configuration was still regretting 'civil–military relations which are seen as a critical element of instability in the country' (UN 2014).

In the context of the European Security Strategy, and writing in 2004, Jorg Faust and Dirk Messner advocated 'a new alliance between development policy and security policy' based on 'moral reasons' and 'enlightened self-interest' (2004: 9). They nonetheless recognized the concern that:

> resources within the development cooperation portfolio could be extensively reallocated in favour of investments of particular relevance to security policy. A close dovetailing of development policy and security policy could, from this perspective, lead to a re-channelling of funds from developing countries or regions with less relevance to security policy to 'risk countries', or from 'classic' fields of development policy e.g. basic education, resource protection to sectors more relevant to security policy e.g. support for police and military (Faust and Messner 2004: 10).

Whilst not dismissing this concern out of hand, Faust and Messner argued that 'traditional' development policies are unlikely to succeed in failed states; they recommend a proactive strategy that 'self-assuredly includes the comparative strengths of development cooperation' (2004: 10). This analysis was borne out by the steady encroachment of the EU into non-traditional areas of development policy, with over thirty security-related operations involving military representatives of EU member states. In 2005, the UK sent a Security Sector Advisory Team to Guinea-Bissau, apparently to canvass the military and police about their perceptions of SSR needs in the country. This exercise was repeated by the EU in 2007. The result was the European Union Mission in Support of Security Sector Reform in Guinea-Bissau (EU SSR Guinea-Bissau) which deployed in 2008. In its framing, the EU SSR was an ambitious step for the EU, emphasizing its holistic intention in its name. The mission aimed to put in place a strategy to reorganize the police and the armed forces, to supply necessary equipment including arms and vehicles, and to amend the existing legal framework (Kohl 2014: 8–9). However, the mission struggled from the onset with the complexities on the ground, coupled with an unenthusiastic response by EU member states to calls for personnel contributions. The rationale for the mission was made clear in the preamble to the joint action that established the mission, stating that 'security sector reform is essential for stability and sustainable development of that country [Guinea-Bissau]' (Council Joint Action 2008). However, once in place it became clear that the 'synergies between the mission and the [European] Commission were far from pronounced' (Koutrakos 2013: 154).

Following an attempted mutiny in 2010 and the subsequent appointment of NaTchuto and Indjai, the EU decided to terminate the mission, having managed to redraw some of the country's legislative texts, such as a new basic law for the police, but having failed in its substantive goals as evidenced by the attempted mutiny. Lack of resources, lukewarm political will and an unwillingness to reform on the part of the Guinea-Bissau army contributed to the mission's ultimate failure. However, the disjunction between its mandate as authorized under the Common Security and Defence Policy (CSDP) and its explicit developmental aims also undermined its effectiveness As a result, as Sebastian Bloching observes, 'the threat by the EU not to keep a CSDP presence in the country in reaction to the military mutiny on 1 April 2010 did not produce sufficient leverage to induce the authorities in Guinea-Bissau to impose the rule of law and the primacy of the civilian democratic power over the military' (2010).

Despite intimations from Angolan President José Eduardo dos Santos that he was willing to help with reform of the Bissau-Guinean armed forces, the official launch of the Angolan Security Mission in Guinea-Bissau (MISSANG) in March 2011 came as a surprise to most stakeholders, and an unwelcome development to most of Guinea-Bissau's senior officers. The mission was costed at a reasonably substantial US$30m and was framed as a technical assistance mission intended to provide SSR for the armed forces, rather than any type of peace support operation. Ultimately, around 600 troops were deployed as part of a mission that was a first for Angola, a complex and risky initiative intended to raise its profile and boost its prestige. The force was headquartered at a high-profile hotel on the road to the airport, a strategic location that was interpreted as a pointed warning to the Bissau-Guinean armed forces not to consider further unconstitutional activities during the upcoming elections (Seabra 2011). Most in the armed forces were under no illusion that the force was neutral, but was there as an external security force to protect Gomes Júnior and his government and to finesse his election as president. There was also an external dimension to the deployment, with suspicion from ECOWAS, notably Nigeria and Senegal, that Angola's ambition was an encroachment into their own sphere of influence. A further, unsubstantiated rumour concerned Angola's supposed acquisitive intentions regarding the country's resources, notably its bauxite and timber assets. Increasingly tense stand-offs between MISSANG troops and the Bissau-Guinean army denoted the possibility of escalation. When the 2012 coup took place, the Angolans kept to their headquarters. Within about six weeks the force had returned to Angola. Although some Bissau-Guinean police officers were given instruction in Luanda as part of a 'train-the-trainer' scheme, there had been few concrete accomplishments in terms of meaningful SSR by the time of the force's hurried withdrawal.

MISSANG's replacement was a force comprising 629 police and army personnel as part of the ECOWAS Mission in Bissau (ECOMIB) with contributions from Nigeria, Senegal and Burkina Faso. ECOMIB deployed in response to an agreement by the 'military command' to step aside for a transitional government and acquiesce to new elections within a year. However, although intended to take over MISSANG's intended SSR function, the unwillingness of the transitional government to include politicians from the PAIGC (the Partido Africano da Independência da Guiné e Cabo Verde), the victors in the annulled March 2012 legislative elections, left ECOMIB in a similar position to its predecessor, perceived as partial and backing one part of the political spectrum. ECOWAS was also at odds with the rest of the international community, including the UN, AU, EU and CPLP, in refusing to recognize the Nhamadjo government (Aubyn 2012). Indeed, Christoph Kohl argues that ECOWAS was 'perceived to be a supporter, even an initiator, of the coup in April 2012' (2014).

Following the 2012 coup, a regime of international travel sanctions and asset freezes was imposed on those military officers involved (UN Security Council 2015). However, it was the sting operation by the DEA in April 2013 that fundamentally shifted the military/political balance, in the first instance in the context of who amongst competing Bissau-Guinean elite personalities controlled the cocaine rents, but potentially in a more substantial and long-term way. Whilst Indjai remained as army commander and other coup leaders kept their military positions, their susceptibility to arrest by US or other international law enforcement agencies had increased markedly. In the run-up to the presidential and legislative elections organized to return the country to constitutionality, Ramos Horta liaised with the US non-resident ambassador, Lewis Lukens, to attempt to thwart the involvement of the armed forces in the electoral process by reassuring Indjai that he would be safe from arrest as long as he remained within Guinea-Bissau's borders and kept his troops in their barracks.

The efforts to limit the role of the military in the political process were broadly successful, and in May 2014 José Mario Vaz of the PAIGC was elected as president in polls held by the international community to be credible. His appointment of Domingos Simões Pereira, also of the PAIGC, as prime minister raised the prospect of Guinea-Bissau's international rehabilitation and the revival of donor assistance, notably from the EU (International Crisis Group 2015). On 25 March 2015 a major conference was held in Brussels organized by the EU in conjunction with the UN Development Programme (UNDP) and the Bissau-Guinean government to launch a strategic and organizational ten-year plan called 'Terra Ranka', or New Start, with the EU pledging €1.3bn in support of the programme, whilst the World Bank and UN pledged $250m and $300m respectively. From this budget, $270m has been set aside for SSR, in particular to pay pensions to the 'veterans' cadre in the armed forces.

The perception of a changed relationship between the newly elected government and the senior military command following the DEA sting operation saw its most concrete expression when Vaz, shortly after taking office, felt sufficiently secure to sack Indjai, agreeing to allow him to retire to his personal estate outside Bissau. For Vaz, this was the first step towards streamlining the number of troops in the army from 5,000 to 2,500. Both Vaz and the international community recognize that a sustainable plan to pay pensions to these retirees is essential if this key policy is to succeed. Moreover, there is also a recognition that, as of September 2015, there is a $20m gap in the pension fund.

The Terra Ranka plan reflects a new optimism amongst the international organizations involved in efforts to address Guinea-Bissau's recurring crises. Speaking at the international conference in March, the EU's High Representative Federica Mogherini praised the country's political trajectory since the elections (EU Commission):

> Guinea-Bissau has achieved important progress made over the past year, starting with the peaceful and credible general elections. We want to encourage the positive trends we see and will support the new government in rebuilding the country,

strengthening its democratic institutions and moving towards stability, reconciliation and economic development (EU Commission).

For the UN, Trovoada hailed the elections as 'a crucial milestone in the return to constitutional order (UN Security Council 2015). However, the Secretary-General's special representative tempered his endorsement with a cautionary warning:

> Guinea-Bissau remains at a crossroads ... the potential for relapse into instability and unconstitutionality will remain high as long as the root causes remain unaddressed. Those root causes lie in a complex interrelation of four main factors: political–military dynamics; ineffective State institutions and the absence of rule of law; poverty and lack of access to basic services (in particular for women and young people); and impunity and human rights violations (UN Security Council).

In August 2015, the country's political fragility was, once more, demonstrated by a further crisis, albeit thankfully without apparent military involvement, following the sacking of Pereira by Vaz and the ensuing stand-off between the president and the National Assembly. Warning that the crisis threatened to unravel the Terra Ranka plan, ECOWAS met at an extraordinary summit that extended ECOMIB's mandate in Guinea-Bissau from January to July 2016.

Conclusion

This chapter has examined how the elite bargain between the political and military elites in Guinea-Bissau was breached by the military. Since then the 'military command' has consistently stymied attempts to reform its dysfunctional structures and practices. This rupture was partially instigated, and has certainly been sustained by the illicit activities of South American cocaine traffickers and the potential for senior military officers (and their political and military accomplices) to gather substantial rents in return for allowing the landing, repackaging and export of cocaine from Guinea-Bissau's territory. The chapter has further explored the relationship between the perceived threat posed by cocaine smuggling and the shift to a securitized agenda being adopted by donors and the broader international community.

There is a general disagreement when it comes to the analysis of the current situation in the country. On one side are those who consider Guinea-Bissau's problems discrete and deep-rooted, with trafficking possibly adding to the country's dilemmas, but ultimately a side issue; on the other are those who believe that the opportunity for easy enrichment that the trafficking offers the military—and to a lesser extent political—elite has fatally undermined the existing structure of elite bargains, which have allowed for previous periods of stability. As the former UN Secretary General's special representative José Ramos Horta argued, the term 'narco-state' is not helpful when seeking to find solutions to the country's complex problems. However, the evidence amassed by law enforcement agencies and scholars conclusively points to South American criminals and their associates operating with impunity, paying for this freedom to use Guinea-Bissau as a trans-shipment hub by bribing the senior 'military command' and their political puppets. That this situation was allowed to develop, however, is the result of zero-sum governance stretching back to the early years of independence, compounded by long-standing ineffective state-building programmes from the gamut of international actors. The pivot to a securitization rationale only further provoked resistance to reform from the military elite.

Arguably, a single event, the DEA sting operation against NaTchuto and Indjai, has the potential to recalibrate this analysis significantly. There is evidence that the traffickers have responded to this partially successful law enforcement intervention by moving or expanding their operations elsewhere along the West African coast, in particular penetrating the political and military elite in neighbouring Guinea-Conakry (cf. Introduction by Green, this volume). Even so, the flexibility afforded by the region's porous borders and the traffickers' own adaptable methods would mean that the revitalization of Guinea-Bissau as a trans-shipment hub could be accomplished in short order.

The impact of what was at its height a significant organized criminal enterprise could be argued to have moved Guinea-Bissau into a new phase in its post-independence political evolution. The need to build the state 'from the ground up', as envisioned by Amílcar Cabral, has as a result of these events been confronted by the desire by international actors to resolve the crisis. Yet successive missions from the outside to reform the military have achieved few concrete results, even though it is in securing the country in part through a military with legitimate—and legal—authority that peace can in the long run be built. Whether the window of opportunity opened by the DEA operation can be seized by the country's politicians, especially Vaz, and by the organization best resourced to support reform, the EU, remains to be seen.

10

GUINEA-BISSAU

THE 'NARCO-STATE' AND THE IMPACT ON INSTITUTIONS IN GUINEA-BISSAU AND COUNTRIES IN THE SUB-REGION

Hassoum Ceesay

In the past fifteen years Guinea-Bissau has slid from an epileptic multi-party democracy led by a reluctant democrat into a short but bloody civil war followed by five coups and several improbable attempts to restore democracy and the rule of law (see chapter by Kohl, this volume). Behind this bewildering mixture of political fortunes has been an unholy alliance of a restive military and a corrupt political class whose shenanigans have weakened the state such that by 2005 Guinea-Bissau was said to have become Africa's first 'Colombia'— a narco-state where the drugs trade had thoroughly corrupted the elite and started to raise disquiet among its neighbours. This chapter looks closely both at the question of whether Guinea-Bissau is as such a 'narco-state', and what the impact of these changes has been for both the country itself and the wider sub-region of which it forms a crucial part.

By the time that the international community's attention turned to the country and talk began of Security Sector Reform in around 2005 (see chapters by Kohl and Massey, this volume), by many accounts the country was now only a few steps from becoming a thoroughbred failed state. In the decade since, it has become clear how Guinea-Bissau's unfortunate recent political upheavals have atrophied its basic institutions such as the judiciary, administration and the security sector, while also threatening to engulf its neighbours, especially The Gambia and Senegal.

There has been much talk of the country as a narco-state, but what does this mean? A close analysis is required of what has actually happened in the country and the effects in the sub-region, to understand to what extent the undeniable institutional decay has turned it into a hub for Andean drug kingpins, and how this political crisis has impacted negatively on its international image and basic sovereign institutions. The chapter begins with a study of the existing literatures on Guinea-Bissau, before contextualizing the relationship of the country with its neighbours in the region. I will then explore the question of whether Guinea-Bissau deserves to be called a 'narco-state', and how the crisis has had both a positive and a negative impact on the diplomacy and security of its neighbours, such as Senegal, Guinea-Conakry and The Gambia. In the final section, the impact of these developments on the state in Guinea-Bissau is discussed, and the relationship between state weakness and the emergence of the drugs trade is seen very clearly.

Introduction and literature review

Although a Portuguese-speaking country, Guinea-Bissau has received very wide attention from scholars writing in English since the mid-1960s at the outbreak of the liberation war led by Amílcar Cabral. The first generation of scholars on Guinea-Bissau, such as Davidson (1969, 1981), Chaliand (1969), Rudebeck (1974), Chabal (1983), Urdang (1979), Chilcote (1972) and Lobban (1973), focused on the armed struggle against Portuguese colonial rule.[1] Much of their work was highly apologetic of Cabral's leadership of the PAIGC. Indeed, Davidson and Rudebeck in particular gained notoriety for their unquestioning support of Cabral's leadership and the PAIGC's conduct of the war. Urdang's oft-cited work (1979) on the role of women in the PAIGC ranks also offers much praise for the women heroes of the liberation war, such as Carmen Pereira.

Later scholars such as Dhada (1993), (Forrest 1987) and Lopes (1987b) dared to break this strain and offered a more obvious critical dissection of not

---

[1] Most of these works, especially those of Challiand and Davidson, are based on such reliable first-hand accounts that they qualify to be seen as primary sources.

only the Cabral phenomenon, but also of the 'unilinear process of liberation' which the first generation always portrayed in their studies.[2] Dhada (1993: 209), for example, moaned that almost all of the works by the first-generation scholars were 'hagiographic' and 'teleologic', portraying the PAIGC's war against the Portuguese as a hitch-less ride to nationhood. By the early 2000s a new group of scholars emerged, who were now less tied to nostalgic musings of a faultless Cabral and a scandal-proof liberation army. Vigh (2006) and Bordonaro (2006) examine the impact of state failure in Guinea-Bissau on youth and society as a whole; Green and Thompson (2011) have dissected the symptoms of state failure as evident in the unwillingness and inability of the state leaders to tackle the drugs trafficking and corruption in the country; Temudo (2009) gives a compelling account of the 'Balantasization' of the state during the three-year rule of Kumba Yalá (2000–3) and its negative impact on the Guinea-Bissau body politic; Gable (2009) discusses the coping strategies of the impoverished Bissau-Guinean citizens such as emigrating to Portugal, while Aguilar and Stenman (1997) dissect the causes and symptoms of the economic collapse of the 1990s and its impact on society.

Thus scholarship on Guinea-Bissau has therefore shifted almost 360 degrees: from hagiography, to reluctant criticism, to a ferocious exposure of a failed social, economic and political entity almost unrecognizable from the highly upbeat and positive studies of the first generation of scholars. Yet throughout, the literature has not adequately addressed the role that Guinea-Bissau's neighbours have played in its rise and fall, and how this decline of the Guinea-Bissau state has impacted on its neighbours. Pre-colonial history tells us that Guinea-Bissau and its neighbours were unified politically in important states such as the Mandinga state of Kaabu, which fell in 1867 under an onslaught by the Fula Confederacy (NCAC OA transcribed cassettes: 170, 171 'Kaabu and Fulladu'). However, the economic links continued in the commerce of the itinerant Mandinga traders called the *dyula*, who fostered strong economic bonds among the peoples of the sub-region, and frequently crossed between Guinea-Bissau, Senegal and The Gambia even under colonial rule (Green 2012: 37). Linguistic affinities added to the unity in the neighbourhood as Mandinga, Fula, Floup and Wolof became trans-boundary languages spoken and understood throughout the sub-region (NCAC OA untranscribed cassettes: 57, 130). Nevertheless, almost no scholarship has

---

[2] Mustafah Dhada was among the first scholars to question the PAIGC-centric scholarship on Guinea-Bissau.

explored these pre-colonial ties which bound Guinea-Bissau to its modern neighbours, nor how its present crises have as a consequence affected the sub-region as a whole. This is an important gap which this chapter addresses, showing how the situation in Guinea-Bissau is interlinked with events and concerns in the whole sub-region: for prospects for Guinea-Bissau and in the region as a whole are deeply intertwined, and the emergence of a 'narco-' or failed state in Guinea-Bissau has important implications for its neighbours.

Background to the 1998 implosion

To understand the genesis of the lingering crisis of state in Guinea-Bissau, we must go back to the November 1980 coup against the regime of Luís Cabral. The coup led by Nino Vieira qualifies as one of the most unnecessary and destructive military takeovers in Black Africa. Not only was it untimely, but it was 'racist', separatist, tribalist and driven by greed for power and title.[3] Scholars such as Carolissen-Essack (1980: 2175) have given the economic, social and political background to the coup of 1980, but have always found it extremely hard to justify adequately the intervention by the army (Chabal (1983: 202). Davidson, an apologist of the PAIGC, called it 'counter-revolutionary' and wondered why 'so powerful and popular a figure as Vieira could not have acted through the National Council (the PAIGC's supreme organ), if required, in order to prevent such developments by democratic means'. The coup was the culmination of a powerful struggle between Vieira and Luís Cabral which, according to Joshua Forrest (1987: 103), started in 1979 when

---

[3] The 'racist' anti-Cape Verdean hue of the coup was explicit in the fact that the coup leader himself in his pronouncements stated that 'the people of Guinea-Bissau are shaking off the domination of the Capeverdeans...' and the fact that the Revolutionary Council which Major Vieira formed soon after the coup did not include a single Cape Verdean. Moreover, Antonio Buscardini, Cabral's Minister of National Security, was one of the few senior government officials who was killed by the coupists. He was of Cape Verdean origins. Forrest (1987: 100) also highlighted the racist and tribalist colour of the coup. He explained that 'President Luiz Cabral lacked a trustworthy base of personal support in either the army or among the peasants; [he] relied heavily on his Cape Verdean colleagues in both the Party and Government', implying therefore that the coupists' fear of Cape Verdean domination was genuine. Vieira's appointment of Victor Saude Maria, noted for his tribalist inclinations, as vice president in the aftermath of the coup also lent credence to the ethnic factor in the coup.

'the two leaders became increasingly hostile towards and at war with one another'.[4] Indeed, the twelve months preceding the coup witnessed a near static state as the major institutions of state, such as the army, civil service and professional classes, took sides in this power struggle, leading to a paralysis which was a foretaste of the current institutional failure in Guinea-Bissau. Fearful of losing his powers and prestige, Vieira resorted to his constituency, the army, and deposed Cabral on 14 November 1980. According to Munslow (1981: 111) the coup was therefore a survival tactic by Vieira and his militaristic and anti-Cape Verdean cohort in the Guinea-Bissau army eager to protect their 'corporate self interest'. However, even more relevant to this study are the immediate and long-term impacts of the coup on the Guinea-Bissau body politic.

The coup led to the split of the PAIGC, as the Cape Verdeans sensed that it was partly directed against them. They formed their own party for Cape Verde, the PAICV, in 1981. The mass departure of Cape Verdean professionals from Guinea-Bissau in the aftermath of the coup deprived the young country of much-needed talent. Moreover, the coup marked the beginning of the militarization of the Guinea-Bissau state with the integration of what Forrest (1987: 105) called 'the peasant backed military into the central decision-making political bodies' of Guinea-Bissau.[5] This was manifested in the entry into the cabinet of army leaders such as Iafai Camara, Paulo Correia and Benghate Na Beate between 1981 and 1985. Yet the cake of patronage could not go round the barracks, such that by 1983 strong disaffection was pervading certain sections of the military which felt left out of promotions or fat jobs. Army disquiet continued to inspire numerous attempted coups in 1982, 1983 and 1985, weakening not only the personal rule of Vieira but also the institutions of the army itself.

Vieira's coup also had negative economic implications for Guinea-Bissau which spiralled into a near collapse of the economy in the early 1990s. From independence to 1980, Cabral had toyed with a centrally planned economy. Indeed, for a brief period in the 1970s scholars such as Galli and Jones (1987: 1) and Rudebeck (1984: 1) held that Guinea-Bissau stood on the cusp of becoming

---

[4] Indeed, when Prime Minister Francisco Mendes (Chico Tie) died in an automobile accident in July 1978, Cabral refused to appoint Vieira to the post immediately; instead he asked Constantino Texeira to act as prime minister for three months before Vieira was given the post, most likely very reluctantly.

[5] It should be noted that until 1979 the Guinea-Bissau army did not have ranks.

'a model for both economic and political development in the African context'.[6] This misplaced optimism was based on the fact that the PAIGC was a peasant-centric liberation movement which sought to canalize the resources of the rural areas and peasant labour to increase agricultural output. Sadly, according to Chabal (1983: 204–5), this sanguine forecast dissolved like salt in water by 1977, due to a cocktail of factors such as drought, poor government produce marketing strategies, urbanization and an inchoate industrialization drive.[7] By 1980, the liberation war watchwords of rural animation and development had been consigned to the trash bins as Bissau, the capital, now devoured the bulk of investment in the productive sectors.[8]

Thus Vieira made an early move towards a more diversified, market-based economy, resumed links with the Bretton Woods institutions and started an Economic Recovery Programme in 1983 to help turn around the stagnant economy (Aguilar and Stenman 1997: 74).[9] With the peso currency devalued and a state privatization body established, the move towards a liberal economy seemed well poised to succeed. However, weak capacity, hesitant privatization of money-losing state enterprises, corruption and graft further weakened the economy, such that by the early 1990s Guinea-Bissau was almost bankrupt.

A weak economy no longer able to take care of the vast network of patronage which helped the regime to cling to power forced Vieira to become a reluctant democrat with multi-party elections in 1994. Rudebeck (1996, 1997: 1) has ably charted the bumpy and hesitant democratic dispensation under Vieira between 1994 and the outbreak of the civil war in 1998. What is clear from his pithy analysis is that this brief phase of multi-party democracy did not pay many dividends to the ordinary people of Guinea-Bissau, who remained mired in poverty. Meanwhile the government 'lacked the internal finance' to run the state. Add an arrogant, despotic and quasi-military leader to this, and the stage was set for an implosion of state. As Kohl's chapter in this

---

[6] These scholars gave a very Marxist-oriented interpretation of the Bissau-Guinean economy and development efforts.

[7] Rapid urbanization in the 1970s was caused by an influx of internally displaced persons fleeing the war in the interior, and demobilized fighters seeking petty jobs in Bissau after the war.

[8] A famous, if not notorious, example of 'grandiose' white elephant industries undertaken by the Cabral regime was the Citroën car assembly plant in Bissau, which produced cars that only a few people could afford.

[9] At this time also, neighbours such as The Gambia had embraced the IMF structural and economic recovery programmes to rescue their lethargic economies.

volume so ably demonstrates, the crises of 1998 helped to put Guinea-Bissau firmly on the route to state decay and becoming a haven for Andean drug cartels which have earned it the sobriquet of a 'narco-state'.

Dateline: Bissau, 7 June 1998, civil war breaks out

On the morning of 7 June 1998, the capital Bissau awoke to the sound of heavy gunfire exploding from a military camp on the north-eastern side of the city (Rudebeck 1998: 484). A section of the army loyal to General Ansumane Mané had rebelled against the regime of Vieira, who in a radio broadcast later that day accused General Mané of an attempted coup. A few hours later General Mané announced the removal of the Vieira regime and the formation of a military junta. The battle went beyond claims and counter-claims. The people of Guinea-Bissau were to suffer an eleven-month armed conflict which destroyed the basic infrastructure and killed many people (see Kohl, this volume)

The media of Guinea-Bissau's neighbours, such as The Gambia, Senegal and Guinea-Conakry, gave the war thorough coverage from its onset to its end, thanks to the newly liberalized airwaves. Local private FM radio stations and independent newspapers gave full coverage to the war, broadcasting to these countries regular updates on its progress.[10] The accessibility of the war made it a topical issue in the sub-region, such that the progress and defeat of the warring factions and the details of halting peace talks were well known to the public. The saturated local media coverage of the conflict helped to galvanize interest and concern across the political leaders, civil society and ordinary people, such that the conflict in Guinea-Bissau became catapulted to centre stage in the discourse about the future of the sub-region.

Scholars such as Massey (2004: 76), Rudebeck (1998: 484) and Sonko (2004: 32) have outlined the background to the conflict and agree that the separatist rebellion led by the MFDC (Mouvement des forces démocratiques de Casamance) the Senegalese province of Casamance was the cause of the personal conflict between President Vieira and General Mané. Massey, for example, describes how an arms shipment from the Guinea-Bissau army,

---

[10] For instance, the newly established Gambia Television regularly sent reporters to Bissau to cover the fighting; the *Daily Observer* newspaper in Banjul also published regular on-the-spot reports of the fighting. The newly established *Sud FM* private radio in Senegal had a team of reporters in Bissau who filed regular reports in French and Wolof.

seized en route to the MFDC separatists, led to a parliamentary inquiry by the Guinea-Bissau legislature. President Vieira heaped blame on General Mané for the arms shipment, which the general denied, in turn blaming Vieira. Vieira acted fast and suspended General Mané; then, even before the parliamentary probe findings were made public, Vieira attempted to dismiss the general, who refused to be made a scapegoat and revolted.

It is noteworthy that this scene playing in Bissau was eerily similar to the one that unfolded in 1980 between Cabral and Vieira. Sonko categorically ascribed the 1998 events to the Casamance arms saga, calling it 'the key reason' for the conflict. The agreement among scholars is therefore that a sub-regional issue, the Casamance conflict, led to a local quarrel, which led to a full-blown war. Meanwhile, even if the fighting was local and confined to Bissau, the conflict became 'immediately regionalized' as 1,200 soldiers from Senegal and 400 troops from Guinea-Conakry entered the war (Rudebeck 2001: 23). Both Senegal and Guinea-Conakry justified their intervention through a defence pact signed with Guinea-Bissau years earlier.[11]

Senegal was severely affected by its intervention in Bissau. Firstly, the high casualties among its soldiers led to a groundswell of opposition to the intervention at home. Indeed, the Diouf government entered the fray only a few days after the results of the parliamentary elections were announced, which gave the opposition forty-seven out of the 140 seats with nine opposition parties represented in the legislature (Ndao 2003: 519). This was the weakest electoral performance of the ruling Parti Socialiste since it came to power in 1960. The strong opposition showing made critics wonder whether in fact President Diouf had the mandate to intervene in Guinea-Bissau (Ndao 2003: 32). Civil society groups started to question the intervention and put pressure on Diouf, with the opposition freshly motivated by its strong showing in the legislative polls and the general public irked by the high casualty of Senegalese soldiers in Bissau, as revealed in the daily bulletins by private FM radio. The intervention continued to give the opposition much ammunition until the February 2000 elections, which Diouf lost. But why did Senegal take the military and not the political option in the Guinea-Bissau conflict?

The current literature points to issues such as the military pact with Guinea-Bissau, and the estimation by Senegal that intervention would work towards 'imposing peace' in the restive Casamance (Massey 2004: 78;

---

[11] For Senegal's justification of intervention, see speech by Jacques Baudin, Foreign Minister, quoted in Massey, above.

Rudebeck 1998: 486). It should be noted, however, that Senegal had had a penchant for military intervention in its neighbourhood since 1980 when it sent troops to Banjul to avert a possible coup against President Sir Dawda Jawara.[12] When the coup materialized in July 1981, Senegal restored President Jawara to power after sending troops to Banjul to quell the rebellion led by Kukoi Samba Sanyang. The intervention saved Sir Dawda's regime, and in return he agreed to the short-lived Senegambia Confederation of 1982–9.

The question could therefore be posed: was Diouf's intervention in Guinea-Bissau in 1998 meant to prop up Vieira in return for concessions of political, military and/or economic nature from Guinea-Bissau, à la Gambia 1981? Scholars have not yet started to explore this theory as a possible reason for the ill-fated Senegalese intervention;[13] but certainly, Senegal's self-image as the 'elder brother' of the region related to the way in which it intervened both in The Gambia in 1981 and in Guinea-Bissau in 1998.

Enter The Gambia

While Senegal opted for the military approach, The Gambia, another neighbour of Guinea-Bissau, took the diplomatic route to end the conflict. The Guinea-Bissau conflict brought about the most ambitious mediation role by The Gambia since its independence in 1965.[14]

The Gambia's foreign policy since independence was based on three primary objectives: 'to strengthen security, promote economic development, and boost national prestige' (Touray 1995: 16). Its mediating role in the Guinea-Bissau crises should be seen through these theoretical lenses.

The inspiration for foreign policy and diplomatic initiative is often the leader. Barely a week after the start of hostilities, Gambian president Yahya A. J. J. Jammeh embarked on shuttle diplomacy to Cape Verde, Guinea-

---

[12] This was the Operation Foday Kabba launched in November 1980 to avert a rumoured coup against the government of President Jawara in the aftermath of the assassination of his Paramilitary Commander Eku Mahoney.

[13] The Senegal intervention was by all accounts ill-fated. Besides the heavy casualties it suffered, the Senegalese army was also blamed for numerous violations, including looting and destruction of heritage sites like the Bissau museum and the archives of the INEP (National Research Institute).

[14] Under President Jawara, The Gambia mediated in the intense Senegal–Guinea-Conakry impasse in the mid-1970s, and in 1990 The Gambia hosted numerous mediation efforts on the Liberian Civil War under the aegis of ECOWAS.

Conakry, Senegal and Mauritania 'in order to canvass regional opinion on the conflict' (Massey 2004: 86). When he returned, he sent his foreign minister, Dr Sedat Jobe, to Bissau to meet General Mané. It was clear from the start that The Gambia was ready to mediate fully in the conflict. However, before we delve further into The Gambia's mediation role and how this impacted on Gambian diplomatic standing in the sub-region and local politics, it is important to digress briefly into the diplomatic relations between The Gambia and Guinea-Bissau.

At the time of The Gambia's attainment of nationhood in 1965, 'Portuguese' Guinea was still in the early stages of liberation. With the attainment of Gambian independence, the PAIGC was further boosted, as a newly independent neighbour emerged as an ally.

The Gambia had critical strategic importance to the PAIGC fighters as a transit point for officials and supplies, and it was a major destination for fleeing civilians and recuperating fighters. As early as March 1966, Chaliand (1969: 29) wrote about a journey he and PAIGC cadres led by Amílcar Cabral made from Dakar into the liberated areas of Guinea-Bissau, passing through Gambian territory. Gambian authorities allowed such movements of PAIGC members and officials, and Cabral's cadres also stocked up on supplies of food and basic necessities while passing through Gambian territory. This was in fact the continuity of a long-standing connection between the two countries, as from the 1930s onwards a huge wave of Manjakos had migrated to The Gambia as 'stranger farmers' and were an important source of labour for groundnut cultivation in the country.[15] The brutalities of the Portuguese colonialists had accentuated this exodus, and then as the war escalated in 1970–3, The Gambia received hundreds of Bissau-Guinean refugees. Indeed, so big and consistent were these migrations that the Manjako now form over 3 per cent of the Gambian population, and constitute the majority in many settlements in the Kombo districts, such as Kombo South, Kombo East and Kombo North.[16]

Meanwhile, The Gambia was a regular and consistent contributor to the OAU (Organization of African Unity) liberation fund, which gave material and financial support to African liberation organizations like the PAIGC. The Fund supported the building of the major PAIGC Solidarity Hospital in

---

[15] For a much cited study on the 'stranger farmers' phenomenon in The Gambia, see Swindell (1978: 3–17).

[16] Major Manjako settlements are found in Tanji, Tujereng, Kitty, and Kartong villages in Kombo South district.

Boke, Guinea-Conakry, in addition to offering military training and hardware to the guerrillas. In June 1972, Jawara met Amílcar Cabral for the first time at the OAU summit in Rabat and reiterated The Gambia's unflinching support for the liberation war; he also supported the OAU's move at Rabat to increase its contribution to the PAIGC by 50% (Dhada 1993: 194).

The Gambia was one of the first countries to give diplomatic recognition to Guinea-Bissau soon after it declared independence in September 1973. Gambia's High Commissioner to Dakar, Sam Sarr, was duly accredited to Bissau and he presented his letters of credence to Luís Cabral in April 1974, deep inside the liberated zone. The PAIGC had earlier also opened a mission in Banjul led by Yaya Kote, and the operating cost of the mission was paid for by the Gambian government. In January 1974, the PAIGC foreign minister, Victor Saude Maria, paid a 'goodwill mission' to The Gambia and was feted by Sir Dawda and other senior Gambian officials, while he extolled the solidarity of The Gambia with the liberation movement.[17]

Soon after Guinea-Bissau's independence was recognized by Portugal, President Jawara visited Bissau and Luís Cabral paid a state visit to Banjul in 1976. These presidential visits heralded a series of ministerial cooperation agreements in agriculture, animal husbandry and forestry between Bissau and Banjul in 1977 and 1978.[18]

However, the 1981 attempted coup in Banjul led to a severe strain on relations between Bissau and Banjul. Firstly, the rebels in Banjul publicly called upon the new Bissau authorities for help to fight the interventionist Senegalese forces sent by President Diouf, and Bissau was too slow to disown the rebels' pronouncements. This must have caused some unease in Banjul. Also, the escaping rebels landed in Guinea-Bissau and when Bissau refused to extradite them to face justice in The Gambia, relations soured further.[19] Even the intervention of a high-powered delegation from The Gambia could not convince the Bissau authorities to hand over the thirteen Gambian fugitives, who included the rebel leader Kukoi Samba Sanyang. Bissau instead facilitated

[17] See 'Guinea-Bissau PM Calls Here', *Gambia News Bulletin*, 8 January 1974, p. 1.
[18] See 'Banjul–Bissau Links Strengthened', *Gambia News Bulletin*, 10 March 1976.
[19] It is suspected by this author, after speaking to many players in this saga, that Jawara did not push for an extradition of the rebels as he was not prepared to have them summarily executed—which many in his cabinet and party ranks were clamouring for in the heated aftermath of the bloody insurrection. Instead, he prevailed on Bissau to expel the rebels to a safe, distant country from which they would not be able to operate.

the rebels' move to a third country, Cuba. This incident left a deep dent in Bissau–Banjul relations, which only healed fully in the mid-1990s when the first Gambian Mission was opened in Bissau.

It is also important to note that at the time of the Gambia's mediation in the Guinea-Bissau conflict in the late 1990s, President Jammeh was already hosting peace talks between the Senegal government and the MFDC rebels in Banjul.[20] Another milestone in Gambian diplomacy at this time was Banjul's occupancy of one of the non-permanent member seats at the UN Security Council from 1998 to 2000. A third important factor in Gambian diplomacy at this time was the personality of its foreign minister, Dr Sedat Jobe, a highly seasoned diplomat and Francophile, who had studied and worked in France, Senegal and in the UN system and therefore had a solid knowledge of France's links with Africa, and strong contacts in the Senegal government.[21] The Gambian president, for his part, had established a solid relationship with both Vieira and General Mané.[22]

The ground was therefore fully set for The Gambia to mediate meaningfully in the crises. Jammeh's whirlwind regional trip and his influence in bringing the two warring parties to the negotiating table should be seen within a wider context, however. Firstly, it followed a failed attempt at local negotiations by Guinea-Bissau's opposition parliamentary group, and the drawing up of contingency plans by Portugal and the USA to evacuate their nationals from Bissau.[23] Thus it was becoming increasingly clear to national and international observers that the hostilities were growing out of control. Secondly, President Vieira was also becoming increasingly stubborn and unyielding as he flatly refused to enter into any negotiations on the conflict.[24] It was obvious that Vieira still believed that the intervention forces from Senegal and Guinea-Conakry would be able to prop up his tottering regime.

---

[20] These talks resulted in a highly publicized but ill-fated Banjul Agreement signed by the MFDC and Dakar in January 1999.

[21] For example, the Sorbonne-trained linguist taught many senior officials in the Senegal government at Dakar University in the 1970s, and was a classmate to many more in Paris in the 1960s.

[22] General Mané was born in the Gambian town of Sukuta, 17 km outside Banjul, of Mandinga parentage. He was among the Gambian youths who crossed the border in the mid-1960s to join the PAIGC fighters. His two-storey house, where he reportedly planned to retire, still stands outside the town.

[23] See 'Mediation Efforts in Bissau', *Daily Observer* (Banjul), 11 June 1998, p. 5.

[24] President Vieira is quoted in the *Daily Observer* (Banjul), 12–14 June 1998, p. 5.

It was this deadlock and intransigence that Jammeh succeeded in breaking through when he got Vieira and General Mané to agree to enter into negotiations. The Gambian president's trump card was his 'close relationship' with both the coup leader and the embattled Vieira.[25] This is in fact why Gambian officials described Jammeh's peace efforts as 'personal'.[26]

But personal contacts aside, Jammeh seemed to have benefited also from the fact that since Guinea-Bissau's two other immediate neighbours were already knee-deep into the crisis, fighting on the side of the despised Vieira, they were therefore neither neutral nor impartial. The Gambia was the obvious acceptable interlocutor in any peace negotiations.[27] The sheer scale of the humanitarian crisis generated by a few days' fighting must also have informed the Gambian resolve to end the crisis through negotiations.[28] It has to be stated that The Gambia also had national interests to protect because thousands of Gambian nationals were trapped in Bissau and rural towns such as Mansoa, most of them engaged in the retail trade and cashew nut production. Their welfare was indeed a preoccupation to Banjul. The re-export trade, which accounts for a sizable chunk of the Gambian GDP, was severely affected by the fighting, as goods could not enter Guinea-Bissau from Banjul.[29] Furthermore, the ethnic, linguistic

[25] See 'Vieira And Mane [*sic*] Accept Jammeh's Offer', *Daily Observer* (Banjul), 16 June 1998, p. 1.

[26] See 'Guinea-Bissau Mediation Efforts Still Holding', *Daily Observer* (Banjul), 30 June 1998, p. 1.

[27] Contrary to some reports, The Gambia was indeed both impartial and neutral. The Gambian leader had developed solid personal relations with the two antagonists in the crisis, which precluded him taking either side. At the same time, The Gambia at this time enjoyed cordial relations with both Guinea-Conakry and Senegal, which is why the Gambian foreign minister Dr Sedat Jobe told the press in Banjul that Senegal and Guinea-Conakry intervened only because they were honouring defence agreements they had with Guinea-Bissau: 'There was no point [during Jammeh's sub-regional shuttle diplomacy in the weekend of 12–13 June 1998] where any of them [Presidents Diouf and Conte] mentioned preference for further military actions'; *Daily Observer* (Banjul), 16 June 1998, p. 2. Moreover, at the end of June rumours were rife in Banjul of the presence of General Mané's men and Vieira himself in Gambian territory pointing to the proximity of both men to Jammeh.

[28] Reports in the Banjul press highlighted that on the first day of fighting thirty people died, and on the third day of fighting 200 people drowned while travelling in an overloaded canoe out of Bissau (*Daily Observer*, op. cit.).

[29] In June alone over 90 tons of goods destined for Guinea-Bissau from Banjul were turned back at the border; *Daily Observer* (Banjul), 15 July 1998, p. 1.

and historic ties between the two countries made it almost inevitable that The Gambia should intervene to end the crisis.[30]

The Gambian mediations led by Dr Sedat Jobe operated under very dangerous conditions. Jobe had to travel by boat to reach the Guinea-Bissau coast as the airspace was closed to all air traffic.[31] He could not land his boat and worked from a French naval ship moored off the coast to evacuate French nationals. His task was described as 'not easy' as heavy fighting was raging in the city.

However, one immediate result of the peace mission was that it secured a ceasefire for the first time since fighting had broken out three weeks earlier. Soon after the ceasefire came into force, multiple negotiations started and culminated in Praia, Cape Verde, where the regional grouping ECOWAS and the lusophone CPLP were able to secure a formal ceasefire in July.[32] In November, the ceasefire was signed in Abuja, Nigeria. The agreement provided for a national unity government, and a peace-monitoring force was authorized by the UN Security Council.[33]

Hence as the foregoing sections clearly show, there had been a long-standing political interconnection at the highest level between events in Guinea-Bissau and those in the wider sub-region. As the last country in the region to achieve independence—and that only after a protracted guerrilla war—political conditions in Guinea-Bissau had always been of the deepest concern and importance to neighbouring countries. This may indeed explain why they were all so keen to intervene following the 1998 *coup d'état*. However, while

---

[30] Important personalities in the Gambian state machinery have Bissau-Guinean roots, including those of the Manjako, Balanta and Mandinga ethnic groups.

[31] The Gambian delegation also included senior security officials: Samba Bah, head of national intelligence; Sankung Badgie, Deputy Head of Police; and Colonel Momodou Badgie of the Gambia National Army—an indication of the desire to get a clear assessment of the security situation in Guinea-Bissau prior to negotiations. They were reportedly in the presidential office in Bissau talking to Vieira's men when it was bombarded by General Mané, forcing the Gambian delegation to retire to the boat; *Daily Observer* (Banjul), 16 June 1998.

[32] Indeed, The Gambia's initial peace overtures opened a Pandora's box of mediation efforts from Portugal, Angola, ECOWAS and the Vatican; Banjul was sanguine that this multiplication of peace initiatives would 'gradually rally round the common interest of a recognition of a ceasefire and a start of dialogue'; *Daily Observer* (Banjul), 30 June 1998, p. 2.

[33] The force deployment was delayed in February as new fighting broke out again in Bissau.

Jammeh's intervention was of short-lived success, the subsequent fifteen years plunged the country into further turmoil and had even greater ramifications for the region as a whole.

Guinea-Bissau's drugs overspill into the sub-region

During the first decade of the 2000s, much evidence suggests that Guinea-Bissau became the place of choice in West Africa for narco-traffickers to set up camp, because of a combination of ecological, political and social factors. Indeed, a close analysis of these factors problematizes the idea that it is the rise of the drugs trade that has turned Guinea-Bissau into a failed 'narco-state'; on the contrary, it was the growing fragility of the state in Guinea-Bissau which made it the ideal hunting ground for drug traffickers, a fragility which their presence has since exacerbated.

Bordanaro (2006: 9) clearly explains the geographical isolation of, for example, the Bijagós archipelago from the rest of the country, which helped make it perfect terrain for landing strips to which the Andean drugs lords could direct their drugs-laden aircraft. This was a legacy in part of the anti-colonial war, when many landing strips were built by both the Portuguese and the Bissau-Guinean rebels over the course of the protracted conflict, some of which were redeployed by the traffickers. With over fifty islands, most of them uninhabited or sparsely inhabited, the Bijagós were the perfect location for drugs operations. It is even reported that Colombian drug cartels have had the temerity to rent or purchase some of these far-flung isles for their activities.

The isolation of these islands means that government authority has always been thin or absent there, in fact appearing to be on permanent holiday from the area. During the 2000s, this offered a conducive environment for drugs to be flown into the country. The absence of the state is explained by the collapse of law and order since the 1998–9 civil war. The divided army and a series of unstable governments, in addition to the weak judiciary, created a huge gap in the public security sector which the narco-traffickers exploited to the fullest (see the evidence in Kohl's chapter, this volume). Bordanaro also describes how these isles shelter groups of highly dispossessed and frustrated youths who feel let down by the state and oppressed by patriarchal culture (ibid.: 60), with a deep sense of 'marginality', easily becoming a link in the drugs chain (ibid.: 31). The constant erosion of state institutions since 1998 was therefore a key factor in accentuating this sense of marginalization, and it created a fertile terrain where the traffickers could take advantage.

The narco-surge in Guinea Bissau appears to have occurred between 2006 and 2008, paradoxically when civilian rule had been restored under Nino Vieira. However, as Kohl's chapter shows in this volume, this development coincided with rumours during the 2005 elections that Vieira had powerful backers who would help him to disburse significant sums of money to his supporters.

The 2006–8 period was marked by record seizures of hard drugs from Andean drugs cartels. UN estimates have since then shown a drop in major seizures, although as O'Regan (2014) argues, this may be misleading: it could be a reflection of 'advancement in the techniques of local groups and their more thorough co-option of key organs of the state' rather than a genuine fall in traffic. This spike in the drugs trade during the civilian rule of Vieira also questions the popular notion that democratic rule offers a solution to the drugs issue in the country; indeed, in this sense, the emergence of the drugs trade in Guinea-Bissau in this period follows closely the pattern of neo-patrimonialism as analysed by Chabal and Daloz in *Africa Works* (Chabal and Daloz 1999). In this analysis, democracy and illicit trade are by no means incompatible.

The rise in drugs seizures in this period prompted much discussion as to whether Guinea-Bissau indeed fitted the sobriquet 'narco-state' or not. Horta (2007) gave a definitive answer that indeed the country was a narco-state; yet by 2014, O'Regan (2014) was not so sure whether Guinea-Bissau still deserved the ignominious title. What is certain is that in the mid, to late 2000s, drugs cartels had control over parts of the territory of the country, mainly some islands; violated its airspace with their nocturnal flights laden with hard drugs; and compromised parts of the security sector, including the highly trained and professional judicial police. This is evidenced by the fact that the army commander at the time is now on trial in the US for drugs offences, and by the fact that evidence related to his trial implicates the highest levels of the Bissau-Guinean government (see chapters by Kohl and Massey, this volume). It can therefore be said that while the narco-traffickers did not seize power, they were indeed extremely close to the centre of power; and while drugs did not run the country, traffickers took advantage of the state's inherent weakness and exacerbated it by their presence.

For her neighbours, this uncertainty in appellation is nothing but academic, as they have all become affected by the narco-surge in Guinea-Bissau. While Bissau is no longer the chief focus, the long period of time when it predominated has had an effect on the region as a whole. To the south, Guinea-Conakry has seen an overspill of narco-trafficking. As recently as June 2015, a ship laden with drugs was seized near Conakry, and several high-ranking officers are under investigation.[34] Recent news reports indicate that Guinea-Conakry is now a drugs 'hotspot'. This is the culmination of growing interest by traffickers in the country since 2009, when a son of the former dictator Lasana Conte was arrested briefly and confessed to having received kickbacks from drug kingpins to 'secure clearance for planes laden with cocaine'.[35]

It is worth comparing here the experiences of these two neighbours, and to ask whether Guinea-Bissau's drugs problem has indeed spilled over into her neighbours' terrain. In both cases, the pre-existing fragility of the state appears to be a prerequisite for the embedding of narco networks. Guinea-Conakry, like Bissau, is undergoing severe political and economic instability, which offers the right conditions for drug traffickers to thrive. It has seen periodic coups, very rapid inflation, and most recently the outbreak of the Ebola virus. Just as in Bissau, there is a widespread belief among Western diplomats that the traffickers have used the unstable political climate to buy the complicity of senior government officials. Thus one can say that the initial problem in both countries and their states is not the question of drugs, but the weakness of state institutions.

Thus even if Guinea-Bissau becomes less important as a drugs hub, this is hardly good news as the cartels may have moved on to new territories. It is worth noting, moreover, that problems are not limited to Guinea-Conakry. Senegal shares a porous border with Guinea-Bissau, much of which is a contested zone between the MFDC separatists and the government. The Casamance region has seen a surge in drugs seizures in the past few years, while there have been reports of MFDC rebels coming to trade drugs at weekly *lumo* markets in Bissau. It is likely that Casamance may offer a transshipment route for the onward trade of cocaine to Europe, but the onward routes from this point remain largely unclear.

As a consequence of these developments, countries in the region such as The Gambia have had to adopt extremely stiff penalties against convicted drug traffickers. In 2010, the Gambian government introduced the death penalty for convicted drug traffickers caught with more than 250 grams of cocaine or heroin. Although seen at the time as high-handed, especially by human rights groups, it received support from both government and opposition MPs, a

[34] See 'Guinea Seizes Gambia Bound Cocaine', *Kairo News*, 6 June 2015, www.kaironews.com.

[35] Lewis, David, 'Surge in cocaine trade undermines Conde's bid to revive Guinea', 31 January 2014, http://www.reuters.com/article/2014/01/31/us-guinea-drugs-insight-idUSBREA0U0EG20140131, accessed 4 February 2016.

measure of the heightened awareness of the drugs menace in the sub-region. The government was pre-empting the proliferation of Andean drug cartels into the country. Efforts have been made to make legislation respond to the dynamics of drugs proliferation in the region. Novak (2012: 63) has highlighted that 'The Gambian legislation instituting the death penalty for drug trafficking was one of a host of legal and policy reforms around the African continent that establish heightened penalties for drug trafficking.' Besides the country-level actions, the pan-continental organization, the African Union, also had its Conference of Ministers for Drug Control and Crime Prevention meet from 28 September to 2 October 2010 in Addis Ababa, Ethiopia, to discuss ways of fighting the drugs trade (ibid.: 63).

In 2012, the Gambian law was repealed, partly as a result of the drop in reported cases of drugs seizures in Guinea-Bissau. Yet Senegal, The Gambia and Mali are among countries in the sub-region which have not let their guard down just yet; all of them have signed agreements to strengthen cooperation with Russia in the fight against drug trafficking. Russia has seized on the notoriety the region is gaining for the drugs trade as a means to strengthen its diplomatic presence through the holding of regular Moscow–Africa anti-drug meetings. The last was held in Banjul in July 2015, attended by ten African countries.[36] The Guinea-Bissau reputation for drugs has therefore caused concern far and wide and has attracted new diplomatic incursions into the sub-region.

O'Regan (2014) has observed that 'drug trafficking, if it is to be analyzed properly, must be treated as a regional rather than national-level phenomenon'. This applies to the countries neighbouring Guinea-Bissau because of porous borders, inadequate enforcement measures and personnel, and the fact that traffickers in the region rarely operate in just one country but spread their business across multiple states. There are large formal and even bigger informal trade and business links between Guinea-Bissau and the countries in the sub-region, such that one investor in Bissau may also be investing in Dakar and Conakry. Such multiplicity of business presence could well be exploited by the cartels to set up shop all over the region. One Achilles heel used by the cartels is the weekly markets, called *lumo*, common in the sub-region, some of which attract traders from four to five countries weekly.[37]

---

[36] See 'Banjul hosts Russia-Africa anti-drug confab', *Standard* (Banjul), 29 July 2015, www.standard.gm.

[37] The Jawbeh *lumo* in eastern Senegal, for example, was banned for weeks in 2014 at

In sum, the region's historical, cultural, economic and political characteristics have lent themselves to the spread of the crisis across the sub-region. While it was Guinea-Bissau that was given the sobriquet of a 'narco-state', the drugs trade has affected every country in the region in one way or another. Drugs have not caused the weakening of the state, but have exacerbated an existing condition: they are, really, a symptom of the fragility of the post-colonial state in much of Africa, and of the urgency of addressing this issue through a more equitable distribution of resources in the region.

Crisis-beaten state machinery

Having seen how the civil conflict has impacted on diplomatic ties between Guinea-Bissau and its neighbours, and how it has created the right conditions for the country to become a choice hub for drugs cartels, it is now pertinent to assess how fifteen years of instability have helped to damage state institutions in Guinea-Bissau, almost beyond repair.

In order to understand this question, it is necessary to consider the role of Kumba Yalá. The December 1999 elections brought Kumba Yalá to power, with the hope that Guinea-Bissau was leaving behind it almost two years of political instability and economic meltdown. Yalá's government was expected to embark on efforts to demilitarize, disarm and demobilize the hundreds of armed youth who had fought on either side of the civil war. Yet the government proved unable to make any tangible efforts. Instead, it busied itself more in 'consumption than construction' (Vigh 2006: 6). Above all, Yalá started a calculated ethnicization of the key institution of state: he started to appoint people from his own ethnic group into positions of responsibility, especially in the army.[38] Indeed, Temudo (2009: 17) aptly states that the institutional crisis worsened during the Yalá presidency:

> The political elites take on multiple identities and shifting allegiances and it tries to instrumentalize ethnic and religious differences... The few resources in the country (fish, bauxite and timber) are being sold for the benefit of the few at the expense of

---

the height of the Ebola crisis as it was seen as a possible conduit for the disease, since it brought together on a weekly basis traders from The Gambia, Senegal, Guinea-Conakry and Bissau. For more on the nature and structure of the weekly markets, see Sanneh, P. Sarjo, 2009.

[38] This was one factor which brought Yalá into open confrontation with General Mané in November 2000, which resulted in the general's death.

the population, which remains impoverished. Kumba Yalá, a highly learned politician, led one of the most instable and corrupt periods in the country's history.[39]

The admixture of graft and nepotism further weakened the state institutions, such that by the time of Yalá's overthrow in late 2003, Guinea-Bissau was close to becoming a failed state (Di John 2011: 1).[40] The political intolerance which went with this erosion of institutions affected the media and civil service. Under Yalá, for example, even journalists in the government-owned radio and TV were harassed with dismissals for simply reporting on activities of the opposition.[41] Under subsequent regimes, media houses were frequently attacked and journalists beaten up by soldiers and thugs under the pay of aggrieved politicians.[42] National TV, created in 1988 and seen at the time as a symbol of Guinea-Bissau's steady progress, has been on and off air for many years since 2008, unable to pay its workers and beset by frequent power outages due to the collapse of the national power grid.

The failures in state institutions in Guinea-Bissau since 1998 remain pervasive and profound. All sectors of the state are in an advanced form of decay, with the war 'almost completely destroying existing infrastructures' (Bordonaro 2006: 206). Bordonaro (ibid.) relates how the civil administration on Bubaque Island ground to a halt as the service became dogged by disputes between cadres of the former ruling PAIGC and the newly elected PRS of Kumba Yalá. Even state officials who survived the struggle had to contend with starvation salaries, which went unpaid for several months. The hospitals existed in structure only, with no drugs, nurses or doctors; usually unpaid, the latter stayed at home or sold the few supplies available on the black market.[43]

---

[39] Vigh, for example, quotes an IMF report which accused the Yalá regime of spending US$1.5m in 'travel expenses' within eight months of its assumption of power.

[40] In my estimation, Guinea-Bissau does meet Zartman's (1995) thesis that state failure occurs 'when the basic functions of the state are no longer performed, as well as referring to a situation where the structure, authority (legitimate power), law, and political order have fallen apart'.

[41] In March 2003, the director of news at the Guinea-Bissau national radio Ensa Seidi was removed for reporting the arrival from exile of former prime minister turned opposition Francisco Fadul. See 'Guinea Bissau: Editor of State radio suspended', *IRIN News*, 13 March 2003, http://www.irinnews.org/report/142067/guinea-bissau-editor-of-state-radio-suspended, accessed 4 April 2014.

[42] See 'Guinea Bissau: Attacks on the media', *Media Alert West Africa* (2006: 30).

[43] In May 2014, the Guinea-Bissau union of civil servants called a nationwide strike over five months of unpaid salaries, while public schools had been closed since February, also due to teachers' unpaid salaries. 'They [Seriff Nhamajo's interim gov-

The most productive segment of the population, the youth, remain disillusioned and disenchanted: losing all hope for their country, they rush to emigrate in search of greener pastures.

Even cultural institutions such as the Bissau Museum and the INEP research institute, once a highly regarded source of information on Guinea-Bissau history and culture, especially for its exhaustive documentation of the liberation war in film and oral testimonies, are in terrible condition, dogged by loss of collections during the war and state neglect.[44] The museum curators have since left for better paid jobs in Praia, Cape Verde, while interference by subsequent ministers has stripped INEP of many of its best research staff, and erratic government subvention has killed what little research work took place there. The appalling erosion of state cultural institutions is particularly depressing because Amílcar Cabral saw culture as a formidable weapon against the colonial rulers, and 'as one of the strengths of the nationalist (PAIGC) movement' (Bordonaro 2006: 112).

One particularly frightful consequence of the crisis brought about by the 1998 civil war is the near collapse of the Guinea-Bissau education sector. The sustained instability has lowered standards. The country has the lowest spend on education in West Africa, and this at one time led to almost 90% of schools closing. Even when they reopened, the schools lacked basic tools such as furniture and textbooks. It is reported that only 22% of students complete secondary school. Thus institutional collapse means that an entire generation of children are losing out on decent education, which will have disastrous impact on the future of the country.[45]

Meanwhile, the ongoing political crises have shown little sign of amelioration (cf. chapter by Kohl, this volume). This crisis in state institutions in

---

ernment] have money to organise elections and buy expensive cars, but they have no money to pay us the workers', a union official told *Radio Bombolon*. These arrears were addressed by the incoming presidency of José Mario Vaz, but the fragility of state employment remains a real concern.

[44] During the war, the Senegalese intervention forces were accused of looting artefacts from the Bissau Museum and used parts of the INEP complex as temporary barracks.

[45] According to media reports, in response to this sad state, parents in some parts of the country have started to contribute money to pay teachers so as to keep their children in school. See 'Guinea Bissau: Still way behind in education', *IRIN News*, http://www.irinnews.org/report/98129/guinea-bissau-still-way-behind-on-education, accessed 1 May 2014.

Guinea-Bissau is epitomized in the chaotic security apparatus which, as this chapter has suggested, has made the country easy prey for the South American narco-traffickers. Mazzetelli (2007: 1072) observes that transnational crime in West Africa, such as drug trafficking:

> represents not only a serious challenge to the balanced and sustainable development of individual countries and the region, but also a threat to the overall stability of these countries, the region and neighbouring regions. The enormous corruptive power of illicit money, coupled with the inner structural weaknesses of states, endangers the very foundations of the fragile democratic institutions.

This holds true for Guinea-Bissau because the state failure has become so acute that neither the political class nor the security apparatus has shown any willingness to tackle the menace. Above all, the ensuing instability has made its territory a safe haven and rearguard base for the various factions in the Casamance insurgency. The MFDC rebels continue to use Guinea-Bissau as a rearguard base in thir thirty-year-old insurgency against Dakar, and the rebels seem to have become bolder in crossing the border into Guinea-Bissau unchallenged after operations in Casamance. Indeed, in May 2013 the MFDC kidnapped a team of twelve de-mining workers in Casamance and hid them in Guinea-Bissau territory until their release was negotiated by the Sant'Egidio organization in Rome.[46] MFDC cadres use Guinea-Bissau territory to cultivate and distribute soft drugs like marijuana, engage in illegal logging and charcoal-burning to raise revenue for their commanders and procure weapons.[47] Most of the MFDC-produced marijuana and illegal timber and charcoal end up in Senegal and The Gambia, where seizures of truckloads of logs and drugs have become common.

Such unwillingness to fight crime has also led to a culture of impunity which manifests in the inability of the state to investigate and punish assassins, coupists, corrupt officials and drug barons. Since the 1998 civil war, political and military leaders including a serving president, two serving army commanders, cabinet ministers and judges have been assassinated or murdered without the perpetrators ever being caught or punished.[48] Thus the collapse of

---

[46] See 'S.African firm says workers freed by kidnappers in Guinea-Bissau', *Chicago Tribune*, 13 July 2013.

[47] See 'Senegal: No end in sight to Casamance conflict', IRIN News, 17 February 2012, www.irinnews.org /report/94895/senegal-no-end-in-sight-to-casamance-conflict.

[48] President Vieira was re-elected in 2005 after he had returned from six years in exile. But in March 2009 he was butchered by still unknown renegade soldiers, a few

the judicial system is symptomatic of a country whose institutions have become severely eroded in the aftermath of the crises which have dogged the country since 1998.

The National Army, once a proud state institution for its manifest valour against the Portuguese colonizers under the command of Amílcar Cabral, has been reduced to a sorry band of marauding gunmen who live in overcrowded barracks, march about in tattered boots and uniforms, and endure hunger and unpaid salaries like the rest of the government workers. The Bissau-Guinean army is over-staffed, over-officered, ill-equipped and ill-paid, not only unable to defend the territorial borders against drug traffickers, but demoralized and rusty.[49]

The inability of the army to execute its most fundamental duty of securing territorial integrity threatens stability in the sub-region. This became even more obvious when it emerged during a recent treason trial in The Gambia that in 2010 a mercenary force was undergoing training somewhere in Guinea-Bissau in readiness to launch a coup against the government of Yahya Jammeh in Banjul. The Guinea-Bissau security apparatus was either unwilling or incapable of apprehending the alleged mercenary band.[50]

Conclusion

It is hard for a keen observer like this writer to offer anything but a negative prognosis for the future: as long as the praetorian army remains unreformed, it is not yet Uhuru for Guinea-Bissau, despite the emergence of a new youth-led civil society, vibrant private FM media, strong-arm, tough-talking diplomacy from the United Nations' representative in the country, Nobel prize laureate José Ramos Horta and the new breed of politicians like the former IMF official, Paulo Gomes.[51]

---

hours after his army commander General Wai had been killed in a bomb attack on his office in Bissau. Leading political leaders like Baciro Dabo (former security minister) and Helder Proença (former defence minister) were subsequently assassinated by untraceable gunmen.

[49] According to a recent study by the African Centre for Strategic Studies, 42% of the army are officers, while its 5,000 strength gives Guinea-Bissau the highest soldier per capita ratio in West Africa: 2.73. See http://www.africacenter.org/security/country/guinea-bissau, accessed 5 April 2014.

[50] See 'Bissau Agent Testifies in Treason Trial', *The Point* (Banjul), 7 April 2010.

[51] In February 2014, prior to the general elections, Ramos Horta told the Chatham

As long as the security forces remain unreformed and are not bent towards respecting the will of the people of Guinea-Bissau, it will be a Herculean task to set the country on the path of stability and growth. This means that its neighbours will remain vulnerable not only to drugs and small-arms trafficking spilling over from Guinea-Bissau, but also to ill-effects of instability and bad governance. Indeed, in many ways the resolution of sub-regional security problems like drugs and small-arms trafficking and the Casamance insurgency depends largely on the return to stability in Guinea-Bissau. The country's southern border with Senegal has become the safe haven for at least two main factions of the Casamance conflict: that of Salif Sadio and César Atoute. One of the costliest attacks on Senegalese soldiers by Salif Sadio's faction in December 2011, which led to the loss of thirteen soldiers, was planned over the border in Guinea-Bissau, and the captured Senegalese soldiers were hidden across the border there.[52] Guinea-Bissau's porous border with Casamance, manned by mostly unpaid and ill-equipped border guards, would always afford the ideal conditions for gun runners, child traffickers and mercenaries.

Indeed, it makes a sobering reflection that in the seven years since 2009, Guinea-Bissau has lost five heads of state, three army chiefs and numerous political leaders, as if the anger of the gods is now also befalling the echelons of state. The words of the Balanta farmer quoted by Temudo (2009: 62) look increasingly relevant:

> Ever since [the war veterans and PAIGC political elite] took power, they are eating at the expense of the population. As long as they will not come to have a ceremony and ask us [the rural population at large] to forgive them, all these killings [among rivals] are not going to stop.

House bulletin: 'The politicians are handling the military, urging them to support one faction or another. The political elites are the main culprits behind the tragic state of affairs, mismanagement, wastefulness, corruption and the impoverishment of the population. The military came in second on my list of entrustment. The military just joined the big heist carried out by political elites who ruled the country since independence. Guinea-Bissau is a failed state in every way: corrupt public services, unpaid salaries to its employees, security forces without control, justice "unable" to judge...' Quoted in *ANGOP* (Angolan News Agency), 17 February 2014, published on www.Gbissau.com.

[52] See 'Senegal: No end in sight to Casamance conflict', op. cit..

CONCLUSION

Toby Green

This book has told a story that has become historical, and which pits local dynamics of agency and change into a global paradigm of economic and political transformation. It analyses how a post-colonial nation-state that emerged from the violent interstices of Portugal's colonial project in West Africa was transformed over four decades into what was labelled the world's first 'narco-state'. To be sure, Bissau-Guineans sometimes lament that their neighbours are better at PR than their rulers, since the drugs trade has been shown to affect the whole region; nevertheless, the conditions which have led to this label and its consequences are unique to the country. These condition are the product of specific historical conjunctures overlapping from pre-colonial, colonial and post-colonial eras; and yet at the same time they speak more widely to issues of governance, security and state-building which have emerged in the era of transnationalism.

At Guinea-Bissau's independence in 1974, it was most certainly a 'micro-state', one which was seen as a hope-filled harbinger of Africa's potential. The country was flooded with fledgling NGOs and their development experts; pedagogical theory was present through dialogue with Paulo Freire, and the agronomical expertise and knowledge of Amílcar Cabral was grafted into the dreams of the nation's future. Scholarships were available aplenty for the nation's young talents to pursue tertiary education in Brazil, Cuba and the

USSR, with the hope of returning to their country and furthering its positive transformation. Neo-colonial or colonial forces may have seen to it that Cabral did not live to see his country's independence, but his ideals lived on. And yet, by 2016, the ideals of the 1970s have atrophied, and the election of José Vaz to the presidency has not much altered the fact that externally the country is seen as a genuine threat to the international community, harbouring drug rings and other avenues for illicit global trade and the fostering of international terrorism.

What happened?

The historical transformation of the state in Guinea-Bissau these past forty years reflects important intersections of long-term trends with immediate historical causation. An immediate cause of the country's initial problems was the oil crisis of the 1970s. As has been shown in many works, the debt crisis in Africa in the 1980s originated directly from the increased energy costs and interest rate hikes associated with the oil crisis of the late 1970s. This was a major source of early instability in Guinea-Bissau, which came to independence at the cusp of these events, only to find both its own economy and the economies of the wider region hampered by these changes. It was certainly a cause of diminishing rents and incomes in the governmental sector in the late 1970s, exacerbating the intra-elite and intra-ethnic tensions which led to the coup in November 1980 by Nino Vieira.

This proximate cause of conflict was, however, exacerbated by the long-term historical fault-lines which had been created by centuries of the slave trade and then formal colonialism. Historically constructed racisms and African–European relations meant that Cape Verdeans had been the administrators of choice for the Portuguese empire in Africa, and indeed that Portuguese Guinea was initially administered from Praia, the capital of Cape Verde. This had brought educational privileges, so that Bissau-Guineans of Cape Verdean extraction tended to dominate the formation of the PAIGC and the revolutionary movement. The construction of ethnic and racial archetypes through both an external slave trade and the anthropological 'sciences' of Portuguese colonialism had created barriers, and these barriers were projected onto the financial crisis of the late 1970s and the oil crisis, so that the immediate and long-term causes of the crisis intersected. The alleged 'stranglehold' of Cape Verdeans on the levers of power provoked the *coup d'état* of Nino Vieira in November 1980, and also triggered the exile of some of the best educated people in the country.

Vieira came to power in the same month in which Ronald Reagan beat Jimmy Carter to the White House in the 1980 US presidential elections; so these transformations took place just at the time when the neo-liberal transformation of the world economy was taking root. These events would become the new paradigm of how local structures intersected with global power, as had occurred already in Guinea-Bissau for many centuries. The increasing inequality between the Global North and the Global South, which was a characteristic of global income distribution in the 1980s and 1990s, structured the increasing disempowerment of state institutions. It is striking, for example, to visit the library of the Instituto Nacional de Estudos e Pesquisas—the national research body in the country—and note from the works on the shelves how all book-buying seems to have ceased in the mid-1980s. With the increasing disempowerment of these institutions came the simultaneous rise of the 'aid industry' to 'address' these inequalities. And so, as Chabal and Daloz noted in *Africa Works* (1999), the state became increasingly an 'empty shell' designed to distribute patronage and administer the parcelling out of national resources for global profit, and also to re-allocate the rents assigned through the aid industry.

Such a pattern of global inequity, intertwined with local injustice, fostered distrust of 'the state' in the country. Resentment festered and first broke out in the civil war of 1998–9, which was a harbinger of things to come: said to have been fought over the parcelling out of rents from an illegal trade (the arms trade to the MFDC rebels in the Casamance), the war brought widespread misery and further emigration of the educated class from the country. Subsequently, even though the increasingly frequent elections of the 2000s saw good voter turnouts, Bissau-Guineans were under no illusions as to the limitations of the governments that would be elected and the lack of real change which they would be able to bring to their lives. The relationship between infighting over the resource distribution from illegal trade and political instability continued: the botched December 2011 coup was said to have been led by the two military personnel identified by the US as key players in the drug trade, Bubu NaTchuto and Antonio Indjai.

By the early 2010s, a new economic and political reality had been shaped in the country. After three decades of neo-liberal revolution, the major resource in Guinea-Bissau was an illegal trade in drugs, while the fiction that the state could foster productivity had long been abandoned in favour of the institutionalized conflict over these illegal rents from an unproductive trade. The consequence of, on the one hand, the recent exponential growth in inequality between the Global South and the Global North and, on the other, the deep historical construction of ethnic and racial division was the emergence of Guinea-Bissau as a potential threat to the international community through the channelling of drugs and money laundering to terrorist networks. In the country itself, however, change was experienced in different ways: as this book has shown, religious attitudes, gender relations, the growing importance of the diaspora, land productivity and relations with the sub-region all changed as a result of the emergence of the new dispensation.

What does this mean for Guinea-Bissau in the twenty-first century? The outlook is rather different depending on perspective. From the perspective of the Global North, there is an imperative for change. The attention of policy-makers has been drawn to the region, and the attempts to drive Security Sector Reform and to bring a global solution to local problems are marked; this is also indicated through the development of other initiatives, such as the UK's All-Party Parliamentary Group on Guinea-Bissau. The 2014 elections were widely seen as a new opportunity for the country, and the signs were initially more positive than before, with talk that the axis for the drugs trade has moved to the south; they were followed by a major donors conference in Brussels in March 2015. However, global powerbrokers were dismayed at the August 2015 crisis in the country, and the signs are that a quick-fix solution is not available.

Alongside the Global North's desire for change, therefore, must come the requirement to understand the seeds of productive change. Productive change requires a productive state, local markets and an acknowledgement of the historical role of the state in constructing markets and trade; drastically reducing the role and power of the state through structural adjustment programmes has in fact hampered economic dynamism in the country, and reduced both state and military to seeking rents elsewhere in order to reproduce themselves; the urgent need for stable rents was clearly a contributing factor to the rise of the drugs trade in the 2000s. Understanding this, and taking steps to renew the state and economic stability, is therefore a key policy aim, for failure to do so may have serious consequences with regard to the drugs trade: while recent reports see other countries such as neighbouring Guinea-Conakry increasingly in the spotlight concerning the drugs trade, this book has shown how the trade does not cause instability, but rather feeds from it, and so continuing instability in Guinea-Bissau will always offer the opportunity for this trade to emerge the stronger.

A more fundamental economic problem relates to the economic balance of the country. A useful comparator here is with the series of mass protests that took place in the country's lusophone counterpart Brazil in 2013, which were attributed by some commentators to the rise of the Brazilian middle class over the preceding decade. Following years of incentives from the Partido dos Trabalhadores under President Lula da Silva, and initiatives such as the *bolsa da família* which encouraged children from poorer families to remain in education, the rise of middle-income families in Brazil produced expectations and subsequent protests which questioned the nature of modern democracy. Hence perhaps it is through the creation and support of a real middle class in post-colonial African nations that democratic and state institutions can be consolidated.

The achievement of this is a long way off in many African countries, as the data examined in the Introduction to this book made clear; and indeed, it was the construction of a strong state in Brazil which facilitated the initiatives of the Lula government. Nevertheless, what is clear is that general stability in countries like Guinea-Bissau requires economic stability, which can only be achieved by both reducing the economic inequalities within the country and also structuring the country's relationship with the world economy. Without such stability, the country will continue to be seen as an 'external threat', the threat of a reinvigorated drugs trade will be present, and the securitization of foreign policy will continue without the core drivers of the perceived threat being resolved through an economic rebalancing and a restructuring of income distribution.

Beyond questions of economics, a further key question that has to be resolved is that of nation-building and the national imaginary. Many of the chapters in this volume have touched in one way or another on the question of 'ethnicity' as it emerges in political and historical detail. What has emerged is that in spite of the attempts by various internal—and external—agencies to instrumentalize ethnicity in the country, the population continues a long tradition of inter-ethnic alliances and collaborations. This is indeed in keeping with the nationalist ideals of Cabral and other lusophone African independence leaders such as Samora Machel in Mozambique and Agostinho Neto in Angola, all of whom argued that in order to construct a lasting post-colonial state it was necessary to move beyond ethnic affiliations and identities. It is instructive to see the lasting influence of this philosophy in Guinea-Bissau today, and it calls to mind the urgent need for an intellectual renewal in the country of philosophical engagements with post-colonial nationalism.

What can be the drivers for such renewal? As this book shows, the role of the Bissau-Guinean diaspora is of increasing importance, with key websites and fora being driven as much if not more by diasporans outside the country as by those still within it. Intellectuals from Guinea-Bissau now work in many institutions across the world, and it may be by harnessing the intellectual 'surplus value' of the diaspora, in tandem with paying close attention to the expansion of tertiary education within the country, that this process could begin to take shape.

Thus, in spite of the gloom which attends any discussion of the country in policy circles, in Guinea-Bissau itself the outlook does not have to be bleak. The country is certainly at a tipping point, and could go either way. If concrete steps are not taken to address the issues outlined in this book, the dangers of further political violence cannot be discounted, with the extra potential to spill over to the civilian population as has occurred in Latin America. Nevertheless, at present, while Human Development Indicators remain among the lowest in the world, the long-standing structures of inter-ethnic collaboration and mutual reliance mean that the people have retained some autonomy and strength even through the worst passages of the political meltdown. It is by renewing these interactions, and strengthening the political and intellectual ties between the country and the diaspora, that positive change can come. Funerals still remain huge gatherings; carnival is still celebrated; palm wine is still tapped and drunk. In spite of everything, Guinea-Bissau is still currently a country that 'works'; and this is surely the most appropriate finding to emerge at the end of this work, which was initially driven forward with such energy by Patrick Chabal.

BIBLIOGRAPHY

Aaby, P. G. J. et al. 1999: 'Nutritional status and mortality of refugee and resident children in a non-camp setting during conflict: follow up study in Guinea-Bissau', *BMJ* 319: 878–81.

Abdenur, A. and de Souza Neto, D. 2013: 'South–South cooperation and democracy in Africa: Brazil's role in Guinea-Bissau', *Africa Review* 5 (2): 104–17.

Abreu, A. 2012: 'Migration and development in contemporary Guinea-Bissau: a political economy approach.' London: University of London, unpublished PhD dissertation.

Adesina, A. A. and Seidi, S. 1995: 'Farmers' perceptions and adoption of new agricultural technology: analysis of modern mangrove rice varieties in Guinea-Bissau', *Quarterly Journal of International Agriculture* 34 (4): 358–71.

AfDB 2015: 'Guinea-Bissau: country strategy paper', Abidjan: African Development Bank.

Aguilar, R. and Stenman, A. 1997: 'Guinea-Bissau: From Structural Adjustment to Economic Integration', *Africa Spectrum* 32 (1): 71–96.

Akyeampong, E. 2005: 'Diaspora and Drug Trafficking in West Africa: A case study of Ghana', *African Affairs* 104 (416): 429–47.

Alvesson, M. 1990: *Assessing the welfare impact of structural adjustment: the case of smallholders in Guinea-Bissau*. Goteborg: Department of Economics, University of Goteborg.

Amselle, J.-L. 1998: *Mestizo Logics: Anthropology of Identity in Africa and Elsewhere*. Stanford: Stanford University Press.

Amselle, J.-L. and M'bokolo, E. (eds) 1999: *Au Coeur de l'Ethnie: Ethnies, Tribalisme et État en Afrique*. Paris: Éditions la Découverte.

Anderson, B. 1992: *Long-Distance Nationalism: World Capitalism and the Rise of Identity Politics, The Wertheim Lecture*. Amsterdam: Centre for Asian Studies.

Anderson, S. and Williams, J. 2011: 'The Securitization of Development Policy or the Developmentalization of Security Policy? Legitimacy, Public Opinion, and the EU

BIBLIOGRAPHY

External Action Service (EAS)', paper presented at the European Union Studies Association Conference, Boston, MA, 2011.

Anonymous, retired Gambian Foreign Ministry Staff, interviewed on 4 March 2014, Banjul.

Arthur, P. 2009: 'Ethnicity and Electoral Politics in Ghana's Fourth Republic', *Africa Today* 56 (2): 44–73.

Aubyn, F. K. 2013: 'Managing Complex Political Dilemmas in West Africa: ECOWAS and the 2012 crisis in Guinea-Bissau', *Conflict Trends* 4: 26–32.

Augel, J. 1993: 'Chão sagrado e mercadoria', in Cardoso, C. and Augel, J. (eds), *Guiné-Bissau vinte anos de independência*. Bissau: INEP: 22946.

Augel, J. 1996: 'Pensar o futuro—religiões na Guiné-Bissau: papel, aspiraçóes, perspectivas', in Augel, J. and Cardoso, C. (eds), *Transição democrática na Guiné Bissau e outros ensaios*. Bissau: INEP: 203–14.

BACIAG (*Boletim Associação Comercial, Industrial e Agrícola da Guiné*) 1958a: 'Reforma Tributária?', in *BACIAG* 1: 6–8.

—— 1958b: 'O Pequeno Comércio', in *BACIAG* 1: 9–11.

—— 1958c: 'A Campanha do Ano Corrente', in *BACIAG* 1: 27–32.

—— 1959: 'Apontamentos sobre o Comércio da Guiné', in *BACIAG* 19: 6–10.

—— 1962: 'A Guiné no Conselho Ultramarino', in *BACIAG* 60: 15–17.

—— 1966: 'Velharias: Indústria e Agricultura', in *BACIAG* 78: 38–45.

Bamyeh, M. A. 1993: 'Transnationalism', *Current Sociology* 41 (3): 1–95.

Bangura, K., Lynch, K. and Binns, J. 2012: 'Coping with the impacts of weather changes in rural Sierra Leone', *International Journal of Sustainable Development and World Ecology* DOI: 10.1080/13504509.2012.740511.

Banks, M. 1996: *Ethnicity: Anthropological Constructions*. London and New York: Routledge.

Baptista, A. M. d'Almeida and Chaves, A. M. L. 1961: 'A Castanha de Cajú: Subsídio para o Estudo da sua Economia', *Ultramar* 4 (2ª série): 70–98.

Baptista, M. M. 1948: 'Problemas Agrícolas Coloniais: a Guiné desconhecida', *Boletim Cultural da Guiné Portuguesa* 12: 881–924; 897–9.

Barker, J. 1977: 'Stability and Stagnation: the State in Senegal', *Canadian Journal of African Studies* 11 (1): 23–42.

Barros, M. de 2012: 'A sociedade civil face ao processo de democratização e o desenvolvimento na Guiné-Bissau (1991–2011)', *Africana Studia* 18: 71–82.

Barry, B. 1985: *Le Royaume du Waalo: Le Sénégal Avant la Conquête*. Paris: Éditions Karthala, 2nd edn.

Barry, B.-S., Creppy, E. and Wodon, Q. 2007: 'Cashew Production, Taxation, and Poverty in Guinea-Bissau', in Barry, B.-S., Creppy, E., Gacitua-Mario, E. and Wodon Q. (eds), *Conflict, Livelihoods and Poverty in Guinea-Bissau*. Washington, DC: World Bank Working Paper 88: 77–88.

Barry, B.-S. and Creppy, E. 2007: *Conflict, Livelihoods, and Poverty in Guinea-Bissau*. Washington, DC: World Bank.

BIBLIOGRAPHY

Bayart, J.-F. 2000: 'Africa in the World: A History of Extraversion', *African Affairs* 99 (1): 217–67.

Bayart, J.-F., Ellis, S. D. K. and Hibou, B. (eds) 1999: *The Criminalization of the State in Africa*. Oxford: James Currey.

Beaver, P. 1805: *African Memoranda: Relative to an attempt to establish a British Settlement on the island of Bulama, on the Western Coast of Africa, in the year 1792*. London: C. and R. Baldwin.

Becker, L. and Diallo, R. 1996: 'The Cultural Diffusion of Rice Cropping in Côte d'Ivoire', *Geographical Review* 86 (4): 505–28.

Bennett, H. 2003: *Africans in Colonial Mexico: Absolutism, Christianity and Afro-Creole Consciousness, 1570–1640*. Bloomington: Indiana University Press.

Berman, B. 1998: 'Ethnicity, Patronage and the African State: the Politics of Uncivil Nationalism', *African Affairs* 97: 305–41.

Bernard, E. 2008: 'Guinea-Bissau: Drug Boom, Lost Hope', *Open Democracy*, 23 October 2008.

Berry, S. 1993: *No Condition is Permanent: The social dynamics of agrarian change in Sub-Saharan Africa*. Madison: University of Wisconsin Press.

Bethke, F. 2012: 'Zuverlässig invalide. Indizes zur Messung fragiler Staatlichkeit', *Zeitschrift für Vergleichende Politikwissenschaft* 6: 19–37.

Biaye, Dalanda 2010: Interview with Aliou Ly, 5 September.

Bigman, L. 1993: *History and Hunger in West Africa: Food Production and Entitlement in Guinea-Bissau and Cape Verde*. Westport, CT: Greenwood Press.

Bloching, S. 2010: 'EU SSR Guinea-Bissau: Lessons Identified', *European Security Review*, 52.

Bocandé, B. 1849: 'Notes sur la Guinée Portugaise ou Sénégambie Méridionale', *Bulletin de la Société de Géographie*, 3ᵉ Série, 11: 265–350 and 12: 57–93.

Boone, C. 1990: 'State Power and Economic Crisis in Senegal', *Comparative Politics* 22 (3): 341–57.

Bordonaro, L. I. 2006: 'Living at the Margins: Youth and Modernity in the Bijago Islands (Guinea-Bissau)'. University Institute for Social Science, Denmark, unpublished PhD thesis.

—— 2009: 'Introduction: Guinea-Bissau Today—The Irrelevance of the State and the Permanence of Change', *African Studies Review* 52 (2): 35–45.

Bordonaro, L. 2010: 'Modernity as marginality: the making and the experience of peripherality in the Bijagó islands (Guinea-Bissau)', *Cadernos de Estudos Africanos* 18–19: 117–37.

Borges, E. S. M. 2009: 'Estudo de caso em Gabú: será que o casamento explica a gravidez precoce das jóvenes islâmicas (Fulas e Mandingas)?' Salvador: Federal University of Bahia, unpublished MA dissertation.

Borszik, A.-K. 2008: 'Régulos in the Gabú Region: Power in non-State Dispute Settlement', *Soronda* Special Issue: 57–90.

BIBLIOGRAPHY

Bowman, J. L. 1987: '"Legitimate Commerce" and Peanut Production in Portuguese Guinea, 1840s–1880s', *Journal of African History* 28 (1): 87–106.

Bowman, J. 1997: *Ominous Transition. Commerce and Colonial Expansion in the Senegambia and Guinea 1857–1919*. Brookfield, VT: Avebury.

Bowman-Hawking, J. 1980: 'Conflict, Interaction, and Change in Guinea-Bissau: Fulbe Expansion and its Impact 1850–1900.' Los Angeles: UCLA, unpublished PhD dissertation.

Brenner, L. 2000: 'Sufism in Africa', in Olupona, J. K. (ed.), *African Spirituality: Forms, Meanings and Expressions*. New York: Crossroad Publishing Co.

Brierley, L. 1955: 'A obra evangélica na Guiné portuguesa', *Portugual d'aquém e d'além mar* 19 (73): 63–4.

Brito, E. 1957: 'Notas sobre a vida religiosa dos Fulas e Mandingas', *Boletim Cultural da Guiné Portuguesa* 12 (46): 149–89.

Brooks, A. 2012: 'Riches from Rags or Persistent Poverty? Inequality in the Transnational Second-hand Clothing Trade in Mozambique.' London: Royal Holloway College, unpublished PhD dissertation.

Brooks, G. 2003: *Euroafricans in Western Africa: Commerce, Social Status, Gender and Religious Observance from the Sixteenth to the Eighteenth Century*. Athens, OH and Oxford: Ohio University Press and James Currey.

Brooks, G. E. 1993: *Landlords and Strangers: Ecology, Society and Trade in Western Africa, 1000–1630*. Boulder, CO: Westview Press.

Brubaker, R. 2004: *Ethnicity without Groups*. Cambridge, MA: Harvard University Press.

Bruce, J., Moura, A. and Tanner, C. 1992: *Uma Nova Lei da Terra para a Guiné-Bissau: Necessidades e Oportunidades. Um Relatório Preparado para a USAID–Guiné-Bissau*. Madison, WI: University of Wisconsin, Land Tenure Center.

Bryceson, D. 2002: 'Multiplex Livelihoods in Rural Africa: recasting the terms and conditions of gainful employment', *Journal of Modern African Studies* 40 (1): 1–28.

Burnham, P. 1996: *The Politics of Cultural Difference in Northern Cameroon*. Edinburgh: Edinburgh University Press for the IAI.

Buzan, B., Waever, O. and de Wilde, J. 1997: *Security: a new framework for analysis*. Boulder, CO: Lynne Rienner.

Bybee, A. 2012: 'The Twenty-first Century Expansion of the Transnational Drug Trade in Africa', *Journal of International Affairs* 66 (1).

Cabral, A. 1954: 'A propósito da Mecanização da Agricultura na Guiné Portuguesa', *Boletim Cultural da Guiné Portuguesa* XIX (34): 389–400.

——— 1956: 'Recenseamento Agrícola da Guiné: Estimativa em 1953', *Boletim Cultural da Guiné Portuguesa* 43: 7–246.

——— 1959/1988: 'A Agricultura na Guiné: algumas Notas sobre as suas Características e Problemas Fundamentais', *Estudos Agrários de Amílcar Cabral*. Lisboa/Bissau: IICT/INEP: 523–35.

BIBLIOGRAPHY

—— 1969a: *Revolution in Guinea*. London: Stage 1.

—— 1969b: 'Guinea: The Power of Arms', *Tricontinental Bimonthly* n. 12.

—— 1969c: 'At the United Nations: Extracts from a Statement made in Conakry in June 1962', in Handyside, R. (ed.), *Revolution in Guinea-Bissau: Selected Texts by Amilcar Cabral*. New York: Monthly Review Press.

—— 1969d: 'The Weapon of Theory', in Handyside, R. (ed.), *Revolution in Guinea-Bissau: Selected Texts by Amilcar Cabral*. New York: Monthly Review Press.

—— 1969e: *Palavras de Ordem Gerais do Camarada Amilcar Cabral aos Responsaveis do Partido*. Conakry.

—— 1972: *Our People Are Our Mountains: Revolutionary Leadership and People's War*. London: Committee for Freedom in Mozambique, Angola and Guiné.

—— 1973: *Return to the Source, Selected Speeches*. New York: Monthly Review Press.

—— 1980: *Unity and Struggle*. London: Heinemann.

Callewaert, I. 2000: *The Birth of Religion Among the Balanta of Guinea-Bissau*. Lund: Department of History of Religions.

Cambon, S. 2003: 'Upgrading the Cashew Nut Value Chain: the Case of the Casamance, Senegal', http://organiccashewnuts.com/research/upgrading-in-the-cashew-nut-value-chain-the-case-of-the-casamance-senegal/

Cardoso, B. 1986: *Guiné Bissau: Evolução Macro-Económica (1974–1985)*. Bissau: INEP.

Cardoso, C. 1990: 'Ki-Yang-Yang: Uma nova religião dos Balantas?' *Soronda: Revista de estudos guineeneses* 10: 3–15.

—— 2004: 'As tendencias actuáis do Islão na Guiné-Bissau', in Gonçalves, A. Custódio (ed.): *O islão na África Subsaariana: actas do 6º Colóquio Internacional Estados, Poderes e Identidades na África Subsariana*. Porto: Centro de Estudos Africanos da Universidade do Porto.

Cardoso, F. L. 2002: 'Subsídios para o estudo dos movimentos migratórios na Guiné-Bissau', *Soronda. Revista de Estudos Guineenses* 3: 29–50.

Caroço, J. V. 1948: *Monjur: O Gabú e a sua História*. Bissau: Centro de Estudos da Guiné Portuguesa.

Carolissen-Essack, A. 1980: 'Coup and After', *Economic and Political Weekly* 15 (52): 2175–6.

Carreira, A. 1947: 'Mandingas da Guiné Portuguesa', *Centro de Estudos da Guiné Portuguesa* (4).

—— 1960: 'População autóctone segundo os recenseamentos para fins fiscais', *Boletim Cultural da Guiné Portuguesa* 58: 241–324.

—— 1961: 'Organização Social e Económica dos Povos da Guiné Portuguesa', *Boletim Cultural da Guiné Portuguesa* 16 (64): 641–736.

—— 1962a: 'População autóctone segundo o recenseamento para fins fiscais', *Boletim Cultural da Guiné Portuguesa* 17 (65): 57–118.

—— 1962b: 'População autóctone segundo os recenseamentos para fins fiscais', *Boletim Cultural da Guiné Portuguesa* 17 (66): 221–80.

BIBLIOGRAPHY

——— 1964: 'A Etnonímia dos Povos de Entre o Gâmbia e o Estuário do Geba', *Boletim Cultural da Guiné Portuguesa* 19 (75): 233–76.

——— 1966: 'Aspectos históricos da evolução do islamismo na Guiné portuguesa (achegas para seu estudo)', *Boletim Cultural da Guiné Portuguesa* 22 (84): 405–55.

——— 1968: 'A Guiné e as Ilhas de Cabo Verde: a sua Unidade Histórica e Populacional', *Ultramar* VIII (32): 70–98.

——— 1984: *Os Portugûeses Nos Rios de Guiné*. Lisbon: Tejo.

Carvalho, B. P. de and Mendes, Henrique 2012: 'A segurança alimentar e a importância da cultura da cajú na Guiné Bissau', *Revista Internacional de Língua Portuguesa*, IIIᵉ Série, 25: 117–40.

Carvalho, C. 1998: 'Ritos de poder e a recriação da tradição: os régulos manjaco da Guiné-Bissau.' Lisbon: ISCTE, unpublished PhD dissertation.

——— 2000: 'A Revitalização do Poder Tradicional e os Regulados Manjaco na Guiné Bissau', *Etnográfica* IV (1): 37–59.

——— 2002: 'Ambiguous Representations: Power and Mimesis in Colonial Guinea', *Etnográfica* 6 (1): 93–111.

——— 2003: 'Local authorities or local power? The ambiguity of traditional authorities from the colonial to the post-colonial period in Guinea-Bissau', paper presented at Cornell University, 2–3 May 2003.

Carvalho, H. D. de 1944: *Guiné: Apontamentos Inéditos*. Lisbon: Agência Geral do Ultramar.

Castanheria, J. 1995: *Quem Mandou Matar Amilcar Cabral?* Lisbon: Ed. Relogio D'Agua.

Castro, A. 1950: 'Notas sobre algumas Variedades de Arroz em Cultura na Guiné Portuguesa', *Boletim Cultural da Guiné Portuguesa* 15 (19): 347–78.

——— 1951: 'Cultura do Amendoim na Guiné Portuguesa', *Boletim Cultural da Guiné Portuguesa* 6 (24): 885–908.

——— 1980: *O Sistema Colonial Português em África (meados do século XX)*. Lisbon: Editorial Caminho.

Chabal, P. 1981: 'The Social and Political Thought of Amílcar Cabral; A Reassessment', *Journal of Modern African History* 19 (1).

——— 1983a: *Amílcar Cabral: Revolutionary Leadership and People's War*. Cambridge: Cambridge University Press.

——— 1983b: 'Party, State and Socialism in Guinea Bissau', *Canadian Journal of African Studies* 17 (2): 189–210.

——— 1996: 'The African Crisis: context and interpretation', in Werbner, R. and Ranger, T. (eds), *Postcolonial Identities in Africa*. London and New Jersey: Zed Books.

——— 2002a: *Amílcar Cabral: Revolutionary Leadership and People's War*. London: Hurst & Co.

—— 2002b: *A History of Postcolonial Lusophone Africa*. London: Hurst & Co.

—— 2002c: 'The Construction of the Nation-State', in Chabal, P. (ed.), *A History of Postcolonial Lusophone Africa*. London: Hurst & Co.

—— 2009: *Africa: The Politics of Suffering and Smiling*. London: Zed Books.

Chabal, P. and Daloz, J.-P. 1999: *Africa Works: Disorder as Political Instrument*. Oxford: James Currey.

Chabal, P. and Vidal, N. (eds) 2007: *Angola: The Weight of History*. London: Hurst & Co.

Chaliand, G. 1969: *Armed Struggle in Africa: With the Guerrillas in 'Portuguese' Guinea*. London: Monthly Review Press.

Chatham House 2013: 'Guinea-Bissau: Rescue from Collapse', Summary of a meeting addressed by José Ramos Horta, Chatham House, London, 29 October 2013. Available at http://www.chathamhouse.org/events/view/194673, accessed 9 February 2016.

Chauveau, J. P. and Richards, P. 2008: 'West African Insurgencies in Agrarian Perspective: Côte d'Ivoire and Sierra Leone Compared', *Journal of Agrarian Change* 8: 515–52.

Chazam, N. 1988: 'Patterns of State–Society Incorporation and Disengagement in Africa', in Rothchild, D. and Chazam, N. (eds), *The Precarious Balance: State and Society in Africa*. Boulder, CO: Westview Press.

Cheneau-Loquay, A. 1991: 'Aperçu de la Situation Foncière en Guinée Bissau: des Tensions Croissantes', *L'Année Africaine* 1990–1: 327–46.

—— 1995: 'Monoculture d'Exportation et Grands Domaines en Guinée Bissau', in *Lusotopie 1999 (Transition en Afrique Lusophone)*: 295–314.

Cheneau-Loquay, A. and Matarasso, P. 1998: *Approche du Développement Durable en Milieu Africain: les Régions Côtières de Guinée, Guinée Bissau et Casamance*. Paris: Harmattan.

Chilcote, R. H. 1972: *Emerging Nationalism in Portuguese Africa: Documents*. Stanford, CA: Hoover Institution Press.

Clapp, J. 1993: 'Interpreting Agricultural Performance in Guinea under Structural Adjustment', *Canadian Journal of African Studies* 27 (2): 173–95.

Có, R. B. 2009: 'Diáspora Guineense Qualificada, uma Rede Periférica no Desenvolvimento do País de Origem', Nº 08/2009, Universidade Técnica de Lisboa, Instituto Superior de Economia e Gestão, Centro de Investigação em Sociologia Económica e das Organizações (SOCIUS), Instituto Nacional de Estudos e Pesquisa (INEP-Bissau).

Cohen, R. 1995: 'Rethinking "Babylon": iconoclastic conceptions of the Diasporic Experience', *New Community* 21: 5–18.

—— 1996: 'Diasporas and the Nation-state: from Victims to Challengers', *International Affairs* 72: 507–20.

Collier, P. 1999: 'On the Economic Consequence of Civil War', *Oxford Economic Papers* 51 (1): 168–83.

BIBLIOGRAPHY

Collier, P. and Hoeffler, A. 2004: 'Greed and Grievance in Civil War', *Oxford Economic Papers* 56 (4): 563–95.

Conducto, J. E. 1965: 'Influência do Islamismo na vida económica dos Fulas'. Lisbon: Escola Superior Colonial, unpublished BA thesis.

Constantine, S. 2006: 'Locating Danger and Negotiating Risk on Manjaco Terrain for Bayu, the Children of Caió, Guinea-Bissau.' Cambridge: University of Cambridge, unpublished PhD dissertation.

Cooper, F. 1981: 'Africa and the World Economy', *African Studies Review* 24 (2/3): 1–86.

—— 2002: *Africa Since 1940: The Past of the Present*. Cambridge: Cambridge University Press.

Cornwall, B. 1972: *Bush Rebels: Personal Account of Black Revolt in Africa*. New York: Holt, Rinehart and Winston.

Cotula L. (ed) 2007: *Changes in 'customary' land tenure systems in Africa*. ISBN 978-1-84369-657-5.

Council Joint Action 2008/112/CFSP on the European Union mission in support of Security Sector Reform in the Republic of Guinea-Bissau [2008] OJ L40/11.

Cravo, T. Paula de Almeida 2012: 'What's in a Label? The Aid Community's Representations of Success and Failure in Mozambique and Guinea-Bissau.' Cambridge: University of Cambridge, unpublished PhD dissertation.

Crick, E. 2012: 'Drugs as an existential threat: An analysis of the international securitization of drugs', *International Journal of Drug Policy* 23: 407–14.

Crowley, E. 2000: 'Institutions, Identities, and the Incorporation of Immigrants within Local Frontiers of the Upper Guinea Coast', in Gaillard, G. (ed.), *Migrations anciennes et peuplement actuel des Côtes guinéennes*. Paris: L'Harmattan: 115–38.

Crowley, E. 1990: 'Contracts with the Spirits: Religion, Asylum and Ethnic Identity in the Cacheu Region of Guinea-Bissau.' New Haven: Yale University, PhD dissertation.

Crowley, E. 1993: *Guinea-Bissau's Informal Economy and its Contribution to Economic Growth*. The Hague: USAID.

Cunningham, J. 1980: 'The Colonial Period in Guiné', *Tarikh* 6 (4): 31–46.

Dahlgren, P. 2005: 'The Internet, Public Spheres, and Political Communication: Dispersion and Deliberation', *Political Communication* 22 (2): 147–62.

Dahou, T. (ed.) 2008: *Libéralisation et Politique Agricole au Sénégal*. Paris: Karthala.

Davidson, B. 1969: *Liberation of Guine, an Aspect of an African Revolution*. Baltimore, MD: Penguin Books.

—— 1981: *No Fist is Big Enough to Hide the Sky: The Liberation of Guinea-Bissau and Cape Verde*. London: Zed Press.

Davidson, J. 2003: 'Native Birth. Identity and Territory in postcolonial Guinea-Bissau, West Africa', *European Journal of Cultural Studies* 6: 37–54.

—— 2007: 'Feet in the Fire: Social Change and Continuity among the Diola of Guinea-Bissau.' Atlanta, GA: Emory University, unpublished PhD dissertation.

BIBLIOGRAPHY

Delfim da Silva, F. 2003: *Guiné-Bissau. Páginas de História política, Rumos da Democracia*. Bissau: Firquidja Editora.

Denis, P. Y. 1976: 'Réalisation Récentes et Perspectives de Développement de la Guinée', *Cahiers d'Outre Mer* 29 (116): 321–47.

Dhada, M. 1993: *Warriors at Work: How Guinea Was Really Set Free*. Niwot, CO: University Press of Colorado.

Di John, J. 2011: '"Failed States" in Sub-Saharan Africa: A Review of the Literature (ARI)', www.realinstitutoelcano.org, accessed 10 April 2014.

Diallo, Cira 2009: Interview with Aliou Ly, Bissau, 12 July.

Diallo, Fatoumata 2009: Interviews with Aliou Ly, Bissau, 27 July and 1 September.

Dias, E. Costa 2008: 'Regulado do Gabú, 1900–1930: a Difícil Compatibilização entre Legitimidades Tradicionais e a Reorganização do Espaço Colonial', *Africana Studia* 9: 99–126.

―――― 1999: 'Protestantismo e proselitismo na Guiné-Bissau: reflexões sobre o insucesso do proselitismo no Oio e na província Leste'. *Lusotopie 1999 (Dynamiques réligieuses en lusophonie contemporaine)*: 309–18.

―――― 2000: 'A Balantização da Guiné-Bissau', *Público* (Lisbon), 5 December 2000.

―――― 2004a: 'A identidade muçulmana kaabunké: um processo de construção identitária sui generis na Senegâmbia', in Gonçalves, A. C. (ed.), *O islão na África Subsariana: actas do 6º Colóquio Internacional Estados, Poderes e Identidades na África Subsaariana*. Porto: Centro de Estudos Africanos da Universidade do Porto.

―――― 2004b: 'A identidade muçulmana kaabunké: um processo de construção identitária sui generis na Senegâmbia', in Gonçalves, A. Custódio (ed.), *O islão na África Subsariana: actas do 6º Colóquio Internacional Estados, Poderes e Identidades na África Subsaariana*. Porto: Centro de Estudos Africanos da Universidade do Porto.

―――― 2005: 'Da escola corânica traditional à escola *arabi*: um simples aumento de qualificação do ensino muçulmano na Senegâmbia?' *Cadernos de estudos africanos* 7–8.

―――― 2008: 'Regulado do Gabú, 1900–1930: a difícil compatibilização entre legitimidades tradicionais e a reorganização do espaço colonial', *Africana Studia* 9: 99–126.

―――― 2013: 'From the Unbearable "Resilience" of Coupism to Ethnicisation: A short Journey for the Armed Forces of Guinea-Bissau', *Nordic Journal of African Studies* 22: 6–22.

Dias, J. R. 1996: 'Agricultura', in Monteiro, A. I. (ed.), *O Programa de Ajustamento Estrutural na Guiné Bissau; Análise dos Efeitos Socio-Económicos*. Bissau: INEP: 317–426.

Diop, A. 1996: *Société Manjak et Migration*. Besançon: Demontrond.

Djaló, T. 2013: *O Mestiço e o Poder: identidades, dominações e resistências na Guiné*. Lisbon: Vega, 2nd edn.

Domingues, M. B. 2000: 'Estratégias femininas entre as bideiras de Bissau'. Lisbon: Universidade Nova de Lisboa, unpublished PhD thesis.

BIBLIOGRAPHY

Drift, R. van der 1992: *Arbeid en Alcohol: de Dynamiek van de Rijstverbouw en het Gezag van de Oudste bij de Balanta Brassa in Guinee Bissau*. Leiden: CNWS.

───── 2000: 'Democracy: Legitimate Warfare in Guinea-Bissau', *Soronda (Número Especial: 7 de Junho)* 4 (New Series): 37–65.

Duarte, F. 1950: 'Os Cabo-Verdianos na Colonização da Guiné', *Boletim Geral das Colónias* 295: 209–11.

Duarte Silva, A. E. 2010: *Invenção e Construção da Guiné-Bissau. Administração Colonial, Nacionalismo, Constitucionalismo*. Lisbon: Almedina.

Easterly, W. and Levine, R. 1997: 'Africa's Growth Tragedy: Policies and Ethnic Divisions', *Quarterly Journal of Economics* 112 (4): 1203–50.

Einarsdóttir, J. 2004: *Tired of Weeping: Mother Love, Child Death, and Poverty in Guinea-Bissau*. Madison, WI: University of Wisconsin Press.

Einarsdóttir, J., Hamadou, B., Gunnlaugur, G. and Geir, G. 2010: 'Child Trafficking in Guinea-Bissau: An Explorative Study'. Reykjavík: UNICEF Iceland.

Ellis, S. 2009: 'West Africa's International Drug Trade', *African Affairs* 108 (431), 171–96.

───── 2012: Review of *Africa and the War on Drugs* by Neil Carrier and Gernot Kantshnig (*African Arguments*, 2012), available at http://africanarguments. org/2012/10/22/africa-and-the-war-on-drugs-a-review-by-stephen-ellis/, accessed 9 February 2016.

Ellis, S. and Shaw, M. 2015: 'Does Organized Crime Exist in Africa?', *African Affairs* 114 (457): 1–24.

Embaló, A. I. 2008: 'Religious and spiritual means of local conflict resolution', *Soronda* (Special Issue 'Experiências locais de gestão de conflitos'): 311–25.

Embaló, B. 2012: 'Civil–Military Relations and Political Disorder in Guinea-Bissau', *Journal of Modern African Studies* 50 (2): 253–81.

Espinosa, M. 1994: 'Ponteiros na Guiné Bissau: o Processo de Concessão de Terras, 1879–1991', *Soronda* 18: 15–38.

Esteves, A. B. 1964: *Castanha de Cajú em Angola*. Lisbon: Missão de Estudo Agronómicos do Ultramar.

European Commission 2015: 'A fresh start for Guinea-Bissau: EU to resume cooperation and provide new support', Brussels, 25 March 2015. Available at http://europa. eu/rapid/press-release_IP-15-4663_en.htm, accessed 9 February 2016.

Faculdade de Direito de Bissau/Instituto Nacional de Estudos e Pesquisa n.d.: *Estudo sobre o Direito Consuetudinário vigente na Guiné-Bissau: Balantas, Fulas, Mancanhas, Manjacos, Mandingas, Papéis*. Bissau: União Europeia/Programa das Nações Unidas para o Desenvolvimento.

Farias, P. F. de Moraes 1985: 'Models of the World and Categorial Models: The "Enslavable Barbarian" as a Mobile Classificatory Label', in Willis, J. (ed.), *Slaves and Slavery in Muslim Africa*, Vol. 1. London: Frank Cass & Co.

Fistein, D. 2011: 'Guinea-Bissau: How a successful social revolution can become an

BIBLIOGRAPHY

obstacle to subsequent state-building', *International Journal of African Historical Studies* 44: 443–55.

Fonseca, D. da 1993: 'A presença da Igreja Católica na Guiné-Bissau depois da Independência', in Cardoso, C. and Augel, J. (eds), *Guiné-Bissau: Vinte Anos de Independencia*. Bissau: INEP.

Fonseca, D. da 1997: *Os Mancanha*. Bissau: Ku Si Mon Editora.

Forrest, J. B. 1987: 'Guinea-Bissau Since Independence: A Decade of Domestic Power Struggles', *Journal of Modern African Studies* 25 (1): 95–116.

——— 1992: *Guinea-Bissau, Power, Conflict and Renewal in a West Africa Nation*. Boulder, CO: Westview Press.

——— 1998: 'State and Peasantry in Contemporary Africa: the Case of Guinea-Bissau', *Africana Journal* XVII: 1–26.

——— 2002: 'Guinea-Bissau', in Chabal, P. (ed.), *A History of Postcolonial Lusophone Africa*. London: Hurst & Co.

——— 2003: *Lineages of State Fragility: Rural Civil Society in Guinea Bissau*. Athens, OH and Oxford: Ohio University Press and James Currey.

——— 2005: 'Democratization in a Divided Urban Political Culture: Guinea-Bissau', in Villalon, L. A. and Von Doepp, P. (eds), *The Fate of Africa's Democratic Experiments: Elites and Institutions*. Bloomington, IN: Indiana University Press.

——— 2010: 'Anatomy of State Fragility: The Case of Guinea-Bissau', in Tschirgi, N., Lund, M. S., and Mancini, F. (eds), *Security and Development: Searching for Critical Connections*. London: Lynne Rienner.

Fosu, A. K. 1992: 'Political Instability and Economic Growth: Evidence from Sub Saharan Africa', *Economic Development and Cultural Change* 40 (4): 829–41.

Franklin, A. B. C. de Sousa 1956: 'A ameaça islâmica na Guiné portuguesa', *Cabo Verde* 7 (86): 34–5.

Funk, U. 1988: 'Land Tenure, Agriculture and Gender in Guinea-Bissau', in Davison, J. (ed.), *Agriculture, Women and Land*. Boulder, CO: Westview Press.

Gable, E. 1990: 'Modern Manjaco: The Ethos of Power in a West African Society.' Charlottesville, VA: University of Virginia, PhD dissertation.

——— 1995: 'The Decolonization of Consciousness: Local Skeptics and the "Will to be Modern" in a West African Village', *American Ethnologist* 22 (2): 242–57.

——— 1996: 'Women, Ancestors, and Alterity Among the Manjaco of Guinea-Bissau', *Journal of Religion in Africa* 26 (2): 104–21.

——— 2009: 'Conclusion: Guinea-Bissau Yesterday ... and Tomorrow', *African Studies Review* 52 (2): 165–79.

Gacitua-Mario, E., Nordang, H. and Wodon, Q. 2007: 'Livelihoods in Guinea-Bissau', in Barry, B.-S., Creppy, E., Gacitua-Mario, E. and Wodon Q., *Conflict, Livelihoods and Poverty in Guinea-Bissau*. Washington, DC: World Bank Working Paper 88: 59–75.

Gaillard, G. 1995: 'Les Yola du Compony: un cas de conversion en Guinée maritime', *Islam et Société au Sud du Sahara* 9: 5–27.

BIBLIOGRAPHY

———— 2002: 'Islam et vie politique en Guiné-Bissau contemporaine', *L'Afrique Politique 2002 (Islams d'Afrique: entre le local et le global)*. Paris: Karthala.

Galli, R. 1986: 'Amílcar Cabral and Rural Transformation in Guinea Bissau: a Preliminary Critique', *Rural Africana* 25–6: 55–73.

———— 1987: 'On Peasant Productivity', *Development and Change* 18(1): 69–98.

———— 1989: *Estratégia de Desenvolvimento na Guiné Bissau: a Contribuição da Comunidade Europeia*. Bissau: Gabinete Representante EU.

———— 1991: 'Liberalization is Not Enough: Structural Adjustment and Peasants in Guinea-Bissau', *Review of African Political Economy* 49–50: 52–68.

———— 1994: 'A Ausência de Capitalismo Agrário na Guiné Bissau durante o Regime do Estado Novo', *Soronda* 17: 107–44.

———— 1995: 'Capitalist Agriculture and the Colonial State in Portuguese Guinea, 1926–1974', *African Economic History* 23: 51–78.

Galli, R. and Jones, J. 1987: *Guinea-Bissau: Politics, Economics and Society*. Boulder, CO: Lynne Rienner.

Garcia, F. 2000: *Guiné 1963–74: os movimentos independentisas, o Islão e o poder português*. Porto and Lisbon: Universidade Portucalense e Comissão Portuguesa de História Militar.

———— 2004: 'O Islão, as confrarias e o poder na Guiné (1963–74)', in *O islão na África Subsaariana: actas do 6º Colóquio Internacional Estados, Poderes e Identidades na África Subsaariana*. Porto: Centro de Estudos Africanos da Universidade do Porto.

Gibert, M. 2009: 'The Securitization of the EU's development agenda in Africa: Insights from Guinea-Bissau', *Perspectives on European Politics and Society* 10 (4): 621–37.

Gibson, R. 1972: *African Liberation Movements; Contemporary Struggles Against White Minority Rule*. London: Oxford University Press.

Girão de Sousa, M. 2013: *A Missão da União Europeia para a Reforma do Sector de Segurança na Guiné-Bissau. Constrangimentos, dificuldades e resultados*. Lisbon: Instituto Superior de Ciências Sociais e Políticas, Universidade de Lisboa, MA thesis.

Glete, J. 2002: *War and the State in Early Modern Europe: Spain, the Dutch Republic and Sweden as Fiscal–Military States, 1500–1650*. London and New York: Routledge.

Gomes, P. 1993: 'O Financiamento Externo e a Liberalização Comercial durante o PAE', in Imbali, F. (ed.), *Os Efeitos Sócio-Económicos do Programa de Ajustamento Estrutural na Guiné Bissau*. Bissau: INEP.

Gonçalves, J. J. 1958: 'O Islamismo na Guiné Portuguesa', *Boletim Cultural da Guine Portuguesa* 13 (52): 397–470.

———— 1960: *Protestantismo em África*. Lisbon: Junta de Investigações do Ultramar (2 vols).

———— 1961: *O Islamismo na Guiné Portuguesa (Ensaio sociomissionológico)*. Lisbon (n.d.).

BIBLIOGRAPHY

—— 1962: *O Mundo Árabo-Islâmico e o Ultramar Português*. Lisbon: Junta de Investigações do Ultramar.

—— 1966: 'A informação na Guiné, em Cabo Verde e em São Tomé e Príncipe (Achegas para o seu estudo)', in *Cabo Verde, Guiné, São Tomé e Príncipe (Curso de extensão universitária)*. Lisbon: Instituto Superior de Ciências Sociais e Politica Ultramarina.

Gordon, D. 1981: 'The problem of women's history', in Carroll, B. A. (ed.), *Liberating Women's History, Theoretical and Critical Essays*. Chicago IL: University of Illinois Press.

Gourevitch, P. 1999: *We Wish to Inform you that Tomorrow we will be Killed with our Families*. London: Picador.

Grands Dossiers 2012: 'Réunion de la CEDEAO à Abidjan: les dirigeants des 15 applaudiront-ils la médiation d'Alpha Condé?' in *Guineexpress*, 26 April 2012, http://www.guineexpress.com/index.php?option=com_content&view=article&i d=136:grands-dossiers—reunion-de-la-cedeao-a-abidjan—les-dirigeants-des-15-applaudiront-ils-la-mediation-dalpha-conde—&catid=2:flahs-news (12.02.2014).

Gray, J. 2014: 'The Dangers of Democracy', *New York Review of Books* 61 (5), 20 March 2014.

Green, T. 2001: *Meeting the Invisible Man: Secrets and Magic in West Africa*. London: Weidenfeld & Nicolson.

—— 2009: 'Architects of Knowledge, Builders of Power: Constructing the Kaabu "Empire", 16th-17th Centuries', *Mande Studies* 11: 91–112.

—— 2011: 'Building Slavery in the Atlantic World: Atlantic Connections and the Changing Institution of Slavery in Cabo Verde, 15th-16th Centuries', *Slavery and Abolition* 32 (2): 227–45.

—— 2012: *The Rise of the Trans-Atlantic Slave Trade in Western Africa, 1300–1589*. Cambridge: Cambridge University Press.

Green, T. and Thompson, P. R. 2011: '"Guinea-Bissau: A Narco-Developmental State?"—A response to Marie Gibert's article', www.africanarguments.org, accessed 2 April 2014.

Guimarães, E. M. 1992: 'O Ajustamento Estrutural na Guiné Bissau: a Experiência dos Anos 80'. Lisbon: ISEG, MA thesis.

Habermas, J. 1989: *The Structural Transformation of the Public Sphere*. Boston: MIT Press.

Hair, P. E. H. 1966: 'The Use of African Languages in Afro-European Contacts in Guinea, 1440–1560', *Sierra Leone Language Review* 5: 5–27.

—— 1967: 'Ethnolinguistic Continuity on the Guinea Coast', *Journal of African History* 8 (2): 247–68.

Handem, A. 2008: 'Guinea-Bissau', in Bryden, A., N'Diaye, B. and Olonisakin, 'F. (eds), *Challenges of Security Sector Governance in West Africa*. Münster: LIT Verlag.

BIBLIOGRAPHY

Hannerz, U. 1992: *Cultural Complexity: Studies in the Social Organization of Meaning.* New York: Columbia University Press.

—— 1996: *Transnational Connections: Culture, People, Places.* London: Routledge.

Hansen, P. 2002: 'European Integration, European Identity and the Colonial Connection', *European Journal of Social Theory* 5 (4): 483–98.

Havik, P. J. 1991: 'As Sociedades Agrárias e a Intervenção Rural na Guiné-Bissau: uma Revista da Literatura Pós-Independência', *Revista Internacional de Estudos Africanos* 14/15: 279–310.

—— 1995: 'Relações de Género e Comércio: Estratégias Inovadoras de Mulheres Comerciantes na Guiné-Bissau', *Soronda* 19: 25–36.

—— 1998: 'Female Entrepreneurship in a Changing Environment: Gender, Kinship and Trade in the Guinea Bissau region', in Risseeuw, C. and Ganesh, K. (eds), *Negotiation and Social Space: a Gendered Analysis of Changing Kin and Security Networks in South Asia and Sub-Saharan Africa.* New Delhi: Sage.

—— 2004: *Silence and Soundbytes: The Gendered Dynamics of Trade and Brokerage in the Pre-Colonial Guinea Bissau Region.* Münster and New York: LIT Verlag and Transaction Publishers.

—— 2007a: 'Ilhas Desertas: Impostos, Comércio, Trabalho Forçado e o Êxodo das Ilhas Bijagós', in CEAUP (ed.), *Trabalho Forçado Africano: articulações com o poder político.* Oporto: CEAUP/Humus.

—— 2007b: 'Kriol Without Creoles: Rethinking Guinea's Afro-Atlantic Connections (Sixteenth to Twentieth Centuries)', in Naro, N., Sansi-Roca, R. and Treece, D. (eds), *Cultures of the Lusophone Black Atlantic.* London: Palgrave Macmillan.

—— 2011a: 'Traders, Planters and Brokers: the Kriston in Portuguese Guinea', *Portuguese Studies Review* (PSR) Special Issue 19 (1/2): 197–226.

—— 2011b: 'Recriar China na Guiné: os Primeiros Chineses, os seus Descendentes e a sua Herança na Guiné Colonial', *Africana Studia* 17: 211–35.

—— 2012: 'Virtual Nations and Failed States: Making Sense of the Labyrinth', in Morier-Genoud, E. (ed.), *Sure Road? Nations and Nationalisms in Angola, Guinea-Bissau and Mozambique.* Leiden: Brill.

Havik, P. J. and Daveau, S. 2010: *Orlando Ribeiro: Cadernos de Campo Guiné 1947.* Oporto: Centro de Estudos Africanos-CEAUP/HUMUS.

Hawthorne, W. 2003: *Planting Rice and Harvesting Slaves: Transformations Along the Guinea-Bissau Coast, 1400–1800.* Portsmouth, NH: Heinemann.

—— 2010: *From Africa to Brazil: Culture, Identity, and an Atlantic Slave Trade, 1600–1830.* Cambridge: Cambridge University Press.

Hendrix, C. and Brinkman, H. 2013: 'Food Insecurity and Conflict Dynamics: Causal Linkages and Complex Feedbacks', *Stability: International Journal of Security and Development* 2 (2). DOI: http://dx.doi.org/10.5334/sta.bm, accessed 9 February 2016.

BIBLIOGRAPHY

Henriques, I. C. 2012: 'Africans in Portuguese Society: Classificatory Ambiguities and Colonial Realities', in Cahen, M. and Morier-Grenoud, E. (eds), *Imperial Migrations: Colonial Communities and Diaspora in the Portuguese World*. Basingstoke: Palgrave Macmillan.

Henry, C. 1994: *Les îles où dansent les enfants défunts: âge, sexe et pouvoir chez les Bijogo de Guinée Bissau*. Paris: CNRS Editions.

Herbert, R. 2003: 'Security Sector Governance: An Analysis of Guinea-Bissau', Netherlands Institute of International Relations 'Clingendael' Working Paper 8.

Herbst, J. 1990: 'Migration, the Politics of Protest, and State Consolidation in Africa', *African Affairs* 89 (355): 183–203.

Heredia, R. C. 1997: 'Ethnicity, Class and Nation: Interrelationships in a Multi-Cultural State', *Economic and Political Weekly* 32 (19): 1010–15.

Heywood, L. M. 2000: *Contested Power in Angola, 1840s to the Present*. Rochester, NY: University of Rochester Press.

Hills, A. 2014: 'Somalia Works: Police Development as State Building', *African Affairs* 113 (450): 88–107.

Hochet, A.-M. 1981: *Étude des Habitudes de Consommation et des Besoins en Produits d'Importation des Populations Rurales de Guinée Bissau*. Bissau: MCEP.

—— 1983: *Paysanneries en Attente Guinée Bissau*. Série d'Études et Recherches 79/80. Dakar: ENDA.

Hoffman, E. 2014: 'Elections Not Enough to Bring Stability to Troubled Guinea-Bissau', *Global Observatory*, 25 March 2014, http://theglobalobservatory.org/analysis/705-elections-not-enough-to-bring-stability-to-troubled-guinea-bissau.html, accessed 9 February 2016.

Hoffman, M. and Lane, C. 2013: 'Guinea-Bissau and the South Atlantic Cocaine Trade', *Center for American Progress Journal*, 22 August 2013: 1–7.

Horta, C. A. P. 1965: 'Análise Estrutural e Conjuntural da Economia da Guiné', *Boletim Cultural da Guiné Portuguesa* 20 (80): 333–495.

Horta, C. A. P. and Sardinha, R. M. 1966: 'A Indústria Transformadora na Guiné Portuguesa', *Boletim Cultural da Guiné Portuguesa* 21 (82): 147–63.

Horta, J. da Silva 2004: 'O Islão nos textos portugueses: noroeste africano (sécs XV-XVII) –das representações à história', in Gonçalves, A. C. (ed.), *O islão na África Subsaariana: actas do 6º Colóquio Internacional Estados, Poderes e Identidades na África Subsaariana*. Porto: Centro de Estudos Africanos da Universidade do Porto.

—— 2011: *A 'Guiné do Cabo Verde': Produção textual e representacões (1578–1684)*. Lisbon: Fundação Calouste Gulbenkian and FCT.

—— 2013: '"Nações", Marcadores Identitários e Complexidades de Representação Étnica nas Escritas Portuguesas de Viagem: Guiné do Cabo Verde (Séculos XVI-XVII)', *Vária Historia* 29 (51): 649–75.

Horta, Loro 2007: 'Guinea-Bissau: Africa's first narco-state', www.africa.upenn.edu/Articles_Gen/guinbisauhorta.html, accessed 10 August 2015.

BIBLIOGRAPHY

Hughes, M. 2009: 'Armed Conflict, International Linkages and Women's Parliamentary Representation in Developing Nations', *Social Problems* 56 (1): 174–204.

Huria, S. 2008: 'Failing and Failed States: The Global Discourse', IPCS (Institute of Peace and Conflict Studies, New Delhi) Issue Brief, 75.

IMF 2011: *Guinea-Bissau: Second Poverty Reduction Strategy Paper*, Country Report 11/353, Washington, DC.

Indjai, B. 2002: 'Solos, Agro-Sistemas e Concessão de Terras na Guiné-Bissau', *Soronda* 5 (nova série): 71–113, 185–246.

Induta, J. Zamora 2001: *Guiné. 24 Anos de Independência 1974–1998*. Lisbon: Hugin Editores.

Infanda, J. Nhaga 2009: 'Participação da Igreja Católica da Guiné-Bissau no conflito político-militar de 1998/99'. Bissau: Seminário Interdiocesano de Bissau, BA thesis.

Iñiguez de Heredia, M. 2013: 'Everyday Resistance in Postconflict Statebuilding: The Case of Eastern Democratic Republic of the Congo.' London: London School of Economics, unpublished PhD dissertation.

Innes, G. 1976: *Kaabu and Fuladu: Historical Narratives of the Gambian Mandinka*. London: School of Oriental and African Studies.

Instituto Nacional de Estatística 2009: *Kantu Djintis, kantu Kasas. Recenseamento Geral da População e Habitação: Característicos Socioculturais*. Bissau.

International Crisis Group 2012: 'Au-delà des compromis: les perspectives de réforme en Guinée-Bissau', *Africa Report* 183.

—— 2014: 'Guinée–Bissau: les élections, et après?', ICG Policy Briefing, 98.

—— 2015: 'La réforme du secteur de la sécurité en Guinée–Bissau: une occasion à saisir', ICG Policy Briefing, 109.

Isaacman, A. and B. 1984: 'The Role of Women in the Liberation of Mozambique', *UFAHAMU* 13 (2–3).

Jacobs, B. 2010: 'Upper Guinea Creole: Evidence in Favor of a Santiago Birth', *Journal of Pidgin and Creole Languages* 26 (3).

Jefremovas, V. 1997: 'Contested Identities: Power and the Fictions of Ethnicity, Ethnography and History in Rwanda', *Anthropologica* 39 (1–2): 91–104.

Jerven, M. 2013: 'For Richer For Poorer: GDP Revisions and Africa's Statistical Tragedy', *African Affairs* 112 (446): 138–47.

Johansen, R. 2008: 'Guinea-Bissau: A New Hub for Cocaine Trafficking', *Perspectives* 5: 4–8.

Johnson, M. C. 2002: 'Being Mandinga, Being Muslim: Transnational Debates on Personhood and Religious Identity in Guinea-Bissau and Portugal.' Urbana, IL: University of Illinois at Urbana-Champaign, unpublished PhD dissertation.

Jong, J. T. de and Reis, R. 2010: 'Kiyang-yang, a West-African Postwar Idiom of Distress', *Culture, Medicine and Psychiatry* 34: 301–21.

Jordan, D. 1999: *Drug Politics: Dirty Money and Democracies*. Norman, OK: University of Oklahoma Press.

Journal of Peasant Studies 2012: 39 (1 and 2).

Journet-Diallo, O. 2007: *Les créances de la terre: Chroniques du pays jamaat (Joola de Guinée–Bissau)*. Paris: Bibliothèque de l'École des hautes études.

Ka, S. 1994: 'Rich entrepreneurs, poor economies: smuggling activities in the Senegambia.' Baltimore, MD: Johns Hopkins University, unpublished PhD dissertation.

Keane, J. 2003: *Global civil society?* Cambridge: Cambridge University Press.

Keese, A. 2007: 'The Role of Cape Verdeans in War Mobilization and War Prevention in Portugal's African Empire, 1955–1965', *International Journal of African Historical Studies* 40 (3): 497–511.

———— 2012: '*Reformist network-building versus authoritarian constraints in the Portuguese late colonial state: forced labour, scandal and calumny in the District of Congo (Angola) 1955–61'.* Paper presented at workshop, 'Formal and informal empire; Portuguese relations with the non-European world', King's College London, 13 January 2012.

Kohl, C. 2008: 'Guinea-Bissau', in Mehler, A., Melber, H. and van Walraven, K. (eds), *Africa Yearbook. Politics, Economy and Society South of the Sahara in 2007*. Leiden and Boston: Brill.

———— 2009a: 'Creole Identity, Interethnic Relations, and Postcolonial Nation-Building in Guinea-Bissau, West Africa.' Halle (Saale): Martin Luther University Halle-Wittenberg, unpublished PhD dissertation.

———— 2009b: 'Guinea-Bissau', in Mehler, A., Melber, H. and van Walraven, K. (eds), *Africa Yearbook. Politics, Economy and Society South of the Sahara in 2008*. Leiden and Boston: Brill.

———— 2009c: 'The Kristons de Gêba of Guinea-Bissau: Creole Contributions to Postcolonial Nation-Building', online working paper, http://wcms.uzi.uni-halle.de/download.php?down=14479&elem=2279195, accessed 9 February 2016.

———— 2010: 'Guinea-Bissau', in Mehler, A., Melber, H. and van Walraven, K. (eds), *Africa Yearbook. Politics, Economy and Society South of the Sahara in 2009*. Leiden and Boston: Brill.

———— 2011: 'Guinea-Bissau', in Mehler, A., Melber, H. and van Walraven, K. (eds), *Africa Yearbook. Politics, Economy and Society South of the Sahara in 2010*. Leiden and Boston: Brill.

———— 2012a: 'Diverse Unity: Creole Contributions to Interethnic Integration in Guinea-Bissau', *Nations and Nationalism* 18: 643–62.

———— 2012b: 'Guinea-Bissau', in Mehler, A., Melber, H. and van Walraven, K. (eds), *Africa Yearbook. Politics, Economy and Society South of the Sahara in 2011*. Leiden and Boston: Brill.

———— 2013a: 'Irrwege und Auswege. Guinea-Bissau nach dem Putsch im April 2012', *HSFK-Standpunkte* (1).

———— 2013b: 'Guinea-Bissau', in Mehler, A., Melber, H. and van Walraven, K. (eds),

Africa Yearbook. Politics, Economy and Society South of the Sahara in 2012. Leiden and Boston: Brill.

———— 2013c: 'Die Reform des Sicherheitssektors in Guinea-Bissau: Zwischen Anspruch und Praxis', *HSFK-Report* (8).

———— 2014a: 'The Reform of Guinea-Bissau's Security Sector', *Peace Research Institute Frankfurt (PRIF) Report*, 126.

———— 2014b: 'Guinea-Bissau', in Mehler, A., Melber, H. and van Walraven, K. (eds), *Africa Yearbook. Politics, Economy and Society South of the Sahara in 2013.* Leiden and Boston: Brill.

Kohl, C. and Schroven, A. 2014: 'Suffering for the nation: Bottom-up and Top-down Conceptualizations of the Nation in Guinea and Guinea-Bissau', Max Planck Institute for Social Anthropology Working Paper 152.

Kohnert, D. 2010: 'Democratization via Elections in an African "Narco-State"? The Case of Guinea-Bissau', Hamburg: German Institute of Global and Area Studies, Working Paper 123.

Kopytoff, I. 1987: 'The Internal African Frontier: the Making of African Political Culture', in I. Kopytoff (ed.), *The African Frontier*. Bloomington, IN: Indiana University Press.

Koudawo, F. 2001: *Cabo Verde e Guiné Bissau: da democracia revolucionária à democracia liberal*. Bissau: INEP.

Koutrakos, P. 2013: *The EU Common Security and Defence Policy*. Oxford: Oxford University Press.

Kriesberg, L. 1997: 'Social movements and global transformation', in Smith, J. et al. (eds), *Transnational Social Movements and Global Politics*. Syracuse, NY: Syracuse University Press.

Kwesi Aning, E. and Pokoo, J. 2013: 'Drug Trafficking and Threats to National and Regional Security in West Africa'. West Africa Commission on Drugs. Available at http://works.bepress.com/kwesi_aning/2, accessed 9 February 2016.

Kyle, S. 2009: 'Cashew Production in Guinea Bissau', Working Paper. Ithaca: Cornell University.

Lea, J. D., Hugo, C. and Cardoso, C. 1990: *A Review of the Cashew Sub-Sector in Guinea Bissau*. Report no. 119. Manhattan, KS: Kansas State University.

Lea, J. D., Hugo, C. and Ribeiro, C. R. 1990: *Rice Production and Marketing in Guinea Bissau: a Contribution for Policy Debate*. Kansas: Kansas State University.

Lewis, D. 2014: 'A Surge in Cocaine Trafficking has Turned Guinea into West Africa's Latest Drug Hotspot', Reuters, 31 January 2014.

Lewis, D. and Valdmanis, R. 2013: 'How U.S. drug sting targeted West African military chiefs', *Wal*, 24 July 2013, http://www.reuters.com/article/2013/07/24/us-guinea-bissau-sting-special-report-idUSBRE96N0AR20130724, accessed 2 September 2015.

Lifton, C. 1991: 'Social soundness and WID analysis: for USAID legal reform project paper'. Bissau: USAID.

BIBLIOGRAPHY

Lima, E. 2007: *O Evangelho de Cristo na Guiné-Bissau: dos primórdios aos nossos dias*. Publidisa.

Lobban, R. 1979: *Historical Dictionary of Guinea Bissau and Cape Verde*. Metuchen, NJ: Scarecrow Press.

Lodge, T. 2014: 'Neopatrimonial Politics in the ANC', *African Affairs* 113 (450): 1–23.

Lopes, C. 1982/1987: 'A Transiçao Historica Na Guiné-Bissau: Do Movimento de Libertação Nacional ao Estado'. Geneva: Institut Universitaire d'Etudes du Développement/INEP.

—— 1982: *Etnia, Estado, e Relações de Poder na Guiné-Bissau*. Lisbon: Edições 70.

—— 1987a: *A Transição Histórica na Guiné-Bissau: do Movimento de Libertação Nacional ao Estado*. Bissau: INEP.

—— 1987b: *Guinea Bissau: From Liberation Struggle to Independent Statehood*. Boulder, CO: Westview Press.

—— 1999: *Kaabunké: espaço, território e poder na Guiné-Bissau, Gambia e Casamance pré-coloniais*. Lisbon: Comissão Nacional para as Comemorações dos Descobrimentos Portugueses.

Lopes, Cátia Nobre 2011: 'O Papel da Mulher no Microcrédito na Guiné-Bissau— Estudo de Caso em Pitche e em Pirada'. Lisbon: Instituto Superior de Economia e Gestão, Universidade Técnica de Lisboa, unpublished MA thesis.

Loureiro Bastos, F. (ed.) n.d.: *Relatório Final do Projecto de Recolha e Codificação do Direito Consuetudinário vigente na República da Guiné-Bissau*. Bissau: EU, UNDP, Faculdade de Direito de Bissau.

Lourenço-Lindell, I. 2002: *Walking the Tightrope: Informal Livelihoods and Social Networks in a West African City*. Stockholm: University of Stockholm.

Luckham, R. and Kirk, T. 2013: 'The Two Faces of Security in Hybrid Political Orders: A Framework for Analysis and Research', *Stability: International Journal of Security and Development* 2 (2): 1–30.

Lundy, B. 2013: 'Ethnic Encounters and Everyday Economics in Kassumba, Guinea-Bissau', *Ethnopolitics* 11 (3): 235–54.

—— 2015: 'Trading on the margins: locating continuities of exchange in Guinea Bissau', *African Identities* 13 (2): 111–28.

Lynn, S. and Jaeger, P. 2004: *Guinea-Bissau Cashew Development Study*. Bissau: Private Sector Rehabilitation and Development Project.

Lyon, J. M. 1980: 'Marxism and Ethno-Nationalism in Guinea-Bissau 1956–79', *Ethnic and Racial Studies* 3 (2).

Lyons, T. 2004: *Guns and Guerrilla Girls; Women in the Zimbabwean Liberation Struggle*. New Jersey: Africa World Press, Inc.

Machado, F. 1998: 'Da Guiné-Bissau a Portugal: Luso-Guineenses e Imigrantes', *Sociologia, Problemas e Práticas* 26: 9–56.

Machado, F. L. 2002: *Contrastes e Continuidades. Migração, Etnicidade e Integração dos*

BIBLIOGRAPHY

Guineenses em Portugal. Oeiras: Celta Editora, Magalhães Ferreira, P. 2004: 'Guinea-Bissau: Between Conflict and Democracy', *African Security Review* 13: 45–56.

Magalhães Ferreira, P. 2005: 'Short Commentary on Guinea-Bissau's Presidential Elections: "Óra na Tchiga!" (It's Time!)', Institute for Security Studies Situation Report.

Maloba, W. O. 2007: *African Women in Revolution.* New York: Africa World Press Inc.

Mamdani, M. 1996: *Citizen and Subject: Contemporary Africa and the Legacy of Late Colonialism.* Princeton, NJ: Princeton University Press.

Mané, Ndalla 2010: Interview with Aliou Ly, Bafatá, 17 July 2010.

Mané, NDo 2010: Interview with Aliou Ly, Boé, 2 August 2010.

Mark, P. and Horta, J. da Silva 2011: *The Forgotten Diaspora: Jewish Communities in West Africa and the Making of the Atlantic World.* Cambridge: Cambridge University Press.

Marks, Z. 2013: 'The Internal Dynamics of Rebel Groups: Politics of Material Viability and Organizational Capacity, RUF Sierra Leone.' Oxford: University of Oxford, unpublished PhD dissertation.

Massey, S. 2001: 'Intervention in Guinea-Bissau', in Furley, O. and May, R. (eds), *African Interventionist States.* Aldershot: Ashgate.

—— 2004: 'Multi-faceted Mediation in the Guinea-Bissau Civil War', *South African Journal of Military Studies* 32 (1): 76–95.

Mathieu, P. 1996: 'La sécurisation foncière entre compromis et conflits: un processus politique?, in Mathieu, P. et al. (eds), *Démocratie, enjeux fonciers et pratiques locales en Afrique.* Paris: Harmattan.

Mazzitelli, A. 2007: 'Transnational Organized Crime in West Africa: The Additional Challenge', *International Affairs* 83 (6): 1071–90.

Mballo, Dianké 2010: Interview with Aliou Ly, Bissau, 20 July 2010.

Mballo, Famara 2010: Group discussion with Aliou Ly, Bissau, 30 July 2010.

Mbembe, A. 2001: *On the Postcolony.* Berkeley, CA: University of California Press.

—— 2010: *Sortir de la Grande Nuit: Essai sur l'Afrique Décolonisée.* Paris: Éditions La Découverte.

McCulloch, J. 1983: *In the Twilight of Revolution. The Political Theory of Amílcar Cabral.* London: Routledge & Kegan Paul.

MDRA 1990a: *Estratégia de Desenvolvimento para o Sector Agrário,* Bissau: Ministério de Desenvolvimento Rural e Agricultura.

—— 1990b: *Résultats du Recensement National de l'Agriculture 1988/1989, V. II: Analyse des Résultats Nationaux et Régionaux.* Bissau: Gabinete de Planificação do Ministério de Desenvolvimento Rural e da Agricultura.

MDRA/FAO/PAM 2007: *Guinée–Bissau: Commerce du Cajou et du Riz et les Implications pour la Sécurité Alimentaire. Bissau/Rome: MDRA/FAO/PAM.*

Mendes, J. M. F. 1970: 'Problemas e Perspectivas do Desenvolvimento Rural da Guiné', *Boletim Cultural da Guiné Portuguesa* 25 (97): 89–144; 25 (98): 273–308.

BIBLIOGRAPHY

—— 1972: 'Acerca do Fomento de Cajú na Guiné', *Boletim Cultural da Guiné Portuguesa* 27 (105): 95–122.

Mendes, P. 2011: 'La dimension des praxis *mandji* dans la dynamique socioculturelle du groupe ethnique Manjak', in Klute, G. and Embalo, B. (eds), *The Problem of Violence. Local Conflict Settlement in Contemporary Africa*. Cologne: Rudiger Koppe Verlag.

Mendy, P. 1990: 'A economia colonial da Guiné-Bissau: "nacionalização" e exploração, 1915–1959', *Soronda* 9: 23–51.

Mendy, P. K. 1994: *Colonialismo Portugûes em África: A Tradição de Resistência na Guiné-Bissau*. Bissau: INEP.

O Militante (Bissau) 5 (November–December), 1997.

Ministério da Administração Interna 1995: *Guiné-Bissau. Constituição, Lei Eleitoral e Legislação complementar*. Vol. III. *Primeiro Encontro Eleitoral. Encontro dos Ministros Responsáveis pela Administração Eleitoral dos Países Africanos de Expressão Portuguesa e de Portugal, Julho de 1994*. Lisbon: Edições 70.

Ministério do Ultramar 1963: *Recenseamento Agrícola de Guiné, 1960–1961*. Lisbon: Comissão para os Inquéritos Agrícolas do Ultramar.

Mokuwa, E., Voors, M., Bulte, E. and Richards, P. 2011: 'Peasant Grievance and Insurgency in Sierra Leone: Judicial Serfdom as a Driver of Conflict', *African Affairs* 110: 339–66.

Morgenthau, R. T. 1964: *Political Parties in French-Speaking West Africa*. Oxford: Clarendon Press.

Munslow, B. 1981: 'The 1980 Coup in Guinea Bissau', *Review of African Political Economy* 21: 109–13.

Nafafé, J. L. 2005: 'Mission and Political Power: Subversive Power Relations in Luso-West Africa (Guinea-Bissau) 1886–1914', in Heyden, Ulrich van der, and Stoecker, H. (eds), *Mission und Macht im Wandel politischer Orientierungen*. Stuttgart: Steiner.

—— 2007a: *Colonial Encounters: Issues of Culture, Hybridity and Creolisation, Portuguese Mercantile Settlers in West Africa*. Frankfurt: Peter Lang.

—— 2007b: 'Lançados, Culture and Identity: Prelude to Creole Societies on the Rivers of Guinea and Cape Verde', in Havik, P. J. and Newitt, M. (eds), *Creole Societies in the Portuguese Colonial Empire*. Bristol: University of Bristol: 65–91.

National Centre for Arts and Culture Oral Archives (NCAC OA), untranscribed cassettes 57, 130; 'Kaabu and Fulladu' transcribed files for cassettes 170, 171, Fajara, The Gambia.

National Institute on Drugs Abuse 2007: 'Monitoring the Future'. Available at http://www.drugabuse.gov/drugpages/MTF.HTML, accessed 9 February 2016.

Ndao, E. I. 2003: *Senegal, Histoire des Conquêtes Democratiques*. Dakar: NEA.

Ndati, Na 2010: Interview with Aliou Ly, Boé, 2 August.

Nhaga, Sandé 2012: Interview with Aliou Ly, Bissau, 28 August 2010, 1 November.

BIBLIOGRAPHY

Nóbrega, Á. 2003a: 'Desejo de "Cambança": O Processo Eleitoral de 1999', *Soronda* 7 (new series): 7–81.

——— 2003b: *A Luta pelo Poder na Guiné-Bissau.* Lisbon: Universidade Técnica de Lisboa, Instituto Superior de Ciências Sociais e Politicas.

Nossiter, A. 2012: 'Leader Ousted, Nation is Now a Drug Haven', *New York Times*, 1 November 2012.

Novak, A. 2012: 'The Abolition of the Death Penalty for Drug Offenses in The Gambia', *Commonwealth Law Bulletin* 38 (1), March 2012.

Nquamé, Theresa 2010: Interview with Aliou Ly, Bissau, 28 July.

Ntephe, P. 2012: 'Does Africa Need Another Kind of Law? Alterity and the Rule of Law in Subsaharan Africa.' London: School of Oriental and African Studies, unpublished PhD dissertation.

O'Regan, D. 2012: 'Narco-States: Africa's Next Menace', *New York Times*, 12 March 2012.

O'Regan, D. and Thompson, P. 2013: 'Advancing Stability and Reconciliation in Guinea-Bissau: Lessons from Africa's first narco-state', Africa Center for Strategic Studies Special Report, June 2013.

O'Regan, H. D. 2014: 'Has Guinea-Bissau become Africa's first narco-state or is it actually losing its importance as a trans-shipment center?' www.isn.ethz.ch/Digital-Library/Articles/Detail, accessed 12 August 2015.

O'Toole, R. 2007: 'From the Rivers of Guinea to the Valleys of Peru: Becoming a Bran Diaspora Within Spanish Slavery', *Social Text* 92, 25 (3): 19–36.

Ogaba Agbese, P. and Klay Kieh Jr, G. 2007: 'Introduction: Democratizing States and State Reconstitution in Africa', in Ogaba Agbese, P. and Klay Kieh Jr, G. (eds), *Reconstituting the State in Africa*. New York: Palgrave Macmillan.

Okafor, F. O. E. 1988: 'The PAIGC and the Economic Development of Guinea Bissau: Ideology and Reality', *The Developing Economies* XXVI (2): 125–40.

Oliveira, J. S. 1966: 'Castanha de Cajú da Guiné Portuguesa: Nota Preliminar', *Garcia de Orta* 14 (4): 503–12.

Ostheimer, A. E. 2001: 'The Structural Crisis in Guinea-Bissau's Political System', *African Security Review* 10: 45–57.

Oteng, J. W. and Sant'Anna, R. 1999: 'Rice production in Africa: current situation and issues', *International Rice Commission Newsletter* (FAO), 48: 41–51, http://www.fao.org/docrep/003/x2243t/x2243t05.htm#P0_0, accessed 9 February 2016.

PAIGC 1973: 'Report on the Politico-Socio-Economic Role of Women in Guinea and the Cape Verde Islands', published in English in *Women in the Struggle for Liberation*. New York; World Student Christian Federation, 1973.

——— 1980: *A Trajectória Económica da Guiné Bissau*. Bissau: Agência Noticiosa da Guiné Bissau.

Paoli, L., Rabkov, I., Greenfield, V. and Reuter, P. 2007: 'Tajikistan: the rise of a narco state', *Journal of Drug Issues* 37 (4): 951–79.

BIBLIOGRAPHY

Parkinson, C. 2013: 'LatAm Drug Traffickers Set Up in Guinea Bissau, Expand in Africa', *Media*, 29 August 2013.

Paulini, T. 1984: *Guinea-Bissau: Nachkoloniale Entwicklung eines Agrarstaates*. Götingen: Edition Herodot.

Pélissier, R. 1989: *Naissance de la Guiné: Portugais et Africains en Sénégambia (1841–1936)*. Orgeval: Ed. Pélissier.

Pereira, J. M. 1986: *Guinea-Bissau Profil*. Bissau: UNESCO.

Pereira, L., Schwartz da Silva, C. and Tavares-Amarante, C. 1992: *Vias para a Modernização da Agricultura—Guiné Bissau*. Bissau: Projecto PASA/Banco Mundial.

Piazza, James 2008: 'Incubators of Terror: Do Failed and Failing States Promote Transnational Terrorism?' *International Studies Quarterly* 52 (3): 469–88.

Piketty, T. 2014: *Capital in the Twenty-First Century*. Cambridge, MA: Harvard University Press.

Poster, Mark 1984: *Foucault, Marxism and History; Mode of Production versus Mode of Information*. Cambridge: Polity Press.

Pratto, F., Sidanius, J., Stallworth, L. A. and Malle, B. 1994: 'Social Dominance Orientation: A Personality Variable Predicting Social and Political Attitudes', *Journal of Personality Psychology* 67 (4): 741–63.

Província da Guiné 1972: *Prospectiva de Desenvolvimento Económico e Social da Guiné*. Lisbon: Junta de Investigações do Ultramar.

Pussetti, C. 2005: *Poetica delle emozioni: I Bijagó della Guinea Bissau*. Rome: Laterza.

Ranger, T. 1993: 'The Invention of Tradition Revisited: The Case of Colonial Africa', in Ranger, T. and Vaughan, O. (eds), *Legitimacy and the State in Twentieth-Century Africa: Essays in Honour of A. H. M. Kirk-Greene*. London: Macmillan Press.

Reinhard, W. (ed.) 1996: *Power Elites and State-Building*. Oxford: Clarendon Press.

Reis, Leonilda Aimé dos 1994: 'Estudo sobre Estruturas Locais Tradicionais de Poupança e Credito'. Bissau: UNDP.

Reitano, T. and Shaw, M. 2013: 'Guinea-Bissau: Arrest of Guinea-Bissau's Drug Lords, Just the First Step in the Battle Against Trafficking', *Institute for Security Studies*, Policy Brief 44, July 2013.

Rema, H. P. 1982: *História das Missões Católicas da Guiné*. Braga: Editorial Franciscana.

RGB 2003: *Análise da Fileira do Arroz*. Bissau: Ministério da Economia e Finanças.

——— 2005: Documento de Estratégia Nacional da Redução da Pobreza (DENARP). Bissau: Ministry of Economy, Planning and Regional Integration (MEPIR).

——— 2011: Segundo Documento de Estratégia Nacional de Redução da Pobreza (DENARP II). Bissau: Ministry of Economy, Planning and Regional Integration (MEPIR)/International Monetary Fund (IMF).

Ribeiro, C. R. 1989: 'Causas da Queda de Produção de Arroz na Guiné-Bissau. A Situação no Sector de Tite, Região de Quínara', *Revista Internacional de Estudos Africanos* 10–11: 227–65.

BIBLIOGRAPHY

Richards, P. 1985: *Indigenous Agricultural Revolution: Ecology and Food Production in West Africa*. London: Hutchinson.

Richards, P. and Ruivenkamp, G. 1997. *Seeds and Survival. Crop Genetic Resources in War and Reconstruction in Africa*. Rome: IPGRI.

Roche, C. 1976: *Histoire de la Casamance: Conquête et Résistance: 1850–1920*. Paris: Éditions Karthala.

Rodney, W. 1966: 'African Slavery and Other Forms of Social Oppression on the Upper Guinea Coast in the Context of the Atlantic Slave Trade', *Journal of African History* 7 (3): 431–43.

—— 1970: *History of the Upper Guinea Coast, 1545–1800*. Oxford: Clarendon Press.

—— 1972: *How Europe Underdeveloped Africa*. London/Dar-es-Salaam: Bogle L'Ouverture Publishers.

Rodrigues, M. M. S. 1948: 'Os maometanos nos futuro da Guiné portuguesa', *Buletin Cultural da Guiné Portuguesa* 3 (9): 220–36.

Rodrigues Zeverino, G. J. 2005: *O Conflito Politico-Militar na Guiné-Bissau (1998–1999)*. Lisbon: Instituto Português de Apoio ao Desenvolvimento.

Roque, S. 2009: 'Peacebulding in Guinea-Bissau: A critical approach', Oslo: Norwegian Peacebuilding Resource Centre Report, 7.

Rudebeck, L. 1974: *Guinea-Bissau: A Study of Political Mobilization*. Uppsala: Scandinavian Institute of African Studies.

—— 1982: *Problèmes de Pouvoir Populaire et Développement: Transition Difficile en Guinée Bissau*. Uppsala: Scandinavian Center for African Studies.

—— 1988: 'Kandadja, Guinea Bissau, 1976–1986: Observations on the Political Economy of an African Village', *Review of African Political Economy* 41: 17–29.

—— 1989: 'Structural Adjustment in a West African Village', in Hermele, K. and Rudebeck, L. (eds), *At the Cross Roads: Political Alliances and Structural Adjustment: Two Essays on Angola, Mozambique and Guinea Bissau*. Uppsala: AKUT.

—— 1990: 'The Effects of Structural Adjustment in Kandjadja, Guinea-Bissau', *Review of African Political Economy* 49: 34–51.

—— 1996: *Buscar a felicidade. Democratização na GuinéBissau*. Uppsala: University to Uppsala.

—— 1998: 'Guinea Bissau: Fighting Breaks Out', *Review of African Political Economy* 25 (77): 484–6.

—— 2001a: *On Democracy and Sustainability: Transition in Guinea Bissau*. Stockholm: SIDA Studies 4.

—— 2001b: *Colapso e Reconstrução política na Guiné-Bissau 1998–2000: Um Estudo de Democratização difícil*. Uppsala: Nordiska Afrikainstitutet.

—— 2010: '"They have Left us in a Hole": Democratisation and Political Power in a West African Village', *Bulletin de l'APAD* 31–32: 2–21.

Russell, A. 2012: 'Talking Politics and Watching the Border in Northern Burundi, *c*.1960–1972.' Oxford: University of Oxford, unpublished PhD dissertation.

258

BIBLIOGRAPHY

Sambu, Segunda 2010: Interview with Aliou Ly, Bissau, 2 August.

Sampil, S. 1969: 'Les Nalous (1865–1900).' Paris: École Pratique des Hautes Etudes (6ème section: sciences économiques et sociales), unpublished dissertation.

Sandoval, A. de 1627: *Naturaleza, Policia, Sagrada, Profana, Costumbres, Ritos, Disciplina, Catchismo Evangelico de Todos Etiopes.* Seville: Francisco de Lira Impressor.

Sané, Fatu 2010: Interview with Aliou Ly, Bissau, 27 July.

Sangreman, C. et al. 2012: *Avaliação do Potencial de Desenvolvimento da Diáspora da Guiné-Bissau em Portugal e França.* Lisbon: IOM Development Fund.

Sanneh, P. S. 2009: 'A Study of Food Insecurity and Rural Development in The Gambia: the Impact of Rural Weekly Markets (*Lumos*).' Manhattan, KS: Kansas State University, unpublished PhD dissertation.

Santos, E. dos 1968: 'Catolicismo, protestantismo e islamismo na Guiné portuguesa', *Ultramar* 8 (32): 112–24.

Schiefer, U. 1987: *Guiné Bissau: Zwischen Weltwirtschaft und Subsistenz.* Bonn: Informationsstelle Südliches Afrika (ISSA).

Schmidt, E. 2002: '"Emancipate Your Husbands!" Women and Nationalism in Guinea, 1953–1958', in Allman, J., Geiger, S. and Nakanyike Musisi (eds), *Women in African Colonial Histories.* Bloomington, IN: Indiana University Press.

Schomerus, M. 2013: 'Dynamics and Challenges of the Juba Peace Talks with the Lord's Resistance Army.' London: London School of Economics, unpublished PhD dissertation.

Seabra, P. 2011: 'Guinea-Bissau: bringing Angola into the fold', IPRIS Viewpoints, April 2011.

SEF portal (Serviço de Estrangeiros e Fronteiras), http://www.sef.pt/portal/V10/EN/aspx/organizacao/index.aspx?id_linha=4167&menu_position=4132, accessed 9 February 2016.

SEF statistics (Relatório de Imigração, Fronteiras e Asilo 2012), http://sefstat.sef.pt/Docs/Rifa%202012.pdf, accessed 9 February 2016.

Seydi, Sano 2010: Interview with Aliou Ly, Gabu, 28 June.

Shaw, M. 2015: 'Drug trafficking in Guinea-Bissau, 1998–2014: the evolution of an elite protection network', *Journal of Modern African Studies* 53 (3): 339–64.

Silva, A. 2013: 'Tensões internas de cunho religioso estalam no PAIGC', in *Ditadura do Consenso*, 12 July 2013, http://ditaduradoconsenso.blogspot.de/2013/07/tensoes-internas-de-cunho-religioso.html, accessed 19 February 2014.

Simo, J. 2011: 'Land grabbing, governance and social peace-building issues in Cameroon'. Paper presented at the International Conference on Global Land Grabbing, organized by LDPI, Sussex, 6–8 April 2011.

Sissoko, F. D. 1945: *Profession de Foi.* Bamako: French-Soudan Imprimerie.

Smith, M. 1974: *Corporations and Society: The Social Anthropology of Collective Action.* London: Duckworth.

Smoltczyk, A. 2013: 'Africa's Cocaine Hub: Guinea-Bissau, A Drug Trafficker's Dream', *Der Spiegel*, 8 March 2013.

Sonko, B. 2004: 'The Casamance Conflict: A Forgotten Civil War', *CODESRIA Bulletin* 3–4: 30–35.

Souaré, I. 2014: 'The African Union as a norm entrepreneur on military coups d'état in Africa (1952–2012): an empirical assessment', *Journal of Modern African Studies* 52 (1): 69–94.

Stiglitz, J. 2012: *The Price of Inequality: How Today's Divided Society Endangers our Future*. London/New York: Penguin.

Stoleroff, M. 2013: *Social Boundaries, Political Elite Bargains and (Dis)order in Guinea-Bissau, 1974–1998*. London: School of Oriental and African Studies, University of London, 2013, unpublished PhD thesis.

Stolte, C. 2012: 'Brazil in Africa: Just Another BRICS Country Seeking Resources?' Chatham House Briefing Paper, November 2012.

Sweet, J. H. 2006: *Recreating Africa: Culture, Kinship and Religion in the African Portuguese World. 1441–1770*. Chapel Hill, NC: University of North Carolina Press.

Swindell, K. 1978: 'Family Farms and Migrant Labour: The Stranger Farmers of the Gambia', *Canadian Journal of African Studies (Revue Canadienne des Études Africaines)* 12 (1): 3–17.

Sy, Adama 2010: Group discussion with Aliou Ly, Bissau, 30 July.

Tambiah, S. J. 1990: 'Presidential Address: Reflections on Communal Violence in South Asia', *Journal of Asian Studies* 49: 741–60.

Tanner, C. 1991: 'Relations between Ponteiros and Tabancas: Implications for a New Land Law in Guinea-Bissau'. Consultant Report. Cambridge: Cambridge SEPR Associates.

Teeken, B., Nuyten, E., Temudo, M. P., Okry, F., Mokuwa, A., Struyk, P. C. and Richards, P. 2012: 'Maintaining or Abandoning African Rice: Lessons for Understanding Processes of Seed Innovation', *Human Ecology* 40: 879–92.

Teixeira da Mota, Avelino/Teixeira da Mota, A. 1954: *Guiné Portuguesa*. Lisbon and Bissau: Agência Geral do Ultramar (2 vols).

——— 1958: Speech as MP for Portuguese Guinea in Portuguese National Assembly, *Diário das Sessões da Assembleia Nacional* 42, 23–04–1958: 911–15.

——— 1970: *Fulas e Beafadas no Rio Grande do Século XV: Achegas Para a Etnohistória da África Ocidental*. Lisbon: Junta de Investigações do Ultramar.

Teixeira, M. 2001: *Rituels divinatoires et thérapeutiques chez les Manjak de Guinée Bissau et du Senegal*. Paris: L'Harmattan.

Temudo, M. P. 1998: 'Inovação e Mudança em Sociedades Rurais Africanas: Gestão dos Recursos Naturais, Saber Local e Instituições de Desenvolvimento Induzido', Vol. I. Lisbon: Universidade de Lisboa, unpublished PhD dissertation.

——— 2005: 'Western beliefs and local myths: A case study on the interface between farmers, NGOs, and the state in Guinea-Bissau Rural Development Interventions', in Igoe, J. and Kelsall, T. (eds), *Between a Rock and a Hard Place: African NGOs, Donors, and the State*. Durham, NC: Carolina Academic Press: 253–77.

BIBLIOGRAPHY

—— 2008: 'From "People's Struggle" to "This War Today": Entanglements of Peace in Guinea-Bissau', *Africa: Journal of the International African Institute* 78 (2): 245–63.

—— 2009: 'From the Margins of the State to the Presidential Palace: the Balanta Case in Guinea Bissau', *African Studies Review* 52 (2): 47–67.

—— 2011: 'Planting Knowledge, Harvesting Agro-Biodiversity: A Case Study of Southern Guinea-Bissau Rice Farming', *Human Ecology* 39 (3): 309–21.

—— 2012: '"The White Men Bought the Forests": Conservation and Contestation in Guinea-Bissau, West Africa', *Conservation and Society*, 10 (4): 354–66.

Temudo, M. P. and Abrantes, M. B. 2012: 'Changing Policies, Shifting Livelihoods: The Fate of Agriculture in Guinea-Bissau', *Journal of Agrarian Change* 13 (4): 571–89.

—— 2014: 'The Cashew Frontier in Guinea Bissau, West Africa: Changing Landscapes and Livelihoods', *Human Ecology* 42: 217–30.

—— 2015: 'The plow and the pen: Balanta youth and the future of agriculture in Guinea-Bissau', *Development and Change* 46 (3): 464–85.

Temudo, M. P. and Schiefer, U. 2003: 'Disintegration and Resilience of Agrarian Societies in Africa—the Importance of Social and Genetic Resources: A Case Study on the Reception of Urban War Refugees in the South of Guinea-Bissau', *Current Sociology* 51 (3): 393–416.

Tertilt, M. 2006: 'Polygyny, Women's Rights and Development', *Journal of the European Economic Association* 4 (2): 523–30.

Thioub, I., Diop, M.-C. and Boone, C. 1998: 'Economic Liberalization in Senegal: Shifting Politics of Indigenous Business Interests', *African Studies Review* 41 (2): 63–89.

Tilly, C. 2000: *Coercion, Capital and European States, AD 900–1990*. Malden: Blackwell.

Tin, H. 2002: 'O benefício do fracasso: PAM, ajuda alimentar e sobrevivência local na Guiné-Bissau, 1998–1999', *Soronda* 3: 77–144.

Touray, O. 1995: 'The Foreign Policy Problems of Developing Micro-states: The Case of the Gambia, 1975–1990.' Geneva: University of Geneva, unpublished PhD dissertation.

—— 2000: *The Gambia and The World: A History of Foreign Policy of Africa's Smallest State, 1965–1995*. Hamburg: Institute of African Affairs.

Tovrov, D. 2014: 'Guinea-Bissau: Drug Trafficking on the Rise in West Africa's Narco-State', *International Business Times*, 27 March, http://www.ibtimes.com/guinea-bissau-drug-trafficking-rise-west-africas-narco-state-734150, accessed 9 February 2016.

Trajano Filho, W. 2004: 'A constituição de um olhar fragilizado: notas sobre o colonialismo português em Africa', in Carvalho, C. and Cabral, J. de Pina (eds), *A Persitência da História*. Lisbon: ICS.

—— 2010: 'The Creole Idea of Nation and its Predicaments: the Case of Guinea Bissau', in Knörr, J. and Trajano Filho, W. (eds), *The Powerful Presence of the Past: Integration and Conflict along the Upper Guinea Coast*. Boston and Leiden: Brill.

Trouillot, M.-R. 1995: *Silencing the Past: Power and the Production of History*. Boston: Beacon Press.

Tung, M. T. 1968: *Four Essays on Philosophy*. Beijing: Foreign Languages Press.

Turé, Fatu 2010: Interview with Aliou Ly, Bissau, 27 July.

United Nations 2014: 'Summary of the visit of HE Mr Antonio Patriota, Chair of the Guinea-Bissau Configuration, Peacebuilding Commission to Guinea-Bissau', 20–23 January 2014.

United Nations Office on Drugs and Crime 2007: 'Cocaine Trafficking in West Africa. The threat to stability and development (with special reference to Guinea-Bissau)', http://www.unodc.org/documents/data-and-analysis/west_africa_cocaine_report_2007–12_en.pdf, accessed 21 August 2015.

United Nations Security Council 2012: 'Special Report of the Secretary General on the Situation in Guinea-Bissau', 30 April 2012, http://uniogbis.unmissions.org/LinkClick.aspx?fileticket=K5TByBubU6k%3d&tabid=9879&mid=12844&language=en-US, accessed 9 February 2016.

—— 2015: 'Report of the Secretary General on the progress made with regard to the stabilization and restoration of constitutional order in Guinea-Bissau', 12 August 2015.

United States Attorney's Office, Southern District of New York, 2013: 'Manhattan US Attorney Announces Arrests of Drug Kingpin Jose Americo Bubo Na Tchuto, the Former Head of the Guinea-Bissau Navy, and Six Others for Narcotics Trafficking Offenses', Press Release, 5 April 2013, http://www.justice.gov/usao/nys/pressreleases/April13/GuineaBissauArrestsPR.php, accessed 25 April 2014.

United States Department of State, 'US Virtual Presence Post: Guinea-Bissau'. Available at http://guinea-bissau.usvpp.gov.

Urdang, S. 1979: *Fighting Two Colonialisms: Women in Guinea-Bissau*. New York: Monthly Review Press.

—— 1981: 'The Role of Women in the Revolution in Guinea-Bissau', in Steady, F. C. (ed.), *The Black Woman Cross-Culturally*. Cambridge: Schenkman Publishing Co. Inc.

—— 1989: *And Still They Dance: Women, War and the Struggle for Change in Mozambique*. London: Earthscan Publications Ltd.

Uwazurike, C. 1996: 'Ethnicity, Power and Prebendalism: The Persistent Triad as the Unsolvable Crisis of Nigerian Politics', *Dialectical Anthropology* 21 (1): 1–20.

Vaz, N. and Rotzoll, I. C. 2005: 'Presidential Elections in Guinea Bissau 2005: A stabilizing Factor in a Fragile Democracy or only a Spot Test of the State of Affairs?', *Afrika Spectrum* 40: 535–46.

Vertovec, S. 2006: 'The Emergence of Super-Diversity in Britain'. Centre for Migration, Policy and Society Working Paper 25. Oxford: University of Oxford.

BIBLIOGRAPHY

Vicente, J. n.d.: 'O que diferentes missionários da Guiné-Bissau escreveramsobre a própria Guiné-Bissau'. In http://diocese.gbissau.org/Public_missionarios.htm, accessed 5 April 2014.

Vicente, J. 1993: 'Quatro séculos de vida cristã em Cacheu', in Lopes, C. (ed.), *Mansas, escravos, grumetes e gentio: Cacheu na encruzilhada de civilizações*. Guiné-Bissau: Instituto Nacional de Estudos e Pesquisa.

Vigh, H. 2006: *Navigating Terrains of War: Youth and Soldiering in Guinea-Bissau*. New York: Berghahn Books.

Vulliamy, E. 2008: 'How a tiny West African country became the world's first narco-state', *The Observer* 8 March, http://www.theguardian.com/world/2008/mar/09/drugstrade, accessed 9 February 2016.

Wadstrom, C. B. 1794: *An Essay on Colonization, particularly applied to the Western Coast of Africa*. London: Darton and Harvey.

Wallis, H. 1996: *Lus numia na sukuru: storia di igreza ivangeliku di Guine–Bisau 1940–1974*. Bubaque: Evangelical Mission.

Walt, V. 2007: 'Cocaine country', *Time* magazine, 27 June 2007.

Wayland, S. 2004: 'Ethnonationalist networks and transnational opportunities: The Sri Lankan Tamil Diaspora', *Review of International Studies*, 30: 405–26.

Weinar, A. 2010: 'Instrumentalising Diasporas for Development: International and European Policy Discourses', in Bauböck, R. and Faist, T. (eds), *Diaspora and Transnationalism: Concepts, Theories and Methods*. Amsterdam: Amsterdam University Press.

World Bank 1994: *Republic of Guinea-Bissau: Poverty Assessment and Social Sectors Strategy Review*, 3 vols. Washington, DC: World Bank.

—— 2006: 'Guinea-Bissau Land Tenure Issues and Policy Study' (P095319), https://openknowledge.worldbank.org/bitstream/handle/10986/12465/689840 ESW0P0950re0Issues000Policies.txt?sequence=2, accessed 22 August 2013.

—— 2010: *Cashew and Beyond: Diagnostic Trade Integration Study for the Enhanced Integrated Framework for Trade Related Technical Assistance*. Washington DC: Integrated Framework Program.

—— 2014: Report AB 7449, http://www-wds.worldbank.org/external/default/ WDSContentServer/WDSP/IB/2013/12/23/000253539_20131230161601/ Rendered/PDF/GW0P1467460PID0Dec17013.pdf, accessed 9 February 2016.

—— 2015: *Armed forces personnel, total*, http://data.worldbank.org/indicator/ MS.MIL.TOTL.P1, accessed 21 August 2015.

Yalla, Hutna 2010: Interview with Aliou Ly, Bissau, 16 August.

INDEX

INDEX

INDEX

281

INDEX